INVENTING
IDAHO

Also by Keith C. Petersen

Idaho: The Land & Its People

John Mullan: The Tumultuous Life of a Western Road Builder (WSU Press)

River of Life, Channel of Death: Fish and Dams on the Lower Snake

Educating in the American West: One Hundred Years at Lewis-Clark State College, 1893–1993

Company Town: Potlatch, Idaho, and the Potlatch Lumber Company (WSU Press)

This Crested Hill: An Illustrated History of the University of Idaho

INVENTING IDAHO

The Gem State's
Eccentric Shape

KEITH C. PETERSEN

WSU
PRESS

Washington State University Press
Pullman, Washington

Washington State University Press
PO Box 645910
Pullman, Washington 99164-5910
Phone: 800-354-7360
Email: wsupress@wsu.edu
Website: wsupress.wsu.edu

This project was supported by a research fellowship from the Idaho Humanities
Council, the state-based partner of the National Endowment for the
Humanities.

Library of Congress Cataloging-in-Publication Data

Names: Petersen, Keith C., 1951- author.
Title: Inventing Idaho : the Gem State's eccentric shape / Keith C.
  Petersen.
Description: Pullman, Washington : Washington State University Press,
  [2022] | Includes bibliographical references and index.
Identifiers: LCCN 2022033526 | ISBN 9780874224184 (paperback)
Subjects: LCSH: Idaho--Boundaries--History. | Idaho--History, Local.
Classification: LCC F752.B7 P48 2022 | DDC 979.6/03--dc23/eng/20220715
LC record available at https://lccn.loc.gov/2022033526

The Washington State University Pullman campus is located on the homelands
of the Niimíipuu (Nez Perce) Tribe and the Palus people. We acknowledge their
presence here since time immemorial and recognize their continuing connection
to the land, to the water, and to their ancestors. WSU Press is committed to
publishing works that foster a deeper understanding of the Pacific Northwest
and the contributions of its Native peoples

Cover design by Jeffry E. Hipp
Maps courtesy Melissa Rockwood, *Rdesign*, Moscow, Idaho.

To Mary, Usha, and Uma
Again.
Always.

The landscape remained the same for hours....State boundaries marked no change in the landscape from one side to the next of each invisible line, which confounded her into wondering how such boundaries had ever been determined in the first place, how irrational the decision seemed, to have ended and begun two states when the land flowed in the same manner through both.

—Melanie Wallace, *The Girl in the Garden*

The name of this state is Idaho, and its boundaries are as follows: Beginning at a point in the middle channel of the Snake river where the northern boundary of Oregon intersects the same; then follow down the channel of Snake river to a point opposite the mouth of the Kooskooskia or Clearwater river; thence due north to the forty-ninth parallel of latitude; thence east along that parallel to the thirty-ninth degree of longitude west of Washington; thence south along that degree of longitude to the crest of the Bitter Root mountains; thence southward along the crest of the Bitter Root mountains till its intersection with the Rocky mountains; thence southward along the crest of the Rocky mountains to the thirty-fourth degree of longitude west of Washington; thence south along that degree of longitude to the forty-second degree of north latitude; thence west along that parallel to the eastern boundary of the state of Oregon; thence north along that boundary to the place of beginning.

—Constitution of the State of Idaho, Article 17

CONTENTS

MAPS

PREFACE

Idaho's eccentric boundary circumnavigates the state over the course of 1,800 miles. But Idaho did not attain that borderline all at once. Between 1819 and 1868, it took its current shape by means of six separate diplomatic and political accords. I debated the best method of addressing each of those distinct borders. I considered beginning at one boundary and proceeding geographically around the state, but, as a historian, I believe most stories are best told chronologically. The first border chapter focuses on Idaho's oldest boundary, the southern line separating Idaho from Nevada and Utah, established in 1819. The narrative then jumps geographically to the far north and the border with Canada, a demarcation finalized in 1846. Then on to the western boundaries with Oregon (1859) and Washington (1863), and the northeastern with Montana (1864). The final border chapter centers on Idaho's most recent boundary, the line with Wyoming, created in 1868.

When Congress established that final border, Idaho lost the Grand Tetons, Jackson Hole, and much of what became Yellowstone National Park to Wyoming. This is just one example of how borders have enduring consequences. To highlight other examples, I added a "border story" following each of the main chapters. Each story provides a case study of how that borderline impacts people's lives. For example, the 21st-century efforts of Oregonians to secede and join Idaho are the focus of the story "Greater Idaho," which follows Chapter Four. This contemporary movement has long historical roots starting in the 1850s.

When diplomats established the international boundary between Canada and the United States in 1846—the subject of Chapter Three—they set another of Idaho's future borders, in the process isolating members of the Kootenai Tribe of Idaho from relatives in British Columbia. The tribe's declaration of war against the United States in 1974, highlighted in the border story "War," resulted in a federally recognized reservation in far northern Idaho.

I selected the border story subjects to focus on a diversity of ways in which Idaho's boundaries have over time influenced those living within their confines, from settlers and miners to Mormon immigrants and Native Americans. Other writers might have selected different examples, but a verifiable truth remains: Idahoans today continue to creatively face the challenges of boundary decisions made a century and a half ago.

Keith C. Petersen
Pullman, Washington
May 2022

PROLOGUE

Student Special

It seemed the entire town had gathered at the Moscow depot. A band played. Old acquaintances reacquainted. A line of cars waited to chauffeur passengers to their new homes up the hill.

The Student Special, pulled by two locomotives, arrived at the station at 12:50 p.m. on a sunny September day. The crowd cheered as 300 nattily attired University of Idaho students disembarked from the ten passenger cars. People distributed flowers, snapped photos, gave hugs. Another school year would soon begin.

The train had just zigzagged through three states—its only possible route—to deliver students from one part of Idaho to another. Although they did not know it, those townspeople assembled at the depot, the students on board, and the operators of this special train—indeed, the University of Idaho itself—all converged on that day because of decisions made in such faraway places as Madrid, London, and Washington, DC, between 1819 and 1868. That is when diplomats and politicians foisted on Idaho the nation's most peculiar borders. Since then, Idahoans have toiled to unite their geographically challenging state. University of Idaho administrators came up with one innovation: The Student Special.

Late in his life, Norman Maclean gained international acclaim for writing *A River Runs Through It*. Earlier, he had been more drawn to mountains than rivers—particularly Idaho's mountains. As a 17-year-old, he spent the summer of 1919 on a fire lookout in north-central Idaho. Day after day, he gazed in wonder upon vast expanses of mountains, "more mountains in all directions than I was ever to see again." They ran far into the distance, endless ridges matted with dark forests. "The mountains of Idaho, poems of geology stretching beyond any boundaries and seemingly even beyond the world," Maclean rhapsodized.[1]

Northern Idaho is a vast sea of mountains, broken only occasionally by lush prairies. They would eventually prove a boon to tourism officials—and Realtors selling property with breathtaking views. But those mountains—not to mention wild rivers and vast canyons—separated north Idaho from the south, isolating the residents of Idaho's panhandle from the rest of the state.

At the time Congress formally established Idaho's bizarre boundaries in the 1860s, few of its members had ever experienced anything like Idaho's craggy peaks. Fewer still had even seen the place they would name Idaho. Faced with urgent issues surrounding a bloody Civil War, they hastily set Idaho's territorial borders, in the process creating an abomination of a panhandle—spectacularly beautiful, but narrow, jagged, and disconnected from the rest of the state. Members of Congress conceived Idaho, then moved on to momentous national concerns. They left it to Idahoans to figure out how to make the place function.

Initially, it seemed north Idaho would do all right. William Wallace, the territory's first governor, proclaimed Lewiston the capital in 1863. Everything changed two years later when an acting governor confiscated the official territorial records and rode off with them to Boise, which has been the capital since. Was the capital stolen? Rightfully transferred? Take your pick, and whether an Idahoan lives north or south of the Salmon River usually determines their point of view. Regardless, northern Idaho residents learned a lesson when they lost the capital to the south. When delegates met in Boise in 1889 to write a constitution for the State of Idaho, northern representatives saw to it that the document spelled out the site of the new state's college. The University of Idaho would be permanently located in Moscow, protected by constitutional decree. No southern hijinks could displace it.

While northern Idaho gained the university, most of the state's people lived in the south—including most of its college-age students. Between the University of Idaho and that principal audience lay those endless ranges of mountains—not to mention rivers and canyons. University administrators tackled the dilemma of linking two disparate parts of a dissimilar state. They faced the same conundrum as generations of Idahoans who have attempted to create a working commonwealth. The geographically challenged members of Congress who set Idaho's strange borders had done Idahoans no favors.

Moscow's newspaper emphasized the challenge. "Geographical barriers make the trip from one part of the state to the other...embarrassing," concluded the editor of the *Daily Star-Mirror*. "To go from any point in south Idaho to a northern city it is necessary to travel through three states and consume much more time than would be used were there a more direct route." So, University of Idaho officials teamed with the Union Pacific Railroad to create the Student Special, a train connecting northern and southern Idaho—via Oregon and Washington.[2]

The train commenced in Pocatello. From there, the Student Special, made up of coach cars, baggage cars, dining car, and sleeper cars "of the latest type," rolled west, gathering more passengers at American Falls, Shoshone, Gooding, Bliss, Glenns Ferry, Mountain Home, Nampa, Caldwell, and Parma. Spur lines transported students from Idaho Falls, Twin Falls, and Boise to the main UP route. The Special crossed the border into Oregon. At Umatilla, the student cars decoupled and waited on a siding to connect with a "milk train" that would carry them through small eastern Washington towns before arriving at Moscow. Students beginning their journey in Pocatello would have covered 692 miles in a little more than 24 hours, roughly equivalent to traveling from New York City to Indianapolis.[3]

Other states ran trains transporting students to universities, but nothing on the scale of Idaho's Student Special. "It gives Idaho the dubious distinction of having the longest known route for a regular student train," noted geographer Benjamin Thomas, "a long trip for a student attending his 'local' state university." The Student Specials began rolling before World War I and operated until after World War II. They carried students to Moscow in the fall, to and from campus at Christmas, and returned them home in the spring. The train became "a well-established feature of the opening of the University each fall" and provided a lifetime of memories for those who rode. "It was a very exciting experience for all of us," recalled one.[4]

Still, it was a makeshift effort to connect two parts of a state that, logically, had no reason to exist inside the confines of one set of borders. Idaho's boundaries circumvent a rugged landscape of mountains, rivers, canyons, forests, and deserts. Much of Idaho's history is one of accommodating its burdensome borders. With ingenuity and resolve,

Idahoans have endeavored to create a unified state. That process would have been much easier if Idaho had more reasonable borders. But then, Idaho would not be Idaho had it matured without struggle.

Idahoans had virtually no say in the way their state took shape. Had they, they probably would have done things differently. But those decisions were made in places far away, by diplomats, politicians, and schemers. Truthfully, they made a mess of things, and Idaho, coping within its illogical confines, almost ceased to exist even before statehood arrived, a near casualty of its curious configuration. Those students who disembarked in Moscow on that sunny day in September were but one part of the puzzle, part of the long and ongoing story of Idahoans creatively attempting to piece together a workable state.

CHAPTER ONE

Rectangles on the Land

It is, admittedly, unusual to begin a book about Idaho with the French and Indian War. But that seems a good place to start this story, because that 18th-century conflict helped determine Idaho's borders—long before there was an Idaho. Understanding how Idaho got its boundaries is critical to understanding Idaho, for one can make a case that its peculiar borders have influenced Idaho's development more than any other factor in its history.

Look at a map of the western United States. Toss out California and Texas, which entered the union under unusual circumstances, and you have a bunch of rectangles. Some borders accommodate natural features, but the map of the West is essentially a vast expanse of box-like states. And then we have Idaho. What in the world happened here?

To unravel the answer requires some understanding of 18th-century North America. It is fitting that the story of how the nation got its most awkwardly shaped state begins with the continent's most inappropriately named war.

A reasonable person could assume that a conflict called the French and Indian War would have pitted French against Indians. Actually, it was combat between French and Indians on one side and British and Indians—albeit fewer of them—on the other. We could refer to this conflict as the Seven Years War, as Europeans do, except it lasted nine years in America. Notwithstanding its problematic nomenclature, the ramifications of this brutal war dramatically influenced American history, even in a place like Idaho—not yet a figment of anyone's imagination at the time.

The war, like most, began as a dispute over territory. In the 1750s, France claimed a vast tract of North America, from the eastern seacoast of Canada, south through the Great Lakes, and on to the Gulf of Mexico. England had chartered companies to establish colonies in America. Their land grants extended from the Atlantic Ocean to the Pacific. Thus, England claimed all the area south of French Canada and north of Spanish Florida—from sea to sea. England and France, in other words, both laid claim to the region between the Appalachian Mountains and the Mississippi River.

These conflicting claims did not much matter for a long time. Relatively few French citizens resided in North America, and British colonists confined themselves to the eastern seaboard. But as British settlers began traipsing to the west side of the Appalachian Mountains, conflicts occurred, beginning in 1754. What Americans called the French and Indian War bloodily ebbed and flowed until France and England signed the Treaty of Paris in 1763. The treaty granted Canada and the region between the Mississippi and Appalachians to England. In a nutshell, it ensured that, while French culture still thrives in parts of Canada and Louisiana, English language and values would dominate that region.

The French and Indian War saddled England with huge debts. When the British imposed a series of unpopular taxes on American colonists to help alleviate the indebtedness, it touched off an affair called the American Revolution.

The revolution would be immaterial to a story about Idaho's boundaries had the victorious Americans not found themselves the new proprietors of those formerly disputed lands between the Appalachians and the Mississippi. What was a young nation to do with all that extra country? As was often Americans' wont in those days, they assigned Thomas Jefferson the task of figuring things out.

As a consequence of the Revolutionary War, England ceded to America 400,000 square miles of land east of the Mississippi River. Several American states had claims on this land dating back to the colonial era. In 1783, Thomas Jefferson journeyed to Annapolis, Maryland, to represent Virginia in the Congress of the Confederation. All delegates to the Congress understood that the new nation had somehow to transform western lands into manageable jurisdictions. Beyond that, they disagreed on just who should create what order. Should existing states that retained claims on the territory decide that country's future? Land speculators? The nascent federal government? His congressional colleagues appointed Jefferson to devise a plan. Over the course of a few months, he conceived the fundamental foundation of American westward expansion.[1]

Jefferson insisted that existing states relinquish to the federal government all their claims to western lands. National policy would shape western expansion, not the whims of individual states. The land, he asserted, should eventually become new states. These would have the same relationship to the federal government as older ones and would pay their share of federal debts. There would be an orderly process of progressing from territorial status to statehood.

Jefferson also realized that the federal government needed to create geographical order. Surveyors should lay out the land in square grids, with precise north-south and east-west lines. One year later, Congress further refined this concept by establishing the system of dividing land into townships and sections. That became the nation's accepted system as it expanded west.

Another Jeffersonian concept of orderliness initially had less success. He proposed dividing the trans-Appalachian region into a series of territories that would eventually become states. The western boundaries of those lying along the Mississippi would meander with the river. But that was Jefferson's only concession to geography. He conceived other borders as straight lines, proposing a series of side-by-side rectangles stacked up like rows of boxes. When each rectangle filled with enough people, it would qualify for statehood. He gave the places classical-sounding names like Assenisipia and Metropotamia. We would today remember nothing of Jefferson's nod to the classics had he not also proposed naming two of them Michigania and Illinoia.

In May 1784, the Confederation Congress appointed Jefferson Minister to France. He sailed for Europe two months later. Congress approved much of what Jefferson had proposed about western lands, particularly his concept of the progression of frontier territories into states. But in his absence, Congress jettisoned his idea of neat, rectangular territories. Such a division, disregarding natural boundaries, would have produced jurisdictions "inconveniently divided by rivers, lakes and mountains, and many of them must...contain a large proportion of barren and unimprovable lands." Some would never enjoy a sufficient number of inhabitants to form a government and would exist "without laws and without order."[2]

Thomas Jefferson's vision of rectangular states went unrealized in the 18th century. It would gain new life in the 19th-century American West.

Few members of Congress had any knowledge of those western lands. But most had a concept that geography should help determine borders. Thus, the country ended up with interestingly shaped states in that region. They bore little resemblance to Jefferson's orderly boxes. But Jefferson's concept of neat rectangles reemerged as the United States expanded west of the Mississippi.

From the earliest days of America, the country has had a keen interest in the creation of state boundaries. The longest clause in the Articles of Confederation, the 1781 precursor to the United States Constitution, dealt with borders. The Articles granted to the Confederation Congress the authority of "last resort" in all boundary disputes. The Constitution, ratified six years later, gave the United States Congress power to admit new states to the union. Although the Constitution did not specifically assign Congress the right to establish the new states' borders, Congress assumed that authority by claiming sole jurisdiction to determine territorial boundaries. By the time western territories became states, Congress had already established their borders. So, in essence Congress held virtually all power over the creation of state borders.

As a result of the Louisiana Purchase, the War with Mexico, and various treaties, the United States in the first half of the 19th century gained unambiguous rights to western America. Congress now had on its hands more land requiring orderliness. Following the process Jefferson established, Congress would first divide this region into territories and then states—with the exception of Texas and California, which entered the union without first becoming territories. The 19th-century United States Congress had this in common with the 18th-century Congress of the Confederation: its members knew virtually nothing about the western lands they oversaw. The borders of western states often reflect that congressional bewilderment. As historian Herman Deutsch noted, "Few subjects offer greater opportunities to ponder the historical results of man's ignorance than does the history of boundary lines." Congress found straight-line borders a reasonable substitute for its lack of understanding of western geography. Rivers form a number of western state borders, and one boundary—between Idaho and Montana—runs along the crest of mountains. But straight lines predominate. Except for about 25 miles along the Rio Grande, all of New

Mexico's borders follow lines of latitude and longitude. The boundaries of Utah, Colorado, and Wyoming consist entirely of straight lines. Jefferson's affinity for boxes reached its apex in the latter two states, which are nearly perfect rectangles. Every state in the continental United States west of the Mississippi has some straight-line borders.[3]

"Congress had a predilection for symmetry when drawing Western boundaries," noted geographer Malcolm Comeaux. Not only did it pursue straight lines, it also sought to create states of approximately equal size. Kansas, Nebraska, and the two Dakotas are all the same height. Although slightly "taller" than those four, Colorado, Wyoming, and Montana are likewise the same distance from north to south. Washington, Oregon, Colorado, Wyoming, and the two Dakotas are the same width. If he could block out Idaho, Thomas Jefferson would be pleased with how Congress mapped the western United States.[4]

Straight lines were easier to plot on maps than marks adhering to natural features, particularly in the 19th-century American West. That region suffered for years from a paucity of accurately detailed maps showing geographic characteristics. Combined with a general congressional lack of knowledge of the region and the Jeffersonian goal of imposing order on a landscape, it becomes clear why most of the West resembles a conglomeration of rectangular boxes. But those strokes, so easily drawn on a flat map, usually defied the natural landscape, paying little heed to mountains, rivers, and valleys. Still, those lines proved critical to people living in the West and continue to be consequential today. As President—and historian—Woodrow Wilson noted, western states were "whimsically enough formed," having "joined mining communities with agricultural, the mountain with the plain, the ranch with the farm" leaving "neighbors ill at ease with one another."[5]

Much of the congressional decision-making over western borders took place when members of Congress could be excused for paying attention to more pressing issues. Take Idaho, for example. That territory came into existence during the darkest days of the Civil War. Members of Congress had more important matters to contemplate than the boundaries of a strangely named territory in a faraway place. Few members of Congress in the 1860s knew anything about that landscape. So, they were susceptible to influence by men who did know the area and could make convincing arguments for borders that would benefit them personally—but not so much the future residents of Idaho.

Idaho is a product of its time—a time of war and of ignorance of western geography, when Congress created a territory, and then a state, with borders that make very little sense. But Idaho is also a product of the time when Congress largely realized the Jeffersonian ideal of geometric symmetry. That seems an odd statement when discussing such a peculiarly shaped state. But paying closer attention to a map of Idaho reveals this. Three of its borders—north, south, and the boundary with Wyoming—are straight lines. A fourth, the border with Washington, is essentially a straight line, excepting a few squiggly miles on its southern end. The borders with Oregon and Montana incorporate both straight lines and geographic features. Regardless of its overall eccentric appearance, most of Idaho's boundaries are straight.

Despite this adherence to geometric lines, Idaho turned out— well, weird, essentially slapped together by a distracted Congress. Author Vardis Fisher called it a "geographic monstrosity." Michael Trinklein claimed, simply, "Idaho makes no sense," featuring regions that "go together about as well as peanut butter and jellyfish." Historians have agreed. "Idaho's odd shape [is the] result of perhaps the most counterintuitive state boundaries in the country," concluded Laura Woodworth-Ney. Idaho's borders defy "historical, geographical, cultural, and social logic," agreed Carlos Schwantes. They "met the criteria of political expediency only, and that may be about the same as saying [they] had no logic at all." All of which might be humorous if not for such serious aftereffects. As longtime Idaho State Historian Merle Wells wrote, "The choice of boundaries did much to decide what the future state would be like."[6]

Idaho's borders have roots in the French and Indian War, in early American diplomacy, and in a Congress that showed little interest in the repercussions of its boundary-drawing authority. The story of how Idaho got its strange shape is the tale of people with little knowledge of the place imposing boundaries and leaving it to Idaho residents to figure things out—which Idahoans have been attempting to accomplish since. It is a story of how famous Americans rarely associated with Idaho history—Thomas Jefferson, John Quincy Adams, Richard Rush, James K. Polk—had much more influence on Idaho's boundaries than did anyone who ever resided there. It is an account of international negotiations, high-stakes chicanery, and political compromise. Rarely is it a story of logic prevailing over irrationality.

CHAPTER TWO

1819
The Southern Border:
Nevada and Utah

At precisely 11:00 a.m. on Monday, February 22, 1819, Spanish Minister Plenipotentiary to the United States Luis de Onís arrived at a small house on the corner of C and Four-and-a-Half Streets in southwest Washington, DC. The dwelling lacked grandeur, much like the city itself. Washington, laid out on an extensive scale as a planned federal metropolis, had yet to fill in. Noted one observer, "Washington may be said to be rather the site of a city…than an actual city." Some modest houses stood on Four-and-a-Half Street, and American Secretary of State John Quincy Adams had rented one. He resided there more for its proximity to the Capitol than its amenities. Adams complained of spiders in the bedroom causing nights of "exquisite torture." His valet had recently "killed a brownish snake two feet long" on the staircase. Still, on this day, that modest rental house hosted history.[1]

Onís and Adams knew each other well. For two years, they had negotiated the futures of their respective countries. Onís walked to Adams's house to sign a treaty that would transform North America. The event fittingly occurred on George Washington's birthday. Twenty-five years earlier, President Washington had appointed Adams ambassador to the Netherlands, predicting Adams would one day "be at the head of [America's] diplomatic corps." This Adams had achieved, becoming secretary of state in 1817.[2]

Reporting on the treaty signed that day in Adams's house, a local newspaper called it "an important day [that] will mark a great era in the history of the United States." John Q. Adams thought it "perhaps the most important day of my life." And Pulitzer Prize-winning historian Samuel Flagg Bemis proclaimed it "the greatest diplomatic victory won by a single individual in the history of the United States."[3]

The treaty provided borders for distant lands thousands of miles to the west. Neither Adams nor Onís had seen that country. It was little-settled, vast, and wild. But the treaty they sealed had repercussions that reverberate centuries later. Today, the boundary they approved to separate Spain from the United States forms the northern borders of three states in the American West, and the southern borders of two others—including a place called Idaho.

Fifty-five years before Pilgrims ate Thanksgiving dinner in Plymouth, Massachusetts, Spaniards had their own feast of thanks at St. Augus-

tine, Florida, the first European city in North America. Seventeen years
before American Robert Gray "discovered" the Columbia River, Spaniards had already located that Great River of the West. So extensive were
Spain's North American holdings that, at the end of the 18th century,
that country claimed virtually everything west of the Mississippi River.
But by 1817, its control over that far-flung expanse had grown tenuous.

At its peak, Spain's empire was as glorious as any the world has
known. It ruled the seas, sent Columbus on his journeys, and flour-
ished with untold wealth gained after brutally vanquishing native
people in the Americas. But in 1805, British admiral Horatio Nelson essentially destroyed Spain's naval fleet at the Battle of Trafalgar,
hamstringing Spanish efforts to control its sweeping domain. Years of
disorder followed as Spain suffered a protracted civil war. Distracted
by political and military tangles at home, Spain also experienced revolt
in its American colonies, most famously by Simon Bolivar, who led
Venezuela, Colombia, Ecuador, Peru, Panama, and his namesake
Bolivia to independence.

Spain was so weakened that, in 1803, it learned only second-hand
that France had sold the vast Louisiana Territory to the United States.
Spain had just ceded that land to France three years earlier in a treaty
supposedly prohibiting France from transferring it to any country
other than Spain. But Spain could only meekly protest the sale. When
President Thomas Jefferson sent Meriwether Lewis and William Clark
to explore the new territory, Spain objected and dispatched four expeditions to intercept them, claiming they were trespassing on Spanish
land. The pursuit proved so ineffectual that Lewis and Clark did not
know they were being chased.[4]

Though Spain feebly protested, Jefferson's Corps of Discovery
could legally justify its exploration of the Louisiana Purchase, which, at
least as far as the United States was concerned, was now clearly American land. When Lewis led a small advance party up a gentle slope over
Lemhi Pass on August 12, 1805, they became the first Euro-Ameri-
cans to reach Idaho—the last of the 50 states entered by whites. And
from that point on, they journeyed into contested territory, claimed by
several countries. Even discounting the disputed Louisiana, Spain still
legally claimed enormous parts of North America, including Florida,
Texas, California—and the Pacific Northwest that Lewis and Clark
were about to traverse.

In the early 19th century, Spain claimed vast tracts of the American West, including the Oregon Country, which encompassed future Idaho. Great Britain, Russia, and the United States also claimed that disputed region.

Lewis and Clark successfully proceeded through that contested territory, and in 1806 returned triumphantly to St. Louis. While Americans celebrated, Spanish officials recognized the expedition as a serious threat to their western claims. Some encouraged Spain to construct a military post on the Columbia River to thwart future American ventures. But the weakened country proved incapable of such a show of force. Having limited military options, Spanish leaders contemplated the best way of retaining some control of its expansive North American hinterland. Diplomacy provided the best opportunity. In 1809, Spain sent one of its most respected envoys, Luis de Onís, to the United States. But America—remaining neutral in the ongoing Spanish Civil War—refused to acknowledge him. Onís lingered in Washington for six years until the United States finally recognized him in December 1815.[5]

Even after that formal recognition, Onís had to wait out the presidential election of 1816. James Monroe's victory clarified the presidency, but Onís still did not know Monroe's selection for secretary of state, the man with whom Onís would ultimately negotiate. Monroe's choice would be consequential—for Onís as well as for the new cabinet member himself. The office had become a stepping-stone to the presidency. Thomas Jefferson, James Madison, and Monroe all ascended to the nation's highest office after serving as secretary of state. Monroe's nominee could well expect to become a future presidential contender. The president's ultimate selection surprised many. But it made political sense. Critics lambasted Monroe as just another member of the Virginia cabal that had a stranglehold on the presidency. Four of the country's first five presidents came from that state—a streak interrupted only by John Adams of Massachusetts. "I have thought it advisable to select a person from the [north]eastern states," Monroe wrote to Jefferson. He chose as his chief foreign policy advisor President Adams's son, John Quincy. The decision made excellent sense for more than political reasons. No American had more diplomatic experience than John Q. Adams.[6]

The 49-year-old Adams had already served as a United States senator, American minister to the Netherlands, Prussia, Russia, and Great Britain, and had negotiated the Treaty of Ghent, ending the War of 1812 between England and the United States. Still, as a former secretary of state himself, Monroe seemed determined to make his own foreign policy decisions. Indeed, he had little respect for any members of his cabinet and delegated little authority. Likewise, Adams had negligible esteem for Monroe, believing him a career politician of limited intellectual acuity. That Adams spectacularly succeeded in his new post despite these handicaps is remarkable.[7]

The short, bald, stout, and perpetually rumpled Adams took his oath of office in September 1817. He found his cramped State Department office, inside an unassuming wooden building four blocks from the White House, in shambles. Towering piles of documents lay scattered about. Some official United States records had simply disappeared. He had worked at European ministerial offices that bustled with servants, couriers, messengers, and assistants. Adams enjoyed none of that, inheriting a poorly funded State Department that supported a handful of clerks, a maintenance laborer, and a night watchman. From here, Adams was to maintain correspondence with more than 100 consuls abroad, meet with foreign ministers, issue passports, record the names of all foreign passengers arriving in the country, and supervise the patent office. It was a nearly impossible task, even for the tireless Adams—who took much work home to that spider-infested house on Four-and-a-Half Street. Yet from that cluttered State Department office and the confines of his modest rental house, Adams crafted some of the most consequential diplomacy in American history. None proved more significant than his mediation with Luis de Onís.[8]

Adams brought to those negotiations a vision of America's future tied to western expansion. Adams, like his father's political adversary Thomas Jefferson, believed America's extension to the Pacific was "destined by Divine Providence." The continent would be "peopled by one nation, speaking one language." For his part, Luis de Onís viewed his task as doing all within his power to thwart that American expansion, retaining as much Spanish land as possible. That both men would, in their ways, succeed is testimony to the talent of those two experienced negotiators.[9]

Onís could be excused if he believed his negotiations with the new secretary of state would focus on Florida, long a point of contention between the two nations. And for a year the two men did concentrate on Florida, with long, erudite, history-laden letters flowing back and forth. Spain's claims to that region dated to 1513, when Juan Ponce de León sailed to the place he called La Florida, "land of flowers." Three centuries later, the over-extended Spanish monarchy had to devote its meager resources to thwarting growing insurrections in South America. It could neither defend Florida nor meet its treaty commitments to restrain Indian attacks upon American citizens living across the border in Georgia. After months of fruitless negotiating, Adams proposed that Spain simply cede Florida to the United States. Spain, he said, retained "nothing but nominal possession" of that land. But Spain was not yet ready for such decisive action ending its long legacy in Florida, and Onís withdrew from the negotiations in a huff. Adams took advantage of that break to raise the stakes. He now contemplated acquiring even more land from Spain—in the far west.[10]

When Onís returned to the talks, he found that Adams had shifted his emphasis to Louisiana. Spain differed with the United States on Louisiana's western border. Many Americans believed the purchase included Texas. Onís disagreed. Adams and Onís labored for months over just where the Louisiana border lay. Those discussions also stalemated. Then, in October 1818, Adams introduced a bold new demand.

He now sought a border between Spain and the United States that stretched well beyond Louisiana—wherever its disputed boundary might lie. Adams pursued a border all the way to the Pacific Ocean, a line that would split in half Spain's far west holdings. Adams's bombshell overwhelmed Onís. "What you add respecting the extension of the [border] beyond the Missouri…to the Pacific Ocean exceeds by its magnitude and its transcendency, all former demands and pretensions stated by the United States," an astonished Onís wrote Adams.[11]

Yet Onís recognized his dilemma. Spain was too weak to defend its territory. Though infuriated by Adams's ultimatum, he understood his only option was to get the best boundary feasible. "If his majesty can't get the support of any Power and hasn't sufficient forces to make war on this country," he wrote to Madrid, "then I think it would be best not to delay making the best settlement possible." The response from Madrid recognized the inevitable: Just get a boundary "as far north as possible," preserving as much of Spain's North American empire as attainable.[12]

Adams proposed a border starting at the Gulf of Mexico, then stair-stepping north and west along rivers to the southern border of the current state of Wyoming. From there, his boundary would extend straight west along the 41st parallel to the Pacific. Onís countered with a proposed boundary line much farther north and much less straight, following the meandering Snake and Columbia Rivers. The two men haggled for months but could not reach a compromise.

Preoccupied with rebellions in South America, the Spanish government gave Onís authority to settle the boundary dispute the best he could. Backtracking from his initial proposal of a boundary along the Snake and Columbia, Onís next suggested a border a bit farther south—but one that would retain Spanish claims over much of the Pacific Northwest. Adams scoffed.

President James Monroe grew increasingly impatient with the prolonged negotiations. To him, the main prize would always be Florida. He cared much less about the West than Adams. When Onís made another offer—proposing to draw the boundary at the 43rd parallel rather than the 41st—Monroe called together his cabinet. The group unanimously agreed to accept the new offer—with one exception. John Quincy Adams insisted on holding out. Monroe agreed to allow Adams some time to pursue his favored position but limited his parameters. If he could not quickly get a better deal, then settle at the 43rd parallel. Adams fumed about Spain niggling over a "couple degrees of wilderness which never will or can be of any value to her." But he recognized he could not hold out forever.[13]

The negotiations now centered on a relatively narrow slice of an immense landscape. The visions of Adams and Onís differed not over rivers, ports, landmarks, or resources, but rather an unknown wilderness separating two parallels of latitude. As far as they knew, the land in question had little value. Each just wanted to get as much as he could. Finally, on February 15, 1819, Onís suggested that they simply split the difference and draw the border at the 42nd parallel. Adams agreed. Both men by this time were exhausted, Adams writing he "became nauseous" he was so weary. And so, Adams and Onís settled on a border that possessed little logic other than allowing two tired diplomats to proceed to other matters. But their arbitrary compromise had enduring significance in the West.[14]

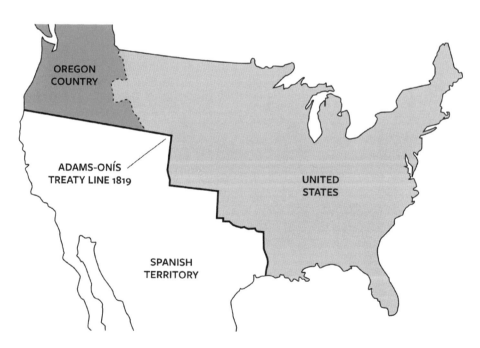

With the Adams-Onís Treaty of 1819, Spain relinquished all claims to the Oregon Country. The 42nd parallel, separating Spain and America, eventually became the southern boundary of Idaho.

To reach the compromise, Spain relinquished to the United States all "rights, claims, and pretensions" to large segments of its western empire, including all of what became the states of Idaho, Washington, and Oregon. Adams also proved willing to relinquish extensive property to reach a deal, trading America's claims to Texas to gain the Pacific Northwest. To many, including some in President Monroe's cabinet, it seemed a dubious exchange. But American rights to Texas were problematic. Forfeiting questionable claims there to gain a border to the Pacific would make America a transcontinental nation, something Adams believed essential to the country's future.[15]

Adams won the prize he sought. Although the settlement the two men reached is commonly known as the Adams-Onís Treaty, it could better be called the Transcontinental Treaty. America had some prior claims to the Northwest through the explorations of people like Robert Gray and Lewis and Clark and the fur-trading outpost established by John Jacob Astor's company at Fort Astoria. But this treaty lent much more validity to America's hold on the Northwest.

While Florida garnered the most attention upon the treaty's signing, ultimately the acquisition of Spanish claims in the West proved equally, if not more, valuable to the nation's future. The treaty's straight-line boundary at the 42nd parallel, from the Rocky Mountains to the Pacific, is still very evident on any map of the country. When Congress divided the West into states, that compromise 19th century international boundary became the southern border of Idaho and Oregon, and the northern border of Utah, Nevada, and California.

And so it was that Luis de Onís marched to John Quincy Adams's modest rental house on George Washington's birthday in 1819. There the two men signed a treaty that would, 71 years later, determine the southern border of the new state of Idaho. Adams, who understood the importance of America stretching from Atlantic to Pacific, labeled the treaty "a great epocha in our history." Just to be sure future Americans recognized who deserved credit for acquiring this land for the United States, he proudly—and accurately—asserted that the concept of obtaining Spanish rights to lands touching the Pacific "as my own." When negotiations bogged down on Florida cession details and Louisiana's borders, Adams initiated a bold new element to the talks. He bulldoggedly held to the vision of a transcontinental America despite Spanish displeasure and tepid presidential support. And Adams won the day.[16]

John Quincy Adams did follow in the tradition of Jefferson, Madison, and Monroe. After serving as secretary of state, he became America's sixth president. His official White House biography states he "was one of America's great Secretaries of State…obtaining from Spain the cession of the Floridas." That, of course, is true, but belies the full significance of his Transcontinental Treaty. An equally important consequence of those long negotiations was the first treaty acknowledging American title to the Pacific Coast.[17]

One can search the indexes of many books about Idaho and find no mention of John Quincy Adams. Indeed, one could probably search them all and not find that entry. That is unfortunate. Not only as secretary of state, but also later as president and as a member of the U.S. House of Representatives, this quintessential Northeasterner never wavered in his belief that the nation's future lay in the West. Until he died, he continued to advocate for unfettered United States control of the Oregon Country.

Adams's steadfast efforts with Spain gave the future state of Idaho its southern border. It would be good for Idahoans of the 21st century to recognize this 19th century man's achievement in shaping their state. He is not a bad choice for respect. As president, he championed the then-unpopular concept of a federal role in advancing the arts and sciences. As a member of Congress, he championed the creation of the Smithsonian Institution and adamantly opposed slavery. He nearly single-handedly struck down the gag rule that prohibited debates about slavery in the House of Representatives, and he successfully argued the Amistad case before the U.S. Supreme Court, freeing the enslaved people who had revolted on board that slave ship and allowing them to return to their African homes. Idahoans could do much worse than elevating this person to an iconic position in their state's archive of significant historical figures.

Charles Francis Adams Jr. certainly appreciated his grandfather's dedication to creating western opportunities. Although John Quincy Adams died before there was an Idaho, his grandson knew the place well. "I regard Idaho as the most promising field of development,"

Charles Francis Adams Jr. wrote in 1887. Then president of the Union Pacific Railroad, he envisioned railway expansion there. Adams headed the UP for only a few years, but as a highly successful businessman he never lost his enthusiasm for Idaho and the Pacific Northwest.[18]

In 1896, he and other entrepreneurs organized the Lewiston Water & Power Company. That business brought irrigation to a piece of flat land across the Snake River from Lewiston, in the State of Washington. Adams and his partners called the place Vineland. Here they envisioned robust vineyards, verdant orchards, and prosperous family farms. The company later platted a nearby community it originally named Concord, after the Massachusetts city where Adams owned property. But Adams, a man with a deep sense of history, proposed changing the name to Clarkston, Washington—an appropriate companion for nearby Lewiston, Idaho—both named for the explorers who had passed through the valley in 1805 and 1806. Adams's company built the first bridge connecting those twin cities.

As Adams's business interests expanded, his two sons, Henry and John, moved to Lewiston in 1899. They built a beautiful home on 450 acres their father had purchased. It overlooked the family's private polo field, with expansive views of the Snake River below. John stayed only briefly, but Henry remained for years, overseeing the family's varied business interests from the Adams Building on Lewiston's Main Street.

Charles Francis Adams Jr.—like thousands of others who ventured to Idaho and the Northwest—caught the vision of his grandfather. That region, the elder Adams insisted, would one day become part of a nation spanning a continent, providing opportunity for untold generations of Americans. He proved to be correct.

John Quincy Adams's diplomacy created the southern border of the future state where his grandson and great-grandsons would one day reside. Along with a good friend—and a political adversary—he would also play a prominent role in establishing Idaho's northern border.

Border Story

FRANKLIN

John Melish, a Scottish orphan born in 1771, moved to the United States in 1810. Fascinated with his new home, he set out to explore. Melish wrote about his wanderings in *Travels in the United States of America,* published in 1812. His work included eight maps. "I have always considered books of travels to be very defective when unaccompanied by maps," he explained. Thus launched his career as one of America's foremost mapmakers. Melish moved to Philadelphia and started the country's first map-publishing company. In 1816, he issued his *Map of the United States with the Contiguous British and Spanish Possessions,* one of the most significant of early American cartographic works. Melish incorporated the reports of Lewis and Clark and Zebulon Pike to determine, as best he could, the contours of the still virtually unknown American West. Even then, he understood so little of that vast area that he simply labeled much of it "unknown country." Melish updated his map in 1818. As Luis de Onís and John Quincy Adams negotiated the future of America, they often had before them Melish's large, three-foot by five-foot, 1818 map. It proved so essential that the Adams-Onís Treaty officially refers to it. After describing the boundary that would separate Spain from the United States, the treaty notes the border will follow geographic references "as laid down in Melish's Map of the United States."[1]

Just two months after Onís and Adams signed their treaty in February 1819, Melish revised his map. It became the first to demark the new boundaries determined by that treaty. Melish drew a straight line from the Arkansas River to the Pacific Ocean, representing the border along the 42nd parallel. The boundary seems obvious on the map. On the ground, it proved to be a bit trickier determining just where it lay.

It was not surprising that American trappers wandered back and forth over the 42nd parallel without recognizing it—or even paying much attention. "None of the mountain men knew where the vague abstraction, the boundary line, really ran," noted historian Dale

Morgan. "Nor did they care." Americans began holding rendezvous in the 1820s. At these raucous affairs, trappers traded furs and replenished supplies. In 1826, they held their rendezvous in the Cache Valley, south of the 42nd parallel in what was then Mexican territory, after that country had secured its independence from Spain and acquired Spanish holdings in North America. If Mexican officials knew of the trespass, they said nothing. The following year, trappers met at Bear Lake, which straddles the parallel. This time Mexico protested. The Americans had slipped south of the line again and Mexico demanded a formal American apology. The United States refused. "Upon examining Melish's Map of North America," the American minister to Mexico replied, it appeared that the Americans had not trespassed. Nothing more came of the protest, but the American minster was wrong. The 1827 Bear Lake rendezvous took place well south of the 42nd parallel, illustrating the difficulty of determining just where borders, so neatly traced on maps, actually lay. Decades later, Mormon settlers encountered a similar dilemma.[2]

When Brigham Young led members of the Church of Jesus Christ of Latter-day Saints into the Salt Lake Valley in July 1847, he knew they were intruding on Mexican territory. But Mexico was at war with the United States, so Young did not worry much about the encroachment. Mexico had greater concerns than religious pioneers trespassing on their far-northern holdings. Some Mormons believed they should establish an independent nation. The time seemed opportune, with the United States and Mexico distracted by war. By 1849, the United States had defeated Mexico. The country the Mormons settled was now part of America, and Mormon officials opted instead to seek American statehood. They petitioned Congress to admit the State of Deseret. A sprawling landmass, it included all of present-day Utah and Nevada, along with parts of Idaho, Oregon, Wyoming, Colorado, New Mexico, Arizona, and California. A proposed sanctuary for a people long persecuted, it derived its borders from natural geographic features, referencing a map published in 1848. That map, based upon

John Fremont's explorations, filled in many of the geographic features missing from Melish's earlier works. The northern border of Deseret ignored the 42nd parallel, instead following ridgelines that separated the Columbia and Great Basin river drainages.

The State of Deseret proposal reached Congress just as it wrestled with several demands for territorial or statehood status in the West. Texas, New Mexico, California, and Oregon also vied for attention. Congress did not totally ignore the request for Deseret but envisioned it instead as the Territory of Utah. Members of Congress expressed skepticism about the accuracy of Fremont's map. Rather than adhering to his geographic contours when creating Utah Territory in 1850, they chose to incorporate straight lines of latitude for the southern and northern borders—the latter being the long-established 42nd parallel. Downsized from Deseret, Utah Territory was still enormous, including all of today's Utah, most of Nevada, and parts of Colorado and Wyoming. It would shrink considerably in coming years, but the 42nd parallel boundary, established by Adams and Onís, would hold.[3]

That straight line paid no heed to natural features. As a result, Bear Lake—the site of the 1827 rendezvous—was eventually split between two states, Utah and Idaho. So was the fertile Cache Valley, the agricultural breadbasket of the Mormon domain.

Brigham Young grew up in a poor farming family. He appreciated fertile ground, and he recognized Cache Valley's potential. "No other valley in the territory is equal to this," asserted the LDS Church president in 1860. "That has been my opinion ever since I first saw this valley." Young hoped to fill Cache Valley "with Saints and not rowdies—not with horse thieves, murderers and rioters." So, he dispatched men to explore the best places to establish communities of upstanding Mormon families. One scouting expedition reported on a favorable site at the valley's northern extremity, a promising place to build a town. In April 1860, Young selected 13 families to settle there. They laid out a village, distributed town lots, constructed cabins side-by-side to form a fortress, planted crops, dug irrigation ditches, and named the place Franklin, after a Mormon apostle.[4]

Brigham Young knew the Mormon colonists he sent north would be running close to the 42nd parallel. So, in June 1855, he ventured out of Salt Lake with a large party to determine just where the northern boundary of Utah lay. Latter-day Saint Apostle Orson Pratt, a talented mathematician and scientist, guided the expedition. Based on Pratt's astrological observations, Young instructed his party to erect a stone at the 42nd parallel. They chiseled a "U" on one side, representing Utah Territory, and an "O" on the other for Oregon, for today's Idaho was then part of that territory. They dug some trenches around the obelisk and retuned to Salt Lake with "the territorial line between Utah [and] Oregon determined."[5]

It is probably not too surprising that those Franklin settlers of 1860 managed to miss Brigham Young's solitary stone. His "official" demarcation could be easily overlooked. Even had they stumbled across it, they would have had a difficult time knowing just where the boundary line extended from that lone marker. And so, as it turned out, they established Franklin about one mile north of the 42nd parallel. Unwittingly, they had just established the first town in what became Idaho. But for several years, the residents of Franklin believed they lived in Utah.

"The founding settlers of Franklin knew they were bumping the... border...when they staked out their town," noted one historian. "But their surveys—admittedly crude—convinced them that they were in Utah." Brigham Young sent out more Saints to establish more towns—receiving no objections from Oregon territorial officials about the possibility that they had crossed into that territory.[6]

But before long, people began suspecting they had passed over the border. "The people...need a surveyor," observed Young in 1864, one year after the formation of Idaho Territory. He recognized that some of his colonists had no doubt crossed the line. "As to whether we are in Utah Territory or Idaho Territory, I think we are now in Idaho," he proclaimed at one meeting of settlers. Idaho legislators agreed. They implored Congress to survey the boundary. "Great difficulties have arisen in administering the laws, and collecting the public revenue, in that portion of our territory bordering upon the territory of Utah," they wrote, "in consequence of our southern boundary line being unsurveyed and unknown."[7]

In 1864, Idaho legislators established Oneida County, which included the northern reaches of Cache Valley. Two years later, Oneida County commissioners ordered their assessor to "place under his assessment roll all the taxable property in the town of Franklin and other settlements lying north of the supposed...boundary line." But they equivocated: The "assessor may omit the collection of...taxes... until he is satisfied regarding the southern boundary line." No one yet knew its exact location.[8]

By the late 1860s, many Mormon settlers realized they had likely established towns in Idaho. But in the absence of an official survey determining the 42nd parallel's location, they continued to live as Utah residents. They had little incentive to become Idahoans, a territory then awash in Mormon harassment. Though Idaho's anti-Mormon bigotry would peak two decades later with passage of the Idaho Test Oath that disenfranchised most Latter-day Saint Church members, it ran virulently in the 1860s as well. The Oneida County sheriff proved the case. The LDS Church, he thundered in 1865, "has lawlessly passed the limits of its own corrupt jurisdiction and dared to pollute the sacred soil of Idaho.... This, however, will not continue. The 'institution,' if allowed to exist at all, shall coil its slimy folds, within its own territorial lines, obtaining sanction from its own corrupt legislation." Small wonder Mormon settlers, though suspecting they had ventured into Idaho, clung to Utah jurisdiction as long as they could. They would "wait until the parallel was finally marked and then adjust."[9]

Mormon pioneers continued pushing north. Idaho officials proved powerless to enforce laws while the official boundary line remained in doubt. Though many Mormon settlers suspected they had ventured north of the border, the residents of Franklin, located far south of most of the newer LDS colonies, genuinely believed they resided in Utah. But it was clear to everyone that the two territories needed a verifiable boundary.

Ideally, surveyors would have marked the 42nd parallel much earlier. The Adams-Onís Treaty of 1819 not only defined the parallel as the boundary between the United States and Spain, but also required the countries to "fix this line with more precision, and to place the landmarks which shall designate exactly the limits of both nations." Surveying was to begin in 1820. That would have saved a lot of frustration for those Franklin pioneers. But international politics overwhelmed the good intentions of Onís and Adams. When Mexico gained independence from Spain, it acquired Spain's lands in the Southwest. The United States now had a boundary with a different country. The nations agreed on the 42nd parallel separating them, but relations between the two grew increasingly heated, surveying was postponed, and finally they found themselves at war in the 1840s. The treaty ending the Mexican-American war gave America title to most of the current western United States. The American government now had little immediate incentive to survey the 42nd parallel, since it was now an internal affair, no longer an international boundary. That worked well until Congress started designating that line as the border between territories. People began settling in those territories—and had no way of determining in just what jurisdiction they had settled. It was time for a survey.[10]

In 1871, the General Land Office hired Daniel George Major to supervise surveying of the Utah-Idaho border. Born in Ireland, Major immigrated to the United States as a toddler in the 1830s. He graduated from Georgetown, became a surveyor, and had previously run boundary lines in Texas and Oregon. His work garnered accolades from the commissioner of the General Land Office who commended his "capacity and faithfulness." For the Utah-Idaho survey, Major hired a crew of 11 men, including his brother John and several axemen and packers. They began surveying in August 1871. At the southeast corner of Idaho Territory—where it met Utah and Wyoming—Major deposited a "glazed white earthen bottle" beneath an eight-foot post surrounded by a pile of stones. From this essential starting point, Major chained the 42nd parallel due west for 153 miles. The survey party left mounds of dirt, small stones, and wooden posts at regular intervals to designate the border. They wanted these markers to last. At one point Major noted that he had "sunk [a] post to within a foot of its top to prevent cattle from rubbing against it." Major completed his work in October, and the General Land Office accepted his report in February 1872. The 42nd parallel between Idaho and Utah had finally been located. Or so people thought.[11]

Daniel Major marked many boundary lines in the West, not all of them accurately. Major "had a difficult time holding an accurate 42nd parallel course." Hired to survey that parallel, which also marked the boundary between California and Oregon, his line "deviated from the 42nd as much as a half mile on either side of the parallel." In the 1980s, the California Attorney General threatened a lawsuit after discovering Oregon claimed 31,000 acres of land that rightfully belonged to California. He balked when California found it had more than 20,000 acres of Oregon. The two states decided just to let Major's wavering line stand.[12]

Major had similar problems hewing the 42nd parallel in Idaho. He got off poorly by setting his crucial starting point more than a half-mile off course. As he continued west, he made more than a half-dozen significant errors. Generally, Idaho gained land at Utah's expense. The "Idaho" town of Strevell, for example, existed for most of the 20th century with a school, hotel, warehouses, and shops, its citizens voting as Idahoans and paying taxes in that state. When modern highways bypassed the community in the 1970s, the last residents exited. Two decades later, modern cartographers calculated that Strevell had, all along, been located in Utah.[13]

Even with Major's inaccuracy, Idaho and Utah finally had a marked border. With the conclusion of Major's survey, the residents of Franklin—along with Ovid, St. Charles, Paris, and some other Mormon outposts—suddenly had sure evidence they lived in Idaho. That territory gained a few thousand residents overnight. It also gained a few deceased residents—graves of people purportedly buried in Utah. Hugh Moon died a year before Major's crew ran its line. A devout Mormon, Brigham Young had sent him north to help colonize the Cache Valley. Moon wished to be buried in Utah. His family honored his request, carrying his body far enough south they believed they were surely in Utah, where they buried him on a hillside. Major's survey determined Moon in fact rests eternally in Idaho—just a few yards north of the border.[14]

Though Major's survey had flaws, it has served as the official boundary between Utah and Idaho since 1872. Still, it took some getting used to, especially for Mormon families accustomed to living under Utah laws. Charles Rich, sent by Brigham Young to establish towns east of Franklin, lived in nearby Paris, another community that turned out to be in Idaho, and yet continued to serve in the Utah legislature into the mid-1870s. His son Joseph resided across the street—and served in the Idaho legislature. Utah officials held out hope that Franklin and other Mormon border towns might one day be "returned" to Utah. When petitioning Congress for statehood in 1872, Utah legislators sought to regain control of the northern Cache Valley, requesting Congress to allow the area to "become a part of this State." Congress refused to act. Utah did not become a state until 1896, and by then officials had given up on annexing land north of the 42nd parallel.[15]

On February 16, 1872, the residents of Franklin, hugging the 42nd parallel, and the inhabitants of Pierce City, more than 350 miles away on the forks of Orofino Creek in north-central Idaho, awoke to a new reality. The previous day, the Commissioner of the General Land Office had accepted Daniel Major's survey report, thereby establishing the border between Idaho and Utah.

Pierce City had emerged in the late fall of 1860, shortly after Elias Pierce, for whom the first residents named the town, discovered gold nearby, setting off the chain of events that led to Idaho becoming a territory three years later. The town boomed quickly, a hodge-podge of plank-sided stores, taverns, hotels, and cabins constructed haphazardly wherever a builder could find an open piece of ground. As the diggings played out, miners moved on, and most business owners followed. Still, a few residents remained in 1872. Probably none of them had heard about Daniel Major's survey, nor would they have cared. They were separated from the people of Franklin by multiple ranges of jagged mountains, miles of whitewater rivers, and a chasm of cultural differences. But in 1872, the residents of Pierce were about to lose status because of Major.

The first residents of Franklin arrived in the spring of 1860, a few months before miners set up camp at Pierce. Though their community also had a rustic feel, it possessed an orderliness Pierce lacked, its cabins erected in neat rows, its town lots laid out in a grid. But they had this in common with the northern town: The residents of Franklin were just as unaware of Pierce as Pierce townspeople were of Franklin.

In accepting Major's survey report, the General Land Office Commissioner noted that "several towns and settlements...which had previously been under the jurisdiction of Utah" now found themselves in Idaho, including Franklin. Overnight, something changed for the residents of that Mormon outpost. Now, rather than being ordinary citizens of just one of dozens of towns founded by Mormons in the 19th-century Great Basin, they discovered their uniqueness. They were now residents of Idaho's oldest city, having beaten Pierce for that honor by about six months. Although the 1872 dwellers of Franklin would have preferred to have found themselves on the Utah side of the border, their 21st-century descendants proudly proclaim their elevated status. As the historical marker in their city center notes, they live in "Idaho's Oldest Town."[16]

CHAPTER THREE

1846
The Northern Border:
Canada

John Quincy Adams spent his life emulating the lofty accomplishments of his father, John Adams, a signer of the Declaration of Independence and second president of the United States. The younger Adams lived up to his father's legacy, becoming a congressman, a United States senator, secretary of state, and president himself. His good friend Richard Rush faced similar familial expectations. His father, Benjamin Rush, America's foremost physician, also signed the Declaration of Independence. And he played a critical role in America's most famous western exploration.

Before Thomas Jefferson sent Meriwether Lewis west, he first directed him to Philadelphia. There Lewis met Benjamin Rush to receive medical advice. Rush outlined the procedures Lewis should follow to ensure the safety of his Corps of Discovery. Lewis proved a quick study. Only one member of the expedition died on that perilous journey. Rush provided Lewis with something else perhaps less helpful in sustaining the Corps: 50 dozen laxative tablets known as "Dr. Rush's Bilious Pills," or more descriptively, "Thunder Clappers." Containing a healthy dose of mercury, their effectiveness as a curative is dubious. But archaeologists owe a debt to Dr. Rush. His mercury-laden capsules have allowed them to track the route of the Corps of Discovery by locating latrines along the way.[1]

Like John Quincy Adams, Benjamin Rush's son Richard also lived up to his family's promise. He became one of America's distinguished diplomats, U.S. attorney general, and a vice presidential candidate when John Q. Adams unsuccessfully ran for reelection as president in 1828. Richard Rush shared Quincy Adams's vision of western expansion. They both believed the Pacific Northwest—the land Lewis and Clark explored—rightfully belonged to the United States. Indeed, had Adams and Rush had their way, Idaho's northern border would have been established much earlier than it was, virtually simultaneously with the creation of its southern border at the 42nd parallel. Instead, it would be nearly three decades before a different president, James K. Polk, signed a treaty officially marking the northern boundary of the future state of Idaho. Those two good friends, Adams and Rush, sons of the nation's founders, lived to see that day. The name Idaho had yet to be invented, but in 1846, through the efforts of Adams, Rush, and Polk, that future state received its second border.

John Quincy Adams sat at his desk in the cramped secretary of state's office and contemplated a country extending to the Pacific Ocean. Attaining that goal would require skillful negotiations with three nations that, like the United States, also claimed the Oregon Country. He personally dealt with Spain, ending its rights to the American Northwest via the Adams-Onís Treaty of 1819. Russia could wait; it had little interest in pressing its claims south of what would become the State of Alaska. That left England. America's rival in two wars posed a more complicated problem for Adams.

In 1814, Quincy Adams had led the American delegation that negotiated the Treaty of Ghent, ending the War of 1812 between the United States and England. That treaty left many issues unresolved, most particularly the border between the United States and British Canada. Diplomats from the two countries agreed to resolve that complex question later. "Later" arrived just as Adams began his tenure as secretary of state.

It took some time for Adams, then serving as minister to Great Britain, to receive notice that President James Monroe had appointed him secretary of state. Word had to travel to Adams by boat, then he had to close his affairs and sail to America. Monroe knew just the person to fill the State Department void while Adams made his way home—Richard Rush. When Adams finally arrived in Washington, DC, in the fall of 1817 to replace Rush, Monroe appointed Rush to take Adams's place as minister to Great Britain. He would negotiate those items from the Treaty of Ghent that had been left until later.

On November 19, 1817, Rush boarded the new man-of-war *Franklin* and sailed from Annapolis for England. He arrived in Portsmouth one month later and made his way to London. Though Great Britain had recently been an adversary, he found much to appreciate about English society. "No language can express the emotion which almost every American feels when he first touches the shores of Europe," he wrote. "This feeling must have a special increase, if it be the case of a citizen of the United States going to England.... In the nursery he learns her ballads. Her poets train his imagination. Her language is his.... In spite of political differences, her glory allures him. In spite of hostile collision, he clings to her lineage." Rush would prove to be a hard bargainer for America. But he always appreciated the bonds he shared with those English diplomats with whom he negotiated.[2]

Rush rented a room near London's Portman Square and marveled at the congested city: "The roll of…carriages of all kinds…was incessant. In all directions they were in motion. It was like a show." He soon settled into business and met with Robert Stewart—Lord Castlereagh—Great Britain's foreign minister. Rush presented his instructions from President Monroe for the upcoming negotiations, including "the question of title to [the] Columbia river" and "the north-western boundary line."[3]

Monroe also sent Albert Gallatin, minister to France, another skilled ambassador, to assist in the diplomacy. English plenipotentiaries John Robinson and Henry Goulburn would represent England, as Castlereagh had been called out of the country. Desiring to start the negotiations before leaving, Castlereagh invited all participants to an extended stay at his country estate. One evening the men walked the expansive grounds, with their gardens of roses and acres of manicured lawns set beside a meandering river. And then, surrounded by all this tranquility, they observed kangaroos, ostriches, and tigers. "Here amidst all that denoted cultivation and art," wrote Rush, "I beheld wild beasts and outlandish birds." Richard Rush had walked into Lady Castlereagh's menagerie. It was a curious site to begin negotiations that would eventually lead to a border for a place far away, a country that would one day be called Idaho.[4]

Following their initial meetings at the Castlereagh estate and zoo, the four primary diplomats settled into negotiations on August 27, 1817, meeting at the Board of Trade at Whitehall, once the site of the ostentatious centuries-old Whitehall Palace. With more than 1,500 rooms, it had for a time been the largest mansion in Europe. A fire destroyed most of it in 1698. Still, the Board of Trade retained enough dazzle to impress Rush and Gallatin. They met Robinson and Goulburn in a room where Edward Gibbon "had often written at the table before us" as he labored on his colossal treatise, *The History of the Decline and Fall of the Roman Empire.*[5]

The negotiators spent the bulk of their time debating Atlantic fishing rights and international commerce. They also argued over "property rights," specifically whether enslaved people held by the British at the end of the war should be returned to their "rightful" American owners. These were all critical matters at that time. But the issue with the longest-lasting significance proved to be the most elusive, settling the international border between the United States and Canada.

Rush and Gallatin advanced a simple concept, one Secretary of State Adams endorsed. They proposed a boundary following the 49th parallel, a straight line all the way west from today's Minnesota to the Pacific Ocean, a proposal elegant in its clarity. Great Britain's diplomats agreed—up to a point.

Both British and American trappers recognized the wealth of beaver and other fur-bearing animals in the Columbia River Basin. The British negotiators proved unwilling to abandon this rich asset to Americans. Robinson and Goulburn suggested that the international boundary follow the 49th parallel west until that line intersected the Columbia River. From that point, the river would become the boundary—meaning Seattle would today be in British Columbia. That proposal did not inspire Richard Rush, who succinctly noted, "to this we could not assent."[6]

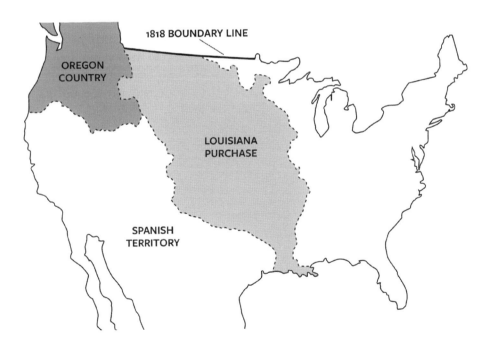

The Treaty of 1818 established the 49th parallel as the international boundary between the United States and British Canada as far the Rocky Mountains. In 1846, that line would be extended farther west.

So, the four negotiators agreed to procrastinate once again. The border would run along the 49th parallel from Lake of the Woods to the Rocky Mountains. The two nations would jointly occupy the country west of that, today's British Columbia, Washington, Oregon, Idaho, and parts of Montana and Wyoming. The countries would settle border issues in that wild land some other day. In the meantime, residents of either country were free to travel through or inhabit land on either side of the 49th parallel. Of course, other than a few trappers and traders, there were few white residents in that vast landscape. That would change.

In 1824, John Quincy Adams's career advanced on the well-traveled path that had led former Secretaries of State Thomas Jefferson, James Madison, and James Monroe to the White House. He won the presidency that year. As he settled into his new office, he had Oregon on his mind. In his last days as secretary of state, he oversaw negotiations leading to the Russo-American Treaty of 1824. Russia had some claims to the Oregon Country, based on exploration and fur trading, but in the 1824 treaty it relinquished its rights to land south of 54 degrees, 40 minutes of north latitude, a line that would become the southern border of Alaska. A year later, England signed a similar treaty with Russia. By the time Adams became president, Spain and Russia had ceded all claims to Oregon, leaving only the United States and England to contest that territory.[7]

The United States based its case for the region south of the 49th parallel on seagoing expeditions, the activity of American fur traders in the region, and the explorations of Lewis and Clark. England based its claims on its own maritime expeditions, the activity of British fur traders in the region, and the explorations of David Thompson who, three years after Lewis and Clark, built the first non-Indian structure in what became Idaho and later became the first white person to navigate the entire Columbia River. Basically, the two nation's claims negated one another.

During Adams's presidency, each side made various proposals to settle the border and end joint occupation. The English wanted the Columbia River and rights to the deep ports of Puget Sound. Americans wanted the same. Although in the 1820s there were more English than Americans in the disputed territory, Richard Rush knew things would change. Americans would eventually settle that country. "In regard to those interests in the remote West," he wrote, "time is for the United States the best negotiator." Adams reluctantly agreed. He had hoped to claim Oregon for the United States during his presidency, but in the end, he yielded to expediency. In 1826, he agreed to renew the joint occupancy accord. Richard Rush proved an accurate prognosticator. Time was the Americans' ally.[8]

The future states of Montana, Idaho, Washington, and Oregon held a few hundred non-Indian residents by 1840. But the region was about to get more.

In May 1841, 60 people gathered in Westport, Missouri. They prepared to follow fur trader Thomas "Broken Hand" Fitzpatrick and Catholic priest Pierre-Jean DeSmet west. The wagon-traveling emigrants, "a curious collection of individuals" in the understated estimation of DeSmet, made it to Soda Springs, in what would become Idaho. There, DeSmet headed north to establish a string of missions. He would eventually authorize the Mission of the Sacred Heart on the St. Joe River. After repeated floods at that location, the mission moved to the Coeur d'Alene River. Popularly known as the Old Mission at Cataldo, the church constructed there in the 1850s would, in the 21st century, be Idaho's oldest building.[9]

The other travelers on the Missouri wagon train split in two parts at Soda Springs. One headed south and became the first American wagon party to cross the Sierra Nevada mountains into California—pioneers of what became the California Trail. The bulk of the emigrants made their way to the Willamette Valley, the vanguard of thousands who would travel over what became the Oregon Trail.

The next year, Lord Alexander Baring made quite a different journey. On April 4, 1842, Baring, the First Baron Ashburton, arrived in Washington, DC, at the head of a special English delegation to meet with Secretary of State Daniel Webster about boundary issues between Canada and the United States. As the two sides considered borders for the Oregon Country, the English had little apprehension over the handful of Americans who had braved their way to Oregon the previous year. They therefore showed little interest in ending the joint occupation agreement. In August, the parties signed the Webster-Ashburton Treaty, which did settle some boundary issues between the United States and Canada, but only from the Great Lakes east. The 49th parallel border to the west remained stuck at the Rocky Mountains. Still, Americans—in the tradition of Richard Rush—believed time to be in their favor. "No matter who owns or governs Oregon, our people will subdue and possess it," boldly asserted the New York *Tribune*.[10]

As Lord Ashburton landed in America to begin his negotiations with Webster, settlers were again gathering in Missouri to trek west. About a hundred made it to Oregon that year; nearly a thousand in "The Great Migration" of 1843. In following years, migrations grew even larger—perhaps 1,500 in 1844 and 2,500 in 1845. England realized its negotiating leverage rapidly diminished as Americans poured into the jointly occupied Oregon. A few years earlier, England had realistic expectations of a boundary on the Columbia River. It now worried about preserving claims north of the 49th parallel before that region, too, swarmed with Americans. In addition to the American hordes, the English had to deal with an aggressive expansionist occupying the White House.

John Quincy Adams had won the presidency in 1824 in a highly contentious race in a divided country. Four men ran for the highest office that year. Andrew Jackson, a Tennessee war hero, received the most popular and electoral votes, but not enough to secure the presidency. Adams came in second. The U.S. House of Representatives determined the outcome. Jacksonians later claimed the House granted Adams the presidency after Henry Clay—who received the fourth most votes—struck a "corrupt bargain" with Adams. Clay would throw his support behind Adams in exchange for becoming Secretary of State. Adams did appoint Clay as Secretary of State. Whether they had struck a nefarious agreement is debatable, but in politics, perception often trumps reality.

A furious Andrew Jackson returned to Tennessee determined to defeat Adams in 1828, and he did. In the years between 1824 and 1828, Jackson nurtured several young politicians resolved to advance their mentor's political cause, including James K. Polk. A few months after Jackson's 1824 defeat, the 29-year-old Polk squeaked out a victory in a five-way race to represent Tennessee in the U.S. House of Representatives, launching his political career. John Quincy Adams harbored no affection for Polk, who Adams believed had "no wit…no gracefulness of delivery, no elegance of language." During his first two terms in Congress, Polk opposed virtually every policy President Adams proposed.[11]

Yet despite their myriad differences, Adams and Polk shared this outlook: an expansionist belief that America would one day span the continent from sea to sea. After losing the presidency, Adams would serve in the House of Representatives, much of that time alongside Polk, a slaveholder whom the abolitionist Adams continued to loathe. But as it turned out, no person did more to fulfill Quincy Adams's vision of a transcontinental America than James Polk.

On the eighth ballot of the bitterly divided Democratic Party's national convention in 1844, Massachusetts delegate George Bancroft placed the name of a compromise candidate before the assembly. Bancroft and most of his fellow delegates had journeyed to Baltimore that May assuming Martin Van Buren would be their nominee. But the former president, through seven contentious ballots, never gained the votes needed. Bancroft suggested the party rally around a little-known Tennessean, James K. Polk. The proposition took off like wildfire among the weary delegates, and on the ninth ballot conventioneers unanimously nominated him.[12]

A few weeks earlier the Whig Party, also meeting in Baltimore, had nominated to head its ticket the much better-known Henry Clay, twice previously a presidential candidate. "Are our Democratic friends serious?" a complacent Clay queried when told the news he would face the obscure Polk in the upcoming election. He anticipated an easy path to the presidency. "Who is James K. Polk?" the Whigs disdainfully mocked. Their celebration proved premature. The 49-year-old Polk became not only the youngest person elected president to that time, but also helped coin a new political term, "dark horse." His protégé's victory over bitter rival Henry Clay also delighted the aging Andrew Jackson.[13]

Most analyses of that election assert Clay lost because he opposed United States annexation of the Republic of Texas. Many Americans believed the Louisiana Purchase of 1803 had given the United States title to Texas. But America renounced whatever claim it had to Texas with the Adams-Onís Treaty of 1819. Some Americans, particularly southerners who viewed Texas as fertile ground for slavery's expansion, renounced the treaty and continued to advocate for Texas annexation. When Mexico won its independence from Spain in 1821, it inherited Texas, but like Spain, had limited ability to defend its interests there. Americans moved into the area and declared Texas's independence in 1836. Mexico refused to recognize an independent Texas, and the United States refused to push for American annexation. But pressure continued to mount in both Texas and the United States. Voters in 1844 preferred Polk's expansionistic views over Clay's caution. They longed for annexation even at the possible expense of war with Mexico.

Texas had loomed large in the election. But so did another part of the continent also long in dispute. The 1844 Democratic Party platform contained only six brief planks, including this one: "Resolved, that our title to the whole of the Territory of Oregon is clear and unquestionable, that no portion of the same ought to be ceded to England or any other power, and that the reoccupation of Oregon and the re-annexation of Texas at the earliest practicable period are great American measures."

Clay and the Whigs disagreed. American settlers should refrain from occupying land west of the Rocky Mountains. The question of what to do with Oregon should be postponed "some thirty or forty years." In an era of expansionistic fervor, that timid position helped hand the election to Polk. In a driving rainstorm on March 4, 1845, the new president assured the crowd gathered at the Capitol for his inauguration that "our title to the country of the Oregon is 'clear and unquestionable.'"[14]

Many in Polk's Democratic Party envisioned Oregon stretching all the way north to latitude of 54 degrees, 40 minutes, the southern border of Russia's American claims. In this scenario, much of British Columbia would today be part of the United States. Advocates of this cause were known as "54-40 Men," and James Polk has drifted through history as seemingly the most powerful of them all. Indeed, history books sometimes describe crowds of Democratic partisans lustily whooping "54-40 or Fight" during the 1844 campaign, exhorting Democratic candidates.

But that is myth. That catchy rallying cry, long erroneously considered one of the most successful political slogans in American election history, played no role in the 1844 campaign. Expansionists coined "54-40 or Fight" more than a year after the votes had been counted.

To Polk, the 54-40 issue was mostly a high-stakes bluff, a tool to help advance diplomatic negotiations with England. Polk wanted Oregon. Just not as far north as 54-40.[15]

Still, America was in an expansionist mood. About the same time "54-40 or Fight" became part of the American parlance, Democratic journalist John O'Sullivan coined another phrase befitting the times. He claimed it America's "manifest destiny" to occupy the entire continent, from Atlantic to Pacific. Democrats knew precisely what they were doing when they linked Oregon with Texas in their brief 1844 party platform. At the time, political agendas advanced or stalled on the issue of slavery and its spread. No one doubted that if Texas entered the union it would do so as a slave state; thousands of enslaved people already lived in the Republic of Texas. Democrats believed they could mollify northerners opposed to slavery by advocating for Oregon, thus maintaining a balance between slave-holding and non-slave regions. Texas and Oregon would remain intricately linked throughout Polk's presidency.[16]

After nearly three decades of joint occupancy, with the English favoring an international border along the Columbia River and the Americans posturing for a line as far north as Alaska, negotiators had backed themselves into corners. What had made so much sense to John Quincy Adams and Richard Rush in 1818—just draw a line to the Pacific along the 49th parallel—would, by the 1840s, seem an ignominious retreat for either side. Somehow, the two countries would have to compromise without either suffering disgrace.

Polk hoped to gain both Texas and Oregon without going to war over either. Certainly, the United States could ill-afford two wars at once. If it came down to one war, much better it be with Mexico than powerful England. Polk needed to resolve the Oregon boundary issue peacefully. A few months into office, he sent a letter to English officials suggesting a border at the 49th parallel, with a possible dip south allowing England to retain all of Vancouver Island. The compromise would allow England to save face as it would gain more land than having as the border a straight line to the Pacific. But many Americans were in no mood for compromise. "Mr. Polk will not fight for Oregon," scoffed Maine's *Portland Advertiser*. England also proved unwilling to concede, and promptly rejected Polk's offer.[17]

Tense brinkmanship followed. Polk withdrew his overture that would have allowed the English to retain Vancouver Island, and refused to submit another proposal. He did something else. The day his cabinet first debated Polk's Oregon policy became the day Polk began writing a daily journal. He wanted to record for posterity the tension over that border dispute in the far Northwest. He kept journaling all the way through his presidency, a bonanza for future historians, one of the most thorough documentations of a presidential administration. Writing in the third person, Polk noted on the first day of his journal in August 1845 that Oregon "had occupied [the President's] thoughts more than any and all others during his administration, and that though he had given his assent to the proposition to compromise at 49° he must say he did not regret that it had been rejected by the British Minister....If we do have war it will not be our fault."[18]

Polk professed to be prepared to "assert and enforce our right to the whole Oregon territory...to 54° 40'." England's rejection of his earlier compromise had clearly angered him. But he found himself in a domestic political bind. Many Americans disagreed with his "warlike tone." Yet expansionists in his own party opposed any compromise. "54-40 or Fight" became their rallying cry. They began a media blitz. As expected, pro-expansion newspapers united behind the cause. But there was more. Advocates went door-to-door in the nation's capital. "In the course of two or three nights," noted one reporter, the figures 54-40 "were written apparently four or five thousand times upon the windows, doors, street-corners, houses, public buildings, stores and fences." Wrote one senator, the numbers appeared "from one end of Pennsylvania Avenue to the other." Clearly, advocates for "all of Oregon" were out to influence Polk.[19]

Polk also had Oregonians to consider. By 1845, a few thousand emigrants had migrated to new homes there. Hundreds more were gathering around Independence, Missouri, to begin their trek west at the time of Polk's inauguration. They were Americans. They looked to the United States government for support and protection. In his first annual message to Congress in December 1845, Polk outlined the situation's complexity. "Beyond all question the protection of our laws...ought to be immediately extended over our citizens in Oregon," he proclaimed. "They have had just cause to complain of our long neglect." Reiterating that he had withdrawn his compromise offer to Great Britain, he reasserted America's right "to the whole Oregon Territory," and concluded: "The national rights in Oregon must either be abandoned or firmly maintained. They can not be abandoned without a sacrifice of both national honor and interest." He had a staunch ally in Congress that day, his old nemesis John Quincy Adams, who resolved "to support my administration on the Oregon question."[20]

Still, it was all bluster, a negotiating tactic. Polk had no interest in warring with England over wild lands north of the 49th parallel. As one senator queried a few days later, would the United States really fight a war over a "strip of territory, almost valueless, and barren, beyond the reach of human comprehension?" Future generations of Pacific Northwest residents would challenge the characterization of the Oregon Country as "barren" or "valueless." But the senator struck a chord with many Americans. So, too, did another senator taking a different view who declared the Polk administration had "no power… to transfer [American] soil…to the dominion, authority, control, and subjection of any foreign prince, state, or sovereignty." Polk found himself squeezed in a political vise.[21]

At the same time, England had problems. As Americans continued moving to Oregon in ever-greater numbers, they soon eclipsed the few British—mostly fur traders—living there. While still confined to an area south of the Columbia River, some would soon make their way north of the river. And there was nothing preventing them from continuing north of the 49th parallel. It would be difficult for England to retain title to that land in the face of increasing American settlement. Ominously for the British, as people began gathering for the 1846 Oregon migration, some had wagons adorned with "54-40," and many expressed a willingness to fight for that line. Public opinion in England provided little support for an aggressive border stance. With the fur trade in decline, most British residents saw little value in that distant land. It did not seem worth a long diplomatic confrontation, let alone a war. Both countries had good reason to reach a settlement over the long-disputed boundary.

England, unable to halt the northern march of Americans, now had little hope for a Columbia River boundary. But it did aspire to retain navigation rights to the river. Polk's aggressive 54-40 feint became untenable in May 1846 when the United States declared war on Mexico over Texas. He could not also wage war with England. The next month, England proposed a new compromise. Polk proved eager to accept. "If I reject it…and make no other proposition the probable result will be war," Polk confided in his journal.[22]

Great Britain essentially offered the identical concept it had rejected the previous year—a 49th parallel boundary that dipped south far enough to grant England all of Vancouver Island. To help preserve some honor after huffily rejecting this Polk proposal earlier, England

The United States and Great Britain jointly occupied the Oregon Country between 1818 and 1846. When they settled the international boundary in the latter year, the future Idaho received its northern border on the 49th parallel.

insisted that the Hudson's Bay Company retain navigation rights to the Columbia River. That proved an easy concession for Polk. The fur trade era was rapidly ending, and the Hudson's Bay Company's Oregon Country charter would expire in a few years. Let England preserve some dignity by retaining short-term Columbia River navigation rights—in exchange for precisely the border Polk had sought just a year earlier. On June 15, 1846, the two countries signed the Treaty of Oregon, ending 28 years of joint occupation. "The state of doubt and uncertainty which has hitherto prevailed respecting the sovereignty and government of the northwest coast of America," the treaty stated, had been "finally terminated." The international border between Canada and what became Idaho would be the 49th parallel.[23]

On July 4, 1848, a crowd gathered in Washington, DC. They witnessed the laying of a cornerstone for the Washington Monument. John Quincy Adams was not there to pay respects to the nation's first president—the man who had appointed him to his first diplomatic post. Though he had lived to see Oregon come fully into the possession of the United States, he died a few months before the Washington Monument ceremonies. Richard Rush did not attend either. The previous year, President James Polk had appointed him minister to France. But President Polk attended. Later that afternoon, after returning to the White House, he received the final version of the Treaty of Hidalgo. That document did much more than end the Mexican War. It also greatly expanded the United States. Mexico ceded to America what became the future states of California, Nevada, and Utah, along with most of Arizona, Colorado, and New Mexico—in addition to giving the United States undisputed control of Texas. The United States thus acquired the land south of the 42nd parallel that Spain had retained in the Adams-Onís Treaty of 1819.

Polk, who did not run for reelection, died less than a year after that momentous 1848 Independence Day. Polk and Adams had long been adversaries. They had little in common and differed dramatically on most political issues. But they shared a common vision of a transcontinental America stretching from Atlantic to Pacific. No two people create a nation. But more than any other two people, these two men bequeathed to America the continental United States.

They also did this: They gave to the future State of Idaho its northern border—a boundary set by diplomatic negotiations long before there was an Idaho.

Border Story

WAR

Isaac Ingalls Stevens lurched into Hellgate, a few miles from present-day Missoula, in July 1855. As Washington's first territorial governor and superintendent of Indian affairs, he was in the midst of a treaty-signing barnstorm. Over the winter of 1854–55, he held multiple councils with tribes in western Washington Territory, finalizing treaties enabling whites to claim millions of acres in exchange for granting Indians small reservations. In May and June, he moved east, negotiating treaties with Nez Perce, Yakama, Umatilla, Cayuse, and other tribes at a massive gathering near Walla Walla. Then he made his way toward Hellgate, accompanied by an Army escort and large pack train. The entourage floundered its way through the Bitterroot Valley, beset by summer storms and delayed by multiple crossings of swollen, zigzagging rivers. Finally, after days of drenching travel, they arrived at Hellgate, where Stevens found Flathead, Pend d'Oreille, and Kootenai Indians waiting patiently. The "hundreds upon hundreds of gaily bedecked Indian warriors" had ridden "over the plains and mountains to powwow," wrote Jesuit priest Adrian Hoecken, whom Stevens asked to translate at the council.[1]

All Stevens's negotiations during that rapid-fire treaty-making season bore the same hallmark. Speaking on behalf of the Great Father, Stevens distributed gifts and promised tribes reservations and long-term federal aid in exchange for taking the bulk of their land. He then invited tribal representatives, many of whom Stevens had self-designated as "headmen," to affix their marks on treaties.

The events occurred in a fog of cultural ignorance and misunderstanding. "Not a tenth of what was said was understood by either side," concluded Hoecken. Few, if any, of the tribal representatives comprehended the treaties' implications for their people. But at least most tribes impacted by the treaties had emissaries at the councils. Not so the Kootenai Tribe of Idaho.[2]

Isaac Stevens traveled the entire distance from Puget Sound to Hellgate without leaving the Territory of Washington, which then consisted of Washington, northern Idaho, and western Montana. He crossed no political borders. Of course, one point of cultural ambiguity between Stevens and tribes arose over the very concept of borders.

The Kootenai ancestral lands spread over a range of more than 300 miles, tracking the course of the Kootenai River. The river starts in the Canadian Rockies, flows into northwestern Montana, cuts west into Idaho, then returns to Canada, where it empties into the Columbia. Obviously, pre-contact Kootenai knew nothing of Canada, Montana, Idaho, or the borders that would come to separate them.

The Kootenai people consisted of several bands, most of whom lived in present-day Canada. One group lived in western Montana, and another in Idaho, at the location of today's city of Bonners Ferry, near the 49th parallel. Generally, the Kootenai are divided into two broad groups, those who live along the upper river, and those, like the Bonners Ferry band, beside the lower. The Bonners Ferry group has long, close economic and familial ties with the other band on the lower part of the river, centered near today's Creston, British Columbia. The Bonners Ferry and Creston Kootenai are essentially one band, separated in 1846 with the creation of the 49th parallel international boundary, a line paying no heed to Indian people's homelands. It is not so much that the border prevented tribal members from interacting as they always had. The border here is not a barricade or a fence. They continued to travel back and forth. But the two groups, located 30 miles apart, witnessed dramatic changes as two distinct white governments—one Canadian, the other American—with different laws and policies toward indigenous people, came to oversee their lives. While each group continued to maintain ancient connections with the other, each had to navigate unique governmental bureaucracies. This separation led to an increasing isolation that would prove arduous, particularly for the smaller group of Kootenai at Bonners Ferry.[3]

The Kootenai have a distinct language unrelated to the Salishan spoken by their neighbors. Indeed, Kootenai is unrelated to any other language. The Kootenai of the lower river—the Bonners Ferry and Creston people—live in a country "covered with wood, and the mountains steep, and intersected with lakes and rivers," as noted by fur trader Alexander Henry, who traveled through in 1811. The lower Kootenai had horses, but they were especially adept at water travel, acclaimed for their sturgeon-nosed canoes. These people guided Canadian fur trader David Thompson through the country in 1809 when his men constructed Kullyspell House, a trading post on Lake Pend Oreille—the first structure built by whites in today's Idaho.[4]

Isaac Stevens knew none of this when he called tribes to Hellgate. Stevens, assuming the Pend d'Oreilles, Flatheads, and Kootenai were all closely intertwined, treated them as three cogs of a single wheel. He insisted that one headman represent each group. He designated a man named Michelle to represent all Kootenai. Michelle, from an upper Kootenai band, seemed reticent to even attend the council, claiming he came only "to listen what they will say; that is why I don't talk." Other tribal members noted the differences between their people and the Kootenai. "I do not know where the land of the Kootenai is," admitted a council representative from another tribe. "It is a long distance off."[5]

The treaty council stretched on for a long, hot week. Army tents fronted Indian tipis on a flat piece of land along the Clark Fork River, a lovely spot surrounded by pines and ringed by mountains. Stevens wanted all three tribes to move to one reservation. Given their cultural differences and attachments to their individual ancestral lands, it is no wonder tribal representatives balked. Frustrated, Stevens finally concluded the council by approving the Flathead Reservation and promising the people of the Bitterroot Valley that the federal government would later survey their land to determine its suitability for another reservation. It is hardly surprising that, in 1871, President Ulysses Grant declared the survey complete—and no land in the Bitterroot Valley had proven suitable for a reservation. All the Flatheads, Pend d'Oreilles, and Kootenai were to move to the Flathead Reservation in today's northwest Montana. In exchange for that reserved land, the tribes ceded 12 million acres in present-day Idaho and Montana. The northern boundary of those relinquished lands was "the forty-ninth parallel of latitude." When Michelle put his "X" on the treaty on July 16, 1855, Stevens unilaterally declared that Michelle represented all Kootenai people.[6]

It is doubtful any of the lower Kootenai knew Michelle. They might not have even been aware of the treaty council. They sent no representative to the proceedings and would have been bewildered to learn that Stevens believed Michelle could represent them—just as surprised as Michelle himself. Even he refused to relocate to the reservation, instead leading a group of Kootenai to Canada. Only one Kootenai band already living near Flathead Lake moved to the reservation. The Bonners Ferry people saw no reason to leave their homeland. The Creator Nupika had made the world, and he gave the Bonners Ferry Kootenai people a very special place. Nupika said, "I have created this beautiful land, to celebrate my Creation here." As long as the Kootenai remained on that ground and kept their covenant with Nupika to protect it, they could live there happily forever. No wonder they had no desire to move to a distant reservation.[7]

At first, the Hellgate Treaty changed little for the Bonners Ferry Kootenai. Then, in 1860, some 200 strangers traipsed through their country packing unusual equipment. These men bivouacked at a site they called Camp Kootenay, at the spot where the lower Kootenai River crosses the 49th parallel into Canada. The Kootenai people welcomed the visitors, helped ferry them across the river, and furnished them guides. These were the surveyors, astronomers, geologists, packers, cooks, artists, naturalists, and laborers sent to survey the international boundary. They were marking the first of Idaho's boundaries to be surveyed, though Idaho did not yet exist. And in truth, they did a poor job of demarcating the line, struggling through the rugged Idaho landscape, unable to stay on track, leaving behind few surveyors' monuments.[8]

Though well aware of the surveyors in their presence, the Kootenai could not have understood the long-term consequences of their work. The 49th parallel would eventually obstruct kinship, trade, and political relationships between the Bonners Ferry and Creston Kootenai. "One band of people, in many ways one family, [was] subjected to tremendous forces of change and dissolution," observed historian Karen Ashton Young. As one Kootenai leader pondered the year surveying began, "What is the meaning of this boundary line? It runs through the middle of my house. My home is on both sides. Why should you, without asking me or considering me, divide my property in two and also divide my children?" When establishing the 49th parallel as the boundary in 1846, neither the United States nor England considered it necessary to discuss things with Indians inhabiting the border regions.[9]

The Bonners Ferry Kootenai at least knew about the parties surveying the international boundary in 1860. They had no knowledge of events in Washington, DC, in 1864 that would further isolate them. In that year, Congress established Montana and created another boundary, this one between that new territory and Idaho. The Bonners Ferry Kootenai were now politically separated not only from their kin in Canada, but also from upper Kootenai in Montana. They found themselves hemmed in on a narrow panhandle in Idaho.

The Idaho Kootenai refused to move to the Flathead Reservation, and the federal government refused to recognize them as an independent tribe. The government marginalized the band, claiming their numbers too small to warrant an official relationship with the United States. Their situation grew increasingly dire as whites settled their lush valley.

In 1890, the Indian agent at the nearby Colville Reservation—across another border in Washington—noted the Kootenai were "in a destitute condition." White residents were unsympathetic. The Bonners Ferry newspaper declared "there is considerable fine ranch land in the locality [but] the Indians claim it all, though under what right we are not informed. We are told that the band number less than a hundred and it would appear to us that they ought to be on some reservation, where Uncle Sam has already donated them the 'fat of the land.'"[10]

In 1892, the United States did allot 80 acres to each head of an Idaho Kootenai family. But the government never delivered promised agricultural assistance. Tribal members continued to suffer. Living in hopeless poverty, many Kootenai abandoned their allotments and moved to British Columbia. Whites invaded to claim their "unused" land. Close familial ties between Bonners Ferry and Creston Kootenai complicated land ownership for those who retained allotments. A Bonners Ferry allottee was likely to have Creston relatives. If they passed their allotted land on to Canadian heirs—who had no legal status in the United States—it often came encumbered with back taxes. More often than not, heirs sold the land to whites to avoid tax payments. The number of allotted acres owned by Bonners Ferry Kootenai shrank precipitously.[11]

A tribal member in 1909 signed a deed to the federal government, requesting that it hold ten acres of his allotted land in trust for the tribe. The government purchased an additional adjoining two-and-a-half acres for an Indian school. The Bonners Ferry Kootenai then concentrated on this 12.5 acres on the outskirts of town. By the 1930s, local sentiment among some white Bonners Ferry residents had softened. They now petitioned the Bureau of Indian Affairs to assist the Kootenai. Idaho Senator William Borah and Congressman Burton French secured funding to construct 18 houses on the 12.5-acre site. Things seemed hopeful until the government again deserted the Kootenai. Forty years later, that inattention sparked one of the most unusual events in the long, sad relationship between Indian people and the United States government.[12]

America's last Indian war began in September 1974. A few months earlier, an elderly Kootenai man died in one of the now-decrepit houses the government had built for the Kootenai in the 1930s. The federal government had provided no maintenance money in the intervening years, and by the 1970s, the tribe had torn down all but two of the 18 original houses, deeming them unlivable. Neither of the two remaining dwellings had heat or running water. Roofs leaked. The tribal elder died of exposure inside his own house. "His water was frozen—there's holes in the roof, it was snowing," recalled Amy Trice, chairwoman of the tribe that had by then shrunk to 67 members. "That's how sad it was. Nobody seemed to care."[13]

But Trice and the other five members of the tribal council cared. The death proved a catalyst, sparking tribal outcry after years of frustration at governmental inertia. The council sent a resolution to Congress and President Gerald Ford. It noted the tribe's aboriginal lands had encompassed thousands of acres in Idaho and Montana. It accurately stated that Isaac Stevens, for whatever reason, had not invited the Bonners Ferry Kootenai to the Hellgate Treaty Council, and that the tribe had no representative there. "Through the gross neglect of the United States," it asserted, "our people have no base for self-security, no hope, no civic pride." The tribe demanded that the federal government recognize the Idaho Kootenai as a sovereign nation, that a portion of its ancestral property be returned, and that the government compensate the tribe for the millions of dollars that had been extracted from its aboriginal lands. Should the government fail to act on the resolution by September 10, 1974, "a declaration of war...will then exist between the Kootenai Nation of Indians and the United States of America and its possessions."[14]

Chairwoman Amy Trice insisted the war would be nonviolent. But that did not mean there would be no action. Tribal members sold "war bonds" to finance their protest. They established roadblocks and requested payment of ten-cent tolls from those entering tribal lands. Although most motorists "zoomed past the roadside solicitors," the action quickly caught the attention of local and national media, which had been Trice's intent from the beginning. Other tribes sent notices of support. Idaho's United States Senators James McClure and Frank Church, along with Representative Steve Symms, introduced a congressional bill to benefit the tribe. Trice and other tribal members journeyed to Washington, DC, to lobby.[15]

The last American Indian war resulted in a rare victory for the Indians. On October 19, President Ford signed the bill sponsored by the Idaho congressional delegation. It provided official federal recognition of the Kootenai Tribe of Idaho and created a 12.5-acre reservation—the land that had been set aside for the Kootenai 66 years earlier. The government also began releasing funds for social welfare programs that helped revitalize the tribe.[16]

Once, the fish were big and plentiful. "William Maughan had the good fortune to catch a sturgeon over nine feet long," read a 1909 news story. "Bonners Ferry is the city for big fish." Indeed. Over the years, newspaper photos captured the thrill of landing fish 11, 12, 13 feet long. As late as 1978, sturgeon fishers diligently set trotlines in the Kootenai River each season, anchored with 150 pounds of metal and dotted with hooks the size of a butcher's, connected to 1,150-pound test line.

But the fishery was playing out. In 1994, Kootenai River white sturgeon officially became an endangered species. Where once there were thousands of fish, now there were perhaps a few hundred adults.

The sturgeon's lineage can be traced back millions of years; they hobnobbed with dinosaurs. White sturgeon can grow up to 19 feet, weigh more than 1,000 pounds, and live to be 100 years old. Kootenai River sturgeon became isolated from their Columbia River cousins more than 10,000 years ago, during the last glacial age. Unlike other Columbia River sturgeon that, like salmon, migrated to the ocean as part of their life cycle, the Kootenai River fish became land-locked, adapting differently.

Scientists attribute the Kootenai River sturgeon's decline to several factors, but the main threat came with the completion of Libby Dam in the mid-1970s. Sturgeon require fast moving water to successfully spawn. The dam reduced spring flows by more than 50 percent. As a result, there has been virtually no natural reproduction since the dam's completion.

But this could end up a success story. Four years before the U.S. Fish and Wildlife Service declared the species endangered, the now federally recognized Kootenai Tribe of Idaho established a sturgeon hatchery outside of Bonners Ferry. "The goal," the tribe states, "is to prevent extinction, preserve the existing gene pool, and begin rebuilding the endangered population until effective habitat restoration measures are implemented." The tribe sees Kootenai River habitat restoration and sturgeon survival as part of its duty to fulfill its covenant with the Creator Nupika, who asked the Kootenai to "honor and guard my creation here." Since 1990, the hatchery released hundreds of thousands of fish.

The time when white sturgeon once again swim in mass along the bottom of Kootenai River could come again. It is just one of many success stories for the Kootenai Tribe of Idaho since the 1974 war.[17]

The tribe worked to return caribou to Idaho. It planted native trees and shrubs along riverbanks to attract insects, improving the food supply for burbot and other fish and started a burbot hatchery to replenish the supply of a game fish that had nearly disappeared from the Kootenai River. It enhanced habitats for native animals, ranging from bald eagles to black bear. The tribe has enlarged its holdings to thousands of acres, often by purchasing former allotment lands held by tribal members in Canada. It opened a health clinic, constructed a tribal center, and provided job training to its members—whose numbers substantially increased after the war.

While the international boundary at the 49th parallel continues to split the Kootenai, the tribe in Idaho has learned to accommodate that barrier. In 1986, it opened the Kootenai River Inn, a beautiful riverside hotel and restaurant in Bonners Ferry. In the 1990s, it officially became the Kootenai River Inn, Casino, and Spa when the tribe gained permission to allow gaming. It is the economic engine of the tribe's renaissance, employing tribal and community members, providing college scholarships, and bankrolling economic development. A good chunk of the income that provides those benefits derives from people driving south from Canada and across the international border.

In 2016, the Kootenai Inn became the first casino in the United States to install dual-currency gaming machines. "Spin and Win in Canadian Dollars!" the casino trumpeted as it branded its dual-currency machines with Canadian flags. No need "to exchange currency to win big here," the promotion boasted, luring Canadians to "stay and play."[18]

The tribe that had warmly greeted the 19th-century survey crews that marked the international boundary did not fully understand the repercussions of the line those men traced. By the 21st century, the tribe understood the nuances of that boundary well. Though squeezed into a fraction of its former homeland, restrained by an international border isolating tribal members from relatives, the Kootenai Tribe of Idaho innovatively discovered ways to capitalize on that boundary to furnish benefits for a people Isaac Stevens had ignored.

CHAPTER FOUR

1859
The Southwestern Border:
Oregon

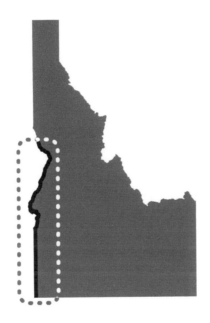

Had Charles Meigs had his way, Idaho would today be much bigger. Meigs hoped to confine Oregon to a narrow corridor between the Cascade Mountains and the Pacific Ocean. That would have provided Idaho with expansive growth potential to its west. Meigs found an enthusiastic ally in Mike McCarter. Their coalition might have worked better had they not lived 163 years apart.

Following the 1846 treaty ending joint occupation, Americans residing in Oregon languished under a provisional government. The United States, so eager to secure the Oregon Country from Great Britain, showed considerably less enthusiasm for authorizing an official territorial administration. In 1836, Marcus and Narcissa Whitman established a Presbyterian mission among Cayuse Indians near the future city of Walla Walla. By 1847, relations between the Whitmans and Indians had soured. Native people accused the missionaries of spreading deadly measles, and abhorred Marcus Whitman's enthusiastic boosterism. They believed he encouraged white settlers to trespass on their land. On November 29, Cayuse and Umatilla Indians killed the Whitmans and a dozen others at the mission. The slayings incited

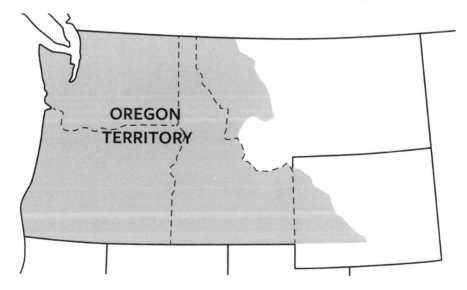

Congress established Oregon Territory in 1848. A huge area, it encompassed all of what became Idaho.

bloody revenge by whites—and finally spurred Congress to establish governmental order in the region. In August 1848, President James K. Polk signed legislation creating Oregon, the first United States territory west of the Rocky Mountains.

The Territory of Oregon was huge—encompassing all of today's Washington, Oregon, and Idaho, along with those parts of Montana and Wyoming west of the Rockies. It was also unmanageable. As settlers migrated north of the Columbia River, distancing themselves from the Willamette Valley, the territory's commercial and governmental center, they demanded the vast territory be divided. It was time for "a legal divorce from the south," thundered the northern country's most influential newspaper. Those northern Oregon residents, most of whom lived around Puget Sound, petitioned Congress for a new territory bounded on the south and east by the Columbia River. In 1853, Congress granted their request for a new government, establishing Washington Territory. But Congress had a different idea about Washington's borders than the one favored by local inhabitants. The Columbia River would indeed form part of the boundary between Washington and Oregon. But rather than arcing north with the Columbia toward Canada, Congress chose to extend the southern boundary of Washington on a straight line along

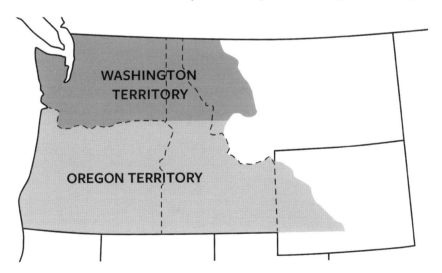

When Congress created Washington Territory in 1853, it split the future Idaho in two. Had the towns then existed, Cottonwood would have been in Washington and neighboring Grangeville in Oregon.

the 46th parallel. The Walla Walla Valley, and the former Whitman mission site, would rest in Washington.[1]

What would eventually become Idaho was now split in two parts, with the north belonging to Washington and the south remaining in Oregon. Had the neighboring Idaho towns then existed, Grangeville would have been in Oregon and Cottonwood in Washington. Washington Territory stretched all the way from the Pacific Ocean, across what became Idaho's panhandle, to the Rocky Mountains. Olympia became the capital. Ten years later, Olympia's awkward location at the far western edge of Washington would play a pivotal role in the formation of another new territory—a place that would take the name Idaho. But before that territory came to be, and before it had any influence over the creation of its own borders, Congress would establish the future Idaho's third boundary when it accepted Oregon into statehood in 1859.

In August 1857, 60 men gathered in the territorial capital at Salem to write a constitution for the proposed new State of Oregon. They faced tough competition for Salem's most newsworthy event of the season. That summer, the town of fewer than a thousand residents also hosted a "mammoth Circus, direct from California," electrifying the local press. At the "largest pavilion ever in this territory," townspeople thrilled to jugglers, tightrope walkers, and Master J. Armstrong performing the "Incredible Act of Throwing a Double Somersault."[2]

Still rough around its edges, Salem nonetheless held lofty pretensions. The town featured a grand public square surrounded by wide, undeveloped avenues with names like Capitol, State, and Court, evidence of Salem's optimistic vision for its future as a seat of state government. A California newspaperman covering the constitutional convention claimed Salem "is to Oregon what Rome is to Christendom—the point from which emanate mandates that are felt to the outward rim of its jurisdiction." Considering Oregon Territory's "outward rim" stretched to the Rocky Mountains, that statement was only slightly exaggerated, though Salem's mandates covered more space than people.[3]

The constitutional convention delegates gathered at the Marion County Courthouse, constructed in 1854. The wooden structure featured an ornate cupola and four majestic Doric columns. Only one of the 60 delegates came from the sparsely populated region east of the Cascade Mountains. Charles Meigs, from Dalles City—later known as The Dalles—represented Wasco County, a fair-sized piece of real estate. Wasco County encompassed all of Oregon east of the Cascades, which included all of today's eastern Oregon, all of southern Idaho, and a good chunk of western Wyoming. Wasco County ran for 130,000 square miles, a little smaller than the current State of Montana. Meigs represented a lot of land, but a place short on people. Aside from Dalles City—incorporated a few months before the convention—only a handful of non-Indians called the enormous county home. Being the only convention delegate from the sparsely populated east side of Oregon, Meigs brought a unique perspective to the proceedings.[4]

Meigs, a lawyer, had moved to Wasco County just two years earlier. He grasped that Oregonians from west of the Cascades shared little with east-siders. "It [is] entirely gratuitous to presume that the interest of the people east of the Cascades would be promoted by being attached to Oregon," he bristled. When he found himself named to the Committee on Boundaries, Meigs channeled his energy into an impassioned—but lonely—effort to lop off Oregon at the crest of the Cascades.[5]

Meigs could point to some precedent in the effort to create a narrow Oregon. In 1855, Congress debated a bill that would have authorized Oregon to form a state constitutional convention, a normal congressional precursor to admitting new states to the union. Many senators, including future presidential candidate Stephen Douglas, believed the Cascades should form the new state's eastern border. "There is your natural boundary," Douglas pronounced while standing before a large map. "This is the line marked by nature as the eastern boundary of your state. Oregon should lie wholly west of the Cascade Mountains."[6]

Congress adjourned before taking action on the Oregon bill. It came up again in 1856, with Congressman John Cadwalader of Pennsylvania the new champion of a slender Oregon. He declared to his colleagues, in justifying the Cascades as his preferred eastern border, "I have a strong objection to the formation of new States of such magnitude that their future influence will unduly preponderate in the scale of power in the Union."[7]

Joseph Lane, Oregon Territory's non-voting congressional delegate, strongly objected. "I am opposed to any division of the Territory
of Oregon by this bill," he admonished. "Divided by the Cascade
Mountains, the portion lying west would make a small State. We want
one great State on the Pacific." He proposed the new state's borders be
left "to the people of the Territory to determine."[8]

Unable to reach agreement, Congress once again failed to pass an
Oregon enabling act. The idea came up again in 1857 when the House
of Representatives passed a bill with a new concept for Oregon's eastern border. Oregon would be slightly wider than having a boundary
at the Cascade crest, but narrower than most Oregonians desired. The
House would have aligned Oregon's border with the eastern boundary
of California, giving both states the same width. Lane again objected,
and when the Senate took up the bill, Douglas's Committee on Territories instead recommended a border much farther east, on the Snake
River. But once again Congress could not agree on the boundary and
failed to pass a bill authorizing an Oregon constitutional convention.[9]

Frustrated by congressional intransigence, Oregonians took the
initiative. Rather than waiting for an enabling act, in June 1857 they
charged ahead without one, electing 60 delegates to a constitutional
convention to convene later that summer. The group included Wasco
County's Charles Meigs. He drifted into Salem with preconceived
notions about Oregon's borders. In 1855, the year Meigs moved to
Dalles City, that town had hosted a different convention. Delegates
to that gathering voted for a new territory, breaking away from Oregon. It would have had its western border at the Cascade Mountains.
Oregon would be narrow; the new territory expansive, ranging from
the Cascades to the Rockies. Nothing came of the proposal, but Meigs
carried to Salem eastern Oregon's fervor for separation from the rest
of the territory that lay west of the Cascades.[10]

Charles Meigs wasted little time making his case. One week after
the constitutional convention convened, he introduced his scheme to
establish Oregon's eastern border along the Cascades. In the debate
over whether straight-line geometry should predominate over natural
geographic borders, Meigs clearly came down as a geography guy. "The
Cascade mountains are the right and natural boundary," he asserted.

"They divide the country east and west....I lay it down as a fixed fact in political science that great natural boundaries are to be observed."[11]

Meigs's proposal came as a minority amendment to the Boundary Committee's report. The rest of his fellow committee members favored an eastern border at the Snake River. Convention delegates promptly defeated Meigs's amendment. Only Meigs voted in favor. When the convention president asked those opposed to Meigs's plan to signify by saying no, the official minutes recorded the "response was very loud."[12]

But Meigs, a persistent fellow, offered his amendment again the next day—and gained twice as many supporters when convention President Matthew Deady joined his cause. Still, the nays overwhelmingly prevailed. Undeterred, Meigs introduced his amendment one last time on September 16, two days before the convention adjourned. While Deady deserted the cause, Meigs picked up two other supporters. Still, their three votes hardly carried the day.[13]

Meigs promptly left town. He provided no official reason for exiting the convention after that final boundary decision, but he was no doubt disgruntled, and failed to appear when convention delegates voted to approve their constitution. That document advocated an eastern border on the Snake River, precisely where the United States Senate had recommended a few months earlier. The middle channel would delineate Oregon's boundary as far as the Snake's confluence with the Owyhee River. From that point, the straight lines favored by so many in Congress would prevail; the southern part of Oregon's eastern border would shoot straight south to the 42nd parallel. Although there was not yet an Idaho, that eastern boundary of Oregon would come to be the southwestern border of that yet-to-be-conceived state.

In Salem, Meigs encountered the same argument Joseph Lane had advanced in Congress: Constitutional convention delegates did not want a small Oregon. "It would be disastrous to the future of the state if we were to confine ourselves," thundered Delazon Smith. "I do not like little states." Thomas Dryer proved even more animated: "If we have a state at all, let us go as far east as we can...to the Missouri line if possible. I would like to take in Utah."[14]

Convention delegates did not endorse annexing Utah. But they did covet a chunk of Washington Territory, eyeing the rich Walla Walla Valley. They proposed, instead of the straight line at the 46th parallel that separated the territories of Washington and Oregon, that the northeast border of the new state should jut farther north. Under this scenario, what is now southeast Washington would today be in Oregon. But delegates did not want that land so desperately they were willing to jeopardize the march to statehood. So, they added a provision to their boundary proposal. If Congress, in its wisdom, thought the border should remain at the 46th parallel, then "Congress...may make [it] the northern boundary." And that is what Congress did, especially after it heard from Washington territorial legislators who were none-too-happy with Oregon's attempted land grab. "The seeking thus to appropriate a valuable portion of the domain of an adjacent Territory without its knowledge or consent, is an act of gross injustice, wanting in courtesy and right," the legislators wrote Congress. Walla Walla would remain in Washington.[15]

Oregonians who hoped to annex Walla Walla had three strikes against them. First, the border between Oregon and Washington had already been set in 1853 when Congress established Washington Territory. Second, Congress had its affinity for straight lines. And third, the Oregon convention delegates had proposed that the border, rather than a straight line, should follow the Snake River as it curved its way into Washington Territory. Congress had issues with rivers as bor-

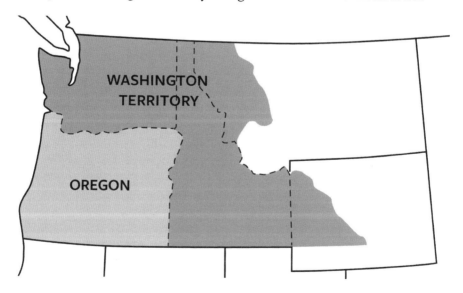

When Congress granted Oregon statehood in 1859, all of the future Idaho became part of an ungainly Washington Territory.

ders. Rivers often wander as they cut new courses. A chunk of land in one state might suddenly find itself on the other side of the river in a different state as waters meandered. As historian Derek Everett concluded, "Rivers…make terrible boundaries."[16]

But there are exceptions. While Congress had no desire for the Snake as the border north of the 46th parallel, the river south of that line is different. There the Snake runs through Hells Canyon, America's deepest river gorge. Rivers do not meander there. Congress proved content to allow Oregon's eastern border to twist with the Snake as it flowed through immovable canyon walls. And thus it transpired that Hells Canyon came to form what may be the most spectacularly beautiful state boundary in the country, dividing Oregon from Idaho.

Many Oregonians, over many years, came to the same conclusion as Charles Meigs: eastern and western Oregon are extravagantly dissimilar. The Cascade Mountains separate Oregon into two distinct landscapes, and that geographical diversity has fostered two different cultures. More than a century-and-a-half after the constitutional convention, Mike McCarter advocated a Meigsian solution to what he considered Oregon's insoluble geographic and cultural dilemma. It is unlikely McCarter had ever heard of Meigs; he is a little-known figure in Northwest history. But just as Meigs in 1857 had advocated a new territory uniting eastern Oregon with what became southern Idaho, in 2020, McCarter began the "Greater Idaho" movement encouraging eastern Oregon to secede and join the Gem State. He was not the first person to believe the constitutional convention delegates had got it all wrong and that Meigs had been correct: Oregon should be a very small state.

Border Story

GREATER IDAHO

Eastern Oregon's Charles Meigs foresaw the urban-rural divide that characterized 21st-century western politics. To the 19th-century Meigs, the Cascade Mountains split urban Oregon from rural. Oregon "west of the mountains will fill up rapidly," he predicted at the 1857 Oregon constitutional convention, "and the possibility is that it will be as densely populated as the Atlantic states—consequently, it would always overbalance us....Our part of the country is not susceptible to a dense population and would best thrive under a government of our own."[1]

Meigs anticipated an Oregon secession movement that would stretch into the 21st century. But he was not alone. Though he was the only delegate from east of the Cascades, others at the constitutional convention advocated separating rural areas from the burgeoning Willamette Valley.

Southern Oregon's Perry Marple offered a resolution during the 1857 convention "that at such time as the electors of that portion of [Oregon] lying south of the Calapooia mountains...shall desire to detach from this state and unite with a portion of California in the formation of a new state...shall be permitted to do so." Southern Oregon residents had complained for years about the "urbanites" of the Willamette Valley. They had held a convention in Jacksonville in 1854 that urged creation of a new Territory of Jackson, carved out of southern Oregon and northern California.[2]

The Jackson movement had several components. There was the emerging urban-rural divide that Meigs observed. There was the difficulty of travel to reach the seat of government in the Willamette Valley—the timeworn complaint of westerners everywhere seeking new territories with government offices closer to home. And there was a racial component. The issue of African American rights in early Oregon history is complicated. The constitutional convention delegates submitted a proposal to voters regarding slavery and free Blacks. Voters overwhelmingly chose to ban slavery in the new state. But they also determined that free Blacks should likewise be excluded. Oregon became the only free state admitted to the union with a constitutional clause excluding Blacks.[3]

On the other hand, supporters of Jackson Territory—named to honor slave owner Andrew Jackson—did not want to discourage Blacks. They just wanted the Blacks in their midst to be enslaved. Jackson Territory would gladly allow slavery.

Nothing came of the 1850s effort to establish Jackson. As Joseph Lane, Oregon's territorial delegate to the United States Congress noted, "a new Territory cannot be made as proposed. The delegation from California does not think of entertaining the idea of clipping their State." In 1860, Lane would run for vice president on the ticket of the pro-slavery wing of the Democratic Party. He had no philosophical qualms about a new slave-holding territory on the West Coast. He was merely a political realist and recognized California would never approve of the Territory of Jackson.[4]

That movement for a new territory died rather quickly. The Oregon constitutional convention delegates soundly defeated Perry Marple's proposal to allow for future consideration of Jackson. And, as Lane observed, members of Congress from California showed no enthusiasm for shrinking their state.[5]

Nearly a century later, the concept of Jackson arose again, this time with a new name honoring another slave owner—Thomas Jefferson. In November 1941, residents of southern Oregon and northern California declared the creation of the State of Jefferson. The movement had a prankish flavor. The state would exist every Thursday; after federal government recognition, it would presumably become a seven-day-a-week affair. Group members established roadblocks and distributed copies of their "Proclamation of Independence." The state flag consisted of two Xs, a symbol for having been double-crossed. *Life* magazine sent reporters. *The New York Times* featured daily articles. Stanton Delaplane, reporting for the *San Francisco Chronicle*, received a Pulitzer Prize for his coverage of the State of Jefferson. The movement had unfortunate timing. After a couple weeks of publicity, Japan attacked Pearl Harbor and Jefferson quickly faded from the national spotlight.[6]

Although something of a lark, the 1941 campaign for Jefferson contained elements of the earlier movement for Jackson. Elected representatives in faraway Sacramento and Salem, according to Jefferson backers, ignored their rural region. Taxes generated from natural resource extraction flowed into state coffers, but little returned for infrastructure improvements back home. The idea of a State of Jefferson never really died. Over the years, it morphed into a cultural movement expressed as a theme of racial identity. By 2020, the drafters of a new State of Jefferson "Declaration of Independence" had lost the sense of humor of their 1940s predecessors. They charged that California was in "open rebellion and insurrection against the government of the United States." The declaration called the governor and other state officials "criminals" for "harboring and shielding illegal aliens." Clearly, the movement for Jefferson had moved well beyond prankishness.[7]

The State of Jefferson had adherents in southern Oregon, but by 2015, it had largely become a California affair. Rural Oregonians advocating splitting away from urban parts of the state found new energy in a different cause. They ditched the effort to create a new state. That would bring two new senators and a congressional delegation, upsetting the congressional balance of power. Such an effort seemed permanently doomed in a politically divided country. Those with rural Oregon angst proposed instead to change state boundary lines. No new state need be created. Rather, rural Oregon—and rural northern California, too, if it wanted to join—would simply secede and become part of "Greater Idaho." Mike McCarter served as Greater Idaho's chief spokesperson, and his 2020 rhetoric sounded a lot like that of Charles Meigs in 1857.[8]

Under the formal name of "Move Oregon's Border for a Greater Idaho," advocates complained of state policy set by a predominantly urban legislature. "It's a movement to try to maintain our rural values," asserted McCarter. "We're afraid of what's coming down legislatively. It'll destroy rural Oregon."[9]

While McCarter shared Meigs's concerns about urban Oregon dominating rural, he drew a different map. Meigs sought a boundary at the Cascade Mountains, splitting Oregon on a north-south crest line. McCarter wanted rural protections for a much larger part of Oregon. Not only would all of eastern Oregon secede to join Idaho, but also southern Oregon. A reconfigured Oregon would then be confined to a small—albeit well-populated—piece of property, essentially the northwest quadrant of the current state. Idaho, on the other hand, would expand all the way to the Pacific Ocean, gaining a port on the sea. "The Oregon/Idaho border was established 161 years ago and is now outdated," declared the Greater Idaho website in 2020. "It makes no sense in its current location because it doesn't match the location of the cultural divide in Oregon."[10]

McCarter and his allies looked across the border to Idaho and perceived much they liked, including a Republican-dominated legislature, stronger gun rights laws, lower taxes, and weaker welfare programs "that preserve state finances." While Idaho enjoyed "less regulation than any other state," the Greater Idaho advocates welcomed some Idaho regulations, such as tougher drug laws, strong abortion restrictions, and schools that refused to "teach kids to hate Americans and Americanism." McCarter also had Idaho's best interests at heart. Noting the potential imminence of civil war, he claimed it would

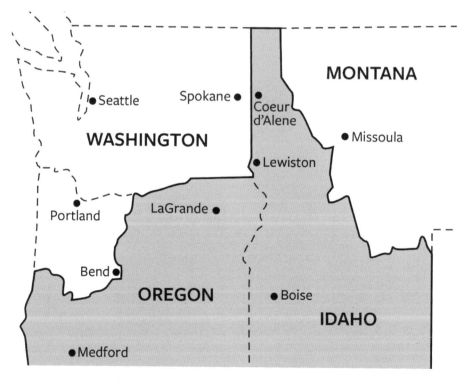

Attracted by Idaho's conservative politics, a 21st-century effort to expand "Greater Idaho" to include most of Oregon gained strength in some rural Oregon counties.

become essential for Idaho to have an ocean port so its "access to the Pacific…would [not] be dependent on good relations with a foreign [possibly enemy] country." McCarter had no doubt about the positive benefits of separating from the urbanite "leftists" who had become "unmoored…from Biblical morality." Charles Meigs, though, might have been disappointed, because by 2020, according to Greater Idaho advocates, Meigs's hometown of The Dalles had been infiltrated with immoral socialists who would despoil Greater Idaho. So, McCarter's maps retained The Dalles in Oregon. But for those few residents of The Dalles who had managed to avoid contamination, McCarter had an easy solution. Once the border shifted, they would have "the option of moving a few miles to experience the freedom of Idaho law."[11]

One does not need to read too closely between too many lines to detect xenophobia in language cloaked as rural-urban angst. In 2020, Idaho's Latino and Hispanic residents made up nearly 13 percent of the population. Still, it was a very white state, with non-Latino whites making up 82 percent. McCarter's crusade appreciated that Idaho did not issue driver's licenses to "immigrants in the country illegally," and prohibited "sanctuary cities" that opposed federal efforts to deport immigrants. Insisting that seceding to Idaho would help protect "our values," McCarter clearly believed a Democratic Oregon legislature that prioritized "one race above another for…program money and in the school curriculum" did not advance those values.[12]

By November 2021, eight Oregon counties had approved initiatives seeking approval to begin efforts to secede. Some counties rejected the initiative. Many people, even in rural Oregon, questioned the utility of a Greater Idaho. Some Idahoans on the other hand, looked more favorably on the potential border change.

When queried by the Greater Idaho movement in 2020, nearly a dozen Republican Idaho legislators claimed to favor the concept—which, in addition to giving Idaho access to the Pacific Ocean would also give it greater congressional representation. In 2021, Idaho legislators invited McCarter to testify. Legislators had been very busy that season, one of the longest in state history. They refused to fund public schools and universities until they were assured teachers would refrain from discussing topics like diversity, racism, and sexism in classrooms. They threatened to withhold money from the Attorney General's budget because he had failed to file legal suits supporting former President

Donald Trump's false allegations that Democrats had stolen the 2020 presidential election. Those who denied climate change failed by only one vote in their effort to defund Idaho Public Television because it aired a children's program that taught the dangers of global warming—a condition many legislators insisted was a hoax. They warned about the health hazards of wearing protective facemasks during the COVID-19 epidemic. This counterintuitive logic not only defied scientific guidance but also surfaced as the nation suffered one of its worst pandemics, which killed thousands of Idahoans. In this type of atmosphere, it is no wonder some Idaho legislators proved so amenable when Mike McCarter and Mark Simmons, a former speaker of the Oregon House of Representatives, came to testify. They shared many beliefs. "We don't need the state breathing down our necks all the time, micromanaging our lives and trying to push us into a foreign way of living," declared Simmons. That sort of thinking inspired Idaho Representative Barbara Ehardt. Greater Idaho is "an intriguing idea," she enthused. "There absolutely are benefits." Ehardt had previously established her xenophobic credentials by blasting Boise State University for hosting campus powwows for its Indian students and providing graduate fellowships for minorities. Accepting equally conservative former Oregonians into Idaho might be just the ticket to preserve values Ehardt espoused. And it would be good for Oregonians, too, as McCarter noted while sealing his case: "Idaho would have the satisfaction of freeing 1.2 million people from immoral blue state laws."[13]

Charles Meigs had predicted clashes between rural and urban lifestyles in the West. Mike McCarter was far from the first person in the Pacific Northwest to catch the secessionist bug. There was, of course, the Jackson/Jefferson effort. And the residents of Idaho's panhandle promoted dozens of secessionist schemes over the course of more than 150 years to try to insulate themselves from the ruling masses of Boise.

The United States Constitution provides for the possibility of state border changes. Indeed, small border adjustments have occurred in the nation's history, and one state, West Virginia, carved itself out of Virginia during the Civil War when insurrectionist Virginians had no say in the matter. The process is onerous, but not impossible. A change of borders requires the approval of the legislatures of the states involved, as well as the United States Congress. However, the possibility of the Oregon legislature approving the secession of nearly three-fourths of its land mass to "Greater Idaho" seems remote. A more viable alternative for disgruntled Oregonians who appreciate Idaho politics would be simply to move to Idaho.

Besides, Idaho already has a seaport at Lewiston.

CHAPTER FIVE

1863
The Northwestern Border:
Washington

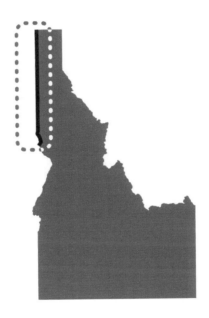

On a hot, dusty August day in 1862, John Mullan rode into Walla Walla. "Thus ended my work in the field, costing seven years of close and arduous attention exploring and opening up a road of six hundred and twenty-four miles," he wrote. Lieutenant Mullan had just led a massive work crew constructing the first engineered highway in the Pacific Northwest, laying a wagon road northeast to Fort Benton. He had now returned via that road to Walla Walla, the place where he began his project four years earlier. It had been a tough slog, building a wagon road over jagged mountains, across churning rivers, through dense forests. But Mullan had succeeded in fulfilling Thomas Jefferson's dream when he had sent Lewis and Clark west. Mullan had connected the headwaters of the Missouri and Columbia Rivers.[1]

Mullan rode into a ragged Washington Territory boomtown. Freight wagons and pack animals crowded along fetid, manure-be-fouled avenues. Rambling one-story frame buildings lined a half-mile-long Main Street. Carpenters scrambled to construct shops and houses to keep pace with the influx of new residents—not all of the best repute. As one observer noted, Walla Walla lay "quite low down the scale of civilization…overrun with thieves, gamblers and women of the demi-mode [sic]." This jerry-built town would soon be Washington's largest city.[2]

A supply center for miners making their way to diggings in what would soon become Idaho, Walla Walla boomed thanks to its favored location at one end of Mullan's new highway. Mullan envisioned even greater things ahead. He planned to resign from the Army and move permanently to Walla Walla. He invested in several businesses, hoping to grow rich along with his adopted town. He thought Walla Walla would become the capital of Washington Territory, and he determined to do all in his power to ensure that development.

Mullan was aware of rumors that Congress would soon establish a new territory, shrinking the huge, ungainly Washington. He believed that when Congress carved out that new territory, it would be in the best interests of Walla Walla citizens if Washington became a long rectangle, stretching from the Pacific Ocean to the Rocky Mountains. In Mullan's vision, land south of the 46th parallel would become the West's as-yet-unnamed newest territory. Walla Walla, just above that parallel, would sit conveniently at the east-west midpoint of the newly shaped Washington, helping to cement its case to become the capital, wresting the seat of territorial government from Olympia, secluded on Puget Sound.

Unfortunately for Mullan, William Wallace—who had business interests in Puget Sound and therefore hoped to retain the capital at Olympia—envisioned a much different Washington. He preferred a smaller, boxier territory with an eastern boundary that lined up with the eastern border of Oregon. It would be a place where Olympia did not rest so ridiculously far off on the western fringe.

Mullan and Wallace would each make their cases about borders to Congress. Wallace would triumph. And the story of how Idaho ended up with an isolated, skinny northern panhandle begins with that William Wallace congressional victory.

When Congress established borders for the new State of Oregon in 1859, it lumped into Washington Territory all of Oregon's former land east of the Snake River. Washington then included all of present-day Washington and Idaho, and parts of Montana and Wyoming—the old Oregon Country minus Oregon. It was an oddly shaped place, with today's southern Idaho resembling a drooping paunch.[3]

In 1859, no one much cared that Washington looked peculiar on a map. Only 11,000 or so non-Indians resided in all that immense tract of land. The majority clustered around Puget Sound. Then Elias D. Pierce appeared on the scene.

The political history of Idaho as we know it begins with E. D. Pierce. In 1852, he opened a trading post in Nez Perce country. Pierce could read a landscape. He suspected the Clearwater region held gold. In February 1860, he set out to explore the possibilities, trespassing on the Nez Perce Reservation. He panned a bit of color and persuaded himself that he had uncovered "a rich and extensive gold field." He believed, accurately, he "had the destiny of that country…at my option."[4]

Pierce kept his find quiet, but a few months later, with eleven other men, he ventured back to "the most dark, dense forest I ever saw." They found much more gold. "I never saw a party of men so much excited," he wrote. This time, word of the discovery quickly made it to Walla Walla and beyond. "The effect…was electrical," reported the *San Francisco Bulletin*, "and awakened a…desire for an immediate stampede to these fields." The gold rush Elias Pierce ignited would transform the Pacific Northwest.[5]

Soon, prospectors were whipsawing lumber for cabins and stores in a brand-new community named Pierce City. A short time later, Lewiston arose, a hodge-podge boomtown of tents and hastily constructed frame buildings at the head of navigation on the Snake River. Miners forged a primitive road linking that scrubby town with Pierce City, and Lewiston became a supply center for Idaho's first mines. The inconvenient fact that Lewiston illegally rested on the Nez Perce Reservation dissuaded no one from trespassing there.

The gold rush dramatically shifted the population center of Washington Territory. By 1861, more people lived east of the Cascades than west. The three men running that year to represent Washington in Congress had many differences. But they agreed on one thing: Whoever won would do their utmost to convince Congress to divide Washington and create a new territory. Everyone could agree on that, particularly those miners far removed from the seat of territorial government. "Of what use to us is a capital located at Olympia?" pondered Lewiston's newspaper publisher. "During four months of the last year no communication could be had with the place at all." Or, as another newspaper put it, Lewiston's residents renounced "any further affiliation with…[the] clam-eating politicians of Olympia." Lewistonians hoped their town would become capital of the new territory. At the same time, Walla Walla aspired to become capital of a newly shaped Washington. And Olympia fought for its capital-city status quo. The destiny of each depended upon the shape of the new territory—a place about to be named Idaho.[6]

William Wallace won the 1861 election as Washington's territorial delegate to Congress. He traveled to Washington, DC, bent upon retaining Washington's capital at Olympia, protecting his Puget Sound business interests. Wallace arrived in the District of Columbia in December 1861. John Mullan left Walla Walla on September 7, 1862, catching a stage out of town, the first leg of a long, jarring trip taking him through Portland and San Francisco and on to the nation's capital. There he would compile the official Army report of his road-building project. And in the winter of 1862–63, Mullan would be drawn into politics, engaging William Wallace in a contest over borders in the far Northwest.[7]

It was an interesting time in the nation's capital. A muddy path led visitors to the entrance of the Smithsonian Institution's red castle-like museum, completed a few years earlier. Cattle grazed in a pasture around the partially completed Washington Monument. Slaughterhouses nearby processed meat for the Union Army during the height of the Civil War. Only the Potomac River separated Washington—the Union's most vulnerable city—from Confederate Virginia. Thousands of troops protected the city, which supported dozens of military hospitals treating sick and wounded soldiers returning from battles that were going poorly for the Union. Thousands of fugitive slaves filled the streets, seeking refuge. A large freedman's village would soon occupy Robert E. Lee's confiscated plantation across the Potomac—a place called Arlington. Scaffolding surrounded the Capitol as laborers worked to complete its massive dome. Inside that Capitol, Congress wrestled to devise ways to finance the ever-more-bloody Civil War. Few members of Congress had time to contemplate something as inconsequential as the shape of a new territory in the faraway West. One who did was Congressman James Ashley.

When James Ashley ran away from home as a teenager, his evangelical preacher father told him, "You're on the straight road to Hell, boy!" Two decades later, Ashley won a seat in Congress representing Ohio. On his first day in office, he penned a letter on official congressional stationery: "Dear Father, I have just arrived." James Ashley became one of the nation's prominent abolitionists, an architect of the Thirteenth Amendment to the Constitution abolishing slavery. He also served as chair of the House of Representatives Committee on Territories. If there were to be a new territory in the Northwest, his committee would help guide the legislation creating it.[8]

Ashley had no knowledge of the squabbling among the residents of Olympia, Lewiston, and Walla Walla over their capital-city aspirations. But he did know about the gold rush E. D. Pierce ignited. And he knew of miners' increasingly strident demands for a new territory with a capital closer to the diggings. When President Abraham Lincoln presented his State of the Union to the 37th Congress in December 1862, it became clear Ashley would soon be paying close attention to matters in the Northwest. Lincoln acknowledged the Civil

War's financial strain on the nation and requested Congress develop "as rapidly as possible" the "immense mineral resources" of Western territories to "improve the revenues of the Government." Effectively harnessing that golden resource would require an efficient government in the mining region. So, on December 15, Representative William Kellogg of Illinois introduced a resolution in the House "that the committee on territories...inquire into the propriety of establishing a Territorial government for that region of country in which are situated the Salmon river gold mines."[9]

Ashley realized the time had arrived to carve a new territory out of unwieldy Washington. But he, like virtually all congressional represen-tatives, knew nothing about that region. It made sense for him to seek the help of a man more familiar with that area than anyone. Ashley turned to John Mullan.

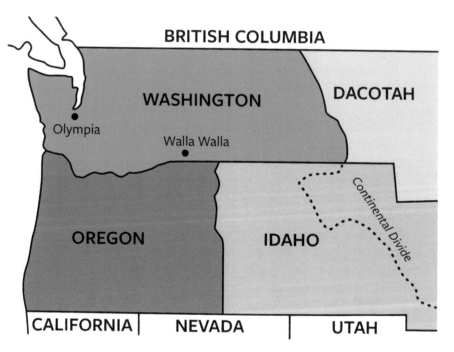

John Mullan's vision for the Northwest recognized the region's east-west orientation. The U.S. House of Representatives approved Mullan's concept in February 1863. Had the Senate agreed, there would be no Idaho panhandle, and centrally located Walla Walla might have wrested Washington's capital from Olympia.

Ashley had a vision for all new western territories. They should be rectangular, a little longer east and west than north and south. Ashley's preference meshed well with Mullan's knowledge of Northwestern geography—as well as Mullan's desire for Walla Walla to become capital of a reshaped Washington Territory.

Mullan took time from writing his Army road report to devise a plan for Northwest territorial boundaries. His map of a revamped Washington Territory featured an east-west rectangle, as Ashley desired. Mullan extended the existing 46th parallel straight-line border that separated eastern Oregon from Washington all the way to the Rocky Mountains. He included all of what became the Idaho panhandle, as well as western Montana, in Washington Territory. In Mullan's map, Olympia sat remotely isolated on the western edge of Washington; Walla Walla was conveniently central. Mullan envisioned that the new territory to be carved from Washington would combine today's southern Idaho with Wyoming. He initially labeled that place Montana on his map.[10]

Ashley introduced legislation creating the new territory and setting boundaries as Mullan proposed. On February 12, 1863, the House of Representatives easily passed the measure. Mullan had triumphed. Or so he thought.

Unbeknownst to Ashley and Mullan, William Wallace was quietly working on a very different scheme with the Senate, particularly with Oregon Senator Benjamin Harding. Wallace had as much interest in protecting Olympia's capital-city status as Mullan had for the aspirations of Walla Walla. Both hoped to benefit financially from economic advantages that accrued to seats of government.

While Mullan worked on his map, Wallace sketched one of his own. He borrowed heavily from Anson Henry. Henry was a close friend of Abraham Lincoln, his political ally, and for a time his personal doctor. Lincoln once wrote of Henry, "What a great, big-hearted man he is...one of the best men I have ever known." Henry moved to Oregon in 1852. In one of Lincoln's earliest presidential appointments, he named his old confidant the surveyor general of Washington Territory. Henry moved to Olympia and, like Wallace, took a keen interest in retaining it as the territorial capital. Henry's close association with the president ensured that his opinion about the territory's borders would have clout. Henry knew of Congress's inclination for straight-line boundaries and rectangular shapes. Given that Congress had already approved the width of Oregon, Henry envisioned Washington as a "sister" of the same width, with an eastern border as straight as possible. Henry's east boundary ran directly north from Lewiston to Canada. That was the concept Wallace had in mind as he began creating his own map of the Northwest. He received a boost when Henry joined him in Washington, DC, to personally lobby Lincoln.[11]

The Wallace-Henry map showed Washington Territory with the same borders as the current Washington State. A huge new territory—one Wallace labeled "Idaho" rather than Mullan's preferred "Montana"—encompassed all of the current states of Idaho and Montana, and virtually all of Wyoming.

Wallace at first did not reveal his proposed boundaries, and Ashley paid him little attention, believing Mullan and Wallace differed principally on what to name the new western territory. Ashley did not really care about the name and believed a conference committee could reconcile such minor differences between the House and Senate versions of the territorial bill. He was unaware that Wallace had proposed to the Senate a very different concept for the new territory's shape, something far more consequential than its name.[12]

The Senate, overwhelmed with Civil War concerns, showed little enthusiasm for a bill creating a new territory, and postponed considering it. "You could make a great many Territories out in that country," observed Senator Lyman Trumbull of Illinois in February. But this was not the time for such frivolity. Even golden resources failed to persuade him. "There are rich mines there, I have no doubt….But at this time in the midst of a Civil War…it seems to me it is an injudicious time" to create a new territory.[13]

The crisis-induced delay worked perfectly for William Wallace. With the help of a key ally, Senator Benjamin Franklin Harding, he laid a skillful trap for Ashley and Mullan. Wallace and Harding sprang it on the final day of the final session of the 37th Congress.

Benjamin Franklin Harding would seem an unlikely congressional power broker. But he had as much influence over setting Idaho's northwest border as Anson Henry or William Wallace. Born in Pennsylvania, Harding moved to Oregon in his twenties and enjoyed a modestly successful political life, even serving briefly as Speaker of the State House of Representatives. One of Oregon's United States senators, Edward Baker, had joined the Union Army and died in battle in 1861. After 30 ballots, a divided state legislature finally settled on Harding to fill the remaining years of Baker's term.

Harding had maneuvered relatively successfully within the parochial confines of local Oregon politics. He arrived in the nation's capital at a time of national calamity and proved largely ineffective at mastering the complexities of national politics in time of crisis. As one contemporary noted, Harding was "devoid of...special accomplishment." Historian John Wunder characterized his "mediocre career in the Senate" as one of "personal embarrassment and failure." Harding introduced only one major piece of successful legislation. But that bill dramatically influenced the history of Idaho.[14]

Congress had a hectic schedule on March 3, 1863. A special session would begin the next day. Bills not passed on March 3, the last day of the 37th Congress, would die, so members of Congress scrambled. They passed the *Habeas Corpus* Suspension Act, enabling President Lincoln to detain prisoners of war, spies, traitors, and others for extended periods without trial. Congress then approved the Enrollment Act, the nation's first federal draft law. Finally, Ashley's House-approved bill to create a new territory came up for debate in the Senate—a group of exhausted men, nearly all ignorant of the bill's specifics, and of the West generally. Senator James Doolittle of Wisconsin marshalled enough energy to make a spirited plea to pass Ashley's bill exactly as it arrived from the House. "It is important that it should be passed.... [It] is an important Territory, with great gold mines in it." Senator James Grimes of Iowa interrupted with a question no doubt on many senators' minds. "Where is it?" he asked.

In this atmosphere of lethargy and confusion, Harding pounced, well aware his colleagues had little regard for or knowledge of the region under consideration. He proposed an amendment to the House bill to change the borders of the territory to those suggested by Wallace rather than the ones advocated by Ashley and Mullan. Since senators had no understanding of the place and little interest in its shape, they deferred to the westerner and passed Harding's amendment with little discussion. Then Harding proposed another amendment, to change the name of the territory to Idaho rather than Mullan's suggested Montana. "I think the name of Idaho is much preferable to Montana," Harding argued. "Montana, to my mind, signifies nothing at all. Idaho, in English, signifies 'the gem of the mountains.'" His frazzled Senate colleagues thought that name just as acceptable as the new borders. They wanted to be done with this seemingly inconsequential piece of legislation. So, they also passed Harding's amendment to change the name.[15]

The Senate action jolted Ashley. When the Senate bill arrived at the House, he vigorously sought a conference committee to hash out what he now knew to be significant differences between the House and Senate versions of the territorial bill. But by then it was near midnight, members of Congress were weary, and time was quickly running out on the 37th Congress. Either the House accepted the Senate version or kill the bill. Over Ashley's loud objections, the House buckled and approved the Senate version. Congress then sent the bill for the new Territory of Idaho—with boundaries carefully crafted by William Wallace, Anson Henry, and Benjamin Harding—to President Lincoln. At dawn on March 4, 1863, Lincoln signed the act creating the new territory. Idaho finally got its name—and its fourth permanent border.[16]

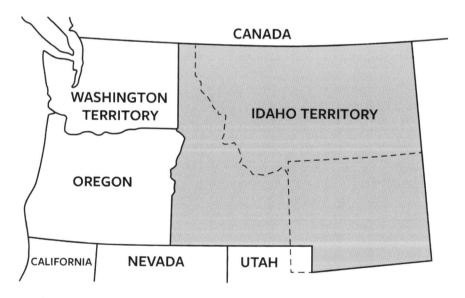

The Senate rejected John Mullan's map and approved William Wallace's vision for the Northwest. Late at night on March 3, 1863, the House of Representatives concurred, creating an enormous Idaho Territory.

The least consequential congressional decision that March 3 came over what name to give the new territory. The name Idaho had been kicking around the halls of Congress for a couple of years. Indeed, Congress came very close to naming Colorado "Idaho" before having a last-minute change of heart. In congressional debate over the Colorado bill in 1861, one senator noted, "Idaho is a very good name. In the Indian language it signifies 'Gem of the Mountains.'" Two years later, William Wallace, well aware of that unused name, fastened it to his map of the new territory. The "Indian origins" of the word appealed to many in Congress.[17]

But the concept of Idaho as an Indian word is nonsense. As Idaho State Historian Merle Wells once noted, "It had the merit of sounding so much like an Indian name that, before long, scarcely anyone would believe that it wasn't."

Not only did people get used to the concept of Idaho as an Indian word. Over time, they embellished the story. Generations of Idaho schoolchildren learned that their state's name came from the Indian word "Ee-da-how," meaning "sunrise" or, more poetically, "sun rising over the mountains." As Wells wrote, "It is far from being the only Indian name which no Indian ever heard of until he got it from a white man."

The fabricated name eventually got attached to a territory and then a state. Whether William Wallace knew of the name's bogus origin is unclear. But the name served Wallace's purposes well, for by attaching it to his map of the Northwest he helped disguise his true intensions, which had everything to do with the shape of the new territory and nothing serious to do with its name. Congress bogged down in semantics, benefitting Wallace. "Is this a mere contest between the two names of Montana and Idaho?" asked bleary-eyed Congressman William Wadsworth of Kentucky as the House contemplated the Senate bill. Ashley tried to convince him that the Wallace-Harding Senate bill had much more serious connotations, but the late hour and overall lack of congressional interest defeated him.[18]

The appellation ultimately had no influence on Idaho's development. It is not a bad name. On the other hand, the border with Washington that Congress imposed had serious aftereffects. Indeed, a case could be made that congressional approval of the Wallace map over Mullan's was the most consequential decision in Idaho history. One year later, Congress would draw another arbitrary border slightly to the east, between Idaho and another new territory named Montana, creating the narrow Idaho panhandle, segregated by mountains and rivers from the rest of the territory. Much of Idaho's political, economic, and cultural history has centered around efforts to connect the north and south, a fractiousness that defined the state into the 21st century. The panhandle's awkward shape can be traced back to that late-night determination in March 1863. That is when a group of men in far-distant Washington, DC—virtually none of whom had any knowledge of the Northwest, and all of whom just wanted to be done with an exhausting legislative session—made a quick decision about a border that would affect the lives of generations of Idahoans to come.[19]

Idaho would have been much better served if Congress had approved John Mullan's plan. His map made greater geographical sense, for it recognized the traditional east-west orientation of the region. Mullan believed the boundaries that Congress defined for Idaho to be absurd. After he lost his struggle with Wallace, Mullan advocated that Congress create a new Northwestern territory, one that combined what are now eastern Washington, northern Idaho, and western Montana, an area with far better geographical logic. Indeed, the concept of a new territory or state encompassing Mullan's vision percolated in that region into the 20th century and continued to find adherents in the 21st.[20]

William Wallace had completely outmaneuvered John Mullan. Not only did Wallace get his way with the border, he also won President Lincoln's appointment as Idaho's first territorial governor—a position Mullan aggressively sought. Mullan lined up an impressive array of politicians to support his appointment, including senators, members of Congress, and a Supreme Court justice. They noted his "great achievements" and "his intimate knowledge of the great North West." Three senators even visited Lincoln in the White House to promote his appointment. Mullan himself wrote the president that his road-building labors had added to "the development of that region to which I am attached and which I desire to make my permanent home."[21]

But on March 10, Congress approved Lincoln's appointment of Wallace as governor. Wallace had rebuffed Mullan again. As the

Sacramento Daily Union mocked, "It would appear that the redoubtable Captain Mullan has beat the bush and somebody else has caught the bird."[22]

William Wallace soon made his way west to assume his new duties as governor of the sprawling Territory of Idaho. It consisted of all of what is now Idaho and Montana, and almost all of Wyoming—an area larger than Texas. Wallace proclaimed Lewiston the capital. A resident had described that new seat of government a year before Wallace arrived: "The town is built of canvas, poles, logs and split boards. Town lots are all the rage....Yet Lewiston is situated upon an Indian reservation, and no one has any title to the lots, save squatter's rights." Still, it was here that Idaho's first territorial legislature met. It immediately requested that Congress shrink the size of the enormous territory. Idaho would soon have another border.[23]

William Wallace would not last long in the ragtag community of Lewiston. He soon won election as Idaho's territorial delegate to Congress and moved back to Washington, DC. He served one term before returning to his business interests in Puget Sound. Nearby Olympia retained its position as capital of Washington thanks largely to him.

John Mullan's return to his businesses in Walla Walla did not work out so well. He went bankrupt and made his way to California where he earned a reputation as a shady lawyer specializing in questionable land deals. He lived long enough to hear reports of the first automobiles traveling on his old wagon road across northern Idaho—a road that would one day go by the name Captain John Mullan Highway, better known as Interstate 90.

Anson Henry had second thoughts about the border between Washington and Idaho. It soon struck him that Walla Walla was gaining influence over Olympia and might yet wrest away the capitol. Like Mullan, he believed the solution lay in creating another new territory in the Northwest. He proposed calling it Columbia. Like Mullan's plan, it would incorporate eastern Washington, northern Idaho, and western Montana. Lewiston and Walla Walla could compete for the capital, leaving Olympia to safely preside over a much smaller Washington. It was a notion that would continue to arise for more than 150 years. But Henry proved no more successful advancing the concept of

Columbia than had Mullan, or would generations of their successors. Henry made his way again to Washington, DC, to make his case for the new territory. But the assassination of his good friend Abraham Lincoln in April 1865 dealt the idea a deathblow. Three months later, Henry drowned in a shipwreck off California.

Benjamin Franklin Harding served only two-and-a-half lackluster years in the United States Senate. He returned to Oregon, retired from public life, and became a farmer. He remains a virtually unknown figure in Idaho history. But his late-night legislating on March 3, 1863, had a powerful influence on a place that—because of him—came to be called Idaho.

Border Story

SURVEY

It is one thing for Congress to create borders. Once Idaho's various boundaries were determined, it proved quite easy to describe them legally. A border, for example, might begin "at a point in the middle channel of the Snake river where the northern boundary of Oregon intersects the same; then follow down the channel of Snake river to a point opposite the mouth of the Clearwater river." Or, more simply, a border might go "east along [the 49th] parallel to the thirty ninth degree of longitude." And once Congress had established the boundaries, it proved uncomplicated to plot them on maps. And with that, Congress had done its work. Someone else would need to translate the legal language into an identifiable boundary on the ground. Someone, in other words, had to survey. In a state like Idaho, rimmed with mountains, pierced with rivers, dense with wilderness—well, in a place like that, the real work had not yet begun. No wonder it took decades to complete the task of marking Idaho's borders.

When Alonzo Richards accepted a contract from the General Land Office in 1873 to survey the boundary between Wyoming and Idaho, he agreed to the following:

> establish at the end of each mile measured…a post at least seven feet long and six inches square, surrounded by a conical mound of Earth or Stone….To receive the post you will make an excavation two feet deep at the bottom of which you will deposit a marked rock or charred block. The mound will be six or seven feet in diameter at the base, and three feet high and the posts will project two feet from the top of the mound.[1]

That sort of job description worked quite well in loamy, flat country. In a place like Idaho, fulfilling such contract demands required excruciatingly hard, time-consuming work. For teams surveying the 49th parallel, just getting to the job site posed problems.

In 1860, topographer Henry Custer struggled through "mountainous and timbered" country attempting to make his way north to the parallel. He tried going part way by boat but found the Pend Oreille River "almost uninterrupted [with] rapids and falls." He then ventured to Priest Lake, assuming he could navigate it to the boundary, but the water did not extend that far. When he ran out of lake, he packed five days of provisions and scrambled north on foot, climbing "the highest mountain I ever ascended." Unable to proceed farther, he surveyed the 49th parallel the best he could from that "splendid and unlimited" viewpoint. He had accomplished a Herculean task, but not exactly the precise on-the-ground survey that officials desired.[2]

That same year, another surveyor attempting to reach the Canadian border tried a route along the shore of Lake Pend Oreille. George Clinton Gardner swam mules in icy rivers, spent precious time building rafts, and precariously made his way north through extensive "boggy ground."[3]

Survey crews had to cut pack trails through nearly impenetrable forests just to reach the northern boundary. Once there, they found it "impossible to follow the 49th parallel continuously," so they ran "the line of the survey...over the nearest practicable route." The Canadian survey crew working simultaneously with the Americans faced similar obstacles. Much of the boundary simply went unsurveyed and unmarked. In 1901, the United States sent another crew to complete the task. Surveyor Amherst Barber, working on the Idaho section, recorded his efforts toiling "terribly in the fallen tree tops on this line in deep snow and thick snow-laden brush along the edge of...monstrous...trees [and]...awful mountain walls."[4]

Given these difficulties along the 49th parallel, it is little wonder that the 1897 surveyors of the Montana-Idaho line had such a tough time even getting started. They hoped to find a boundary marker at the intersection of the Idaho, Montana, and British Columbia borders from which to commence. But that proved impossible "because of the fact that there was no monument on the international boundary within a reasonable distance with which a connection could be made." Former survey crews had been unable to make it to that spot. The 1897 team finally found a monument eight-and-a-half miles distant and plotted their calculations from there.[5]

Idaho's mountainous environment made for grueling work along that Montana line. Surveyors completed the 70 miles of straight-line boundary south from the 49th parallel in 1899 after three years in the field. They encountered conditions ranging from forest-fire smoke "so dense as to render observations impossible" to "snow being so deep as to render practically impossible the ascent of peaks."[6]

In 1904, the General Land Office contracted with Howard Carpenter to complete the survey of the 667 miles of Montana-Idaho boundary along the Bitterroots and Rockies. Carpenter hired a crew of more than 20 men, supported with dozens of horses. There were chainmen, rodmen, mound men, axemen, flagmen, cooks, horse wranglers, and packers. Even with such a large assault team, it took Carpenter four years to complete the task. "One of the greatest difficulties," he reported, "has been the very short season in which the work could be carried forward and the prevalence of storms even during that season."[7]

Yet the difficulties encountered in surveying Idaho's five other borders pale in comparison to the effort to mark the line separating Washington and Idaho.

The Nez Perce call the place Tsceminicum, the meeting of the waters. It is a lovely spot in Lewiston, where the Clearwater River merges with the Snake. But it proved a damnably difficult place from which to begin a survey.

In the summer of 1873, the General Land Office awarded Rollin Reeves of Olympia a contract to mark the boundary between Washington and Idaho. With his $10,800, Reeves hired an astronomer, two transit men, a leveler, four chainmen, four mound builders and axemen, two cooks, and three packers, along with 45 horses. They set out for Lewiston to establish the initial location from which they had been instructed to begin their work, the point "in the middle channel of Snake River, opposite the mouth of Clearwater, as it existed March 3, 1863." They discovered Tsceminicum is not quite as tranquil as it appears from the shore.[8]

To determine the precise middle channel, Reeves interviewed "old citizens and rivermen in Lewiston." He consulted with John Silcott, who operated ferries on the Snake and Clearwater. He met with E. F. Coe, owner of the *Colonel Wright*, the first steamboat on the Snake River. And he sought advice from Thomas Stump who, in 1865, in an effort to determine the navigability of the Snake above Lewiston, captained the *Colonel Wright* 80 miles upstream. The river proved none too navigable. Stump destroyed his boat. After visiting with Stump, Reeves probably had a hunch that the rivers here ran wild. It had taken Stump four-and-a-half days to churn the 80 miles upstream. He made it back to Lewiston in less than five hours, his hull a splintered wreck. As Reeves soon learned, "the terrible force of the water" could complicate things.[9]

Reeves found that his informants had "various interpretations" about the exact spot from which he was to begin, giving him "the greatest...anxiety." He spent two weeks of "considerable embarrassment" attempting to confirm the definitive middle channel. He decided to float a buoy into the river and take measurements from the shore to ascertain the exact spot. The torrential river quickly swept away the buoy. So, he tried another buoy. Same result. He repeated the process five times with "buoys of varied construction and weight." All cascaded down the boiling river before he could make any observations from shore. Then he hammered a heavy stake into the ground, wrapped a thick rope around it, tied the other end to a large keg, and tossed it into the turbulent current. A hundred feet of line played out. Then another hundred. And then the keg disappeared, dragged under by the rope's sodden weight.[10]

After trying "all the appliances we could secure or invent," Reeves gave up. He could not ascertain the middle channel. Even if he had, it would have been "impracticable to plant a visible iron monument at the junction of the two rivers." So, he identified an "approximate location." His team then went to work marking an adjacent place on shore to serve as the official survey starting point. They dug a two-foot hole on the north bank of the river, just above the high-water mark. They filled the bottom with charcoal, erected a six-foot-long stone shaft, and surrounded it with a mound of packed soil. They then dug four pits three feet deep and ten feet long radiating out north, south, east, and west from the marker. Finally, they chiseled "1873" on one side of the stone, and I.T. and W.T. on the other sides, for Idaho and Washington territories. Then Reeves and his crew headed north to run a straight line to Canada and sink boundary posts in the ground at every mile.[11]

The difficulty ascertaining the middle channel portended an arduous trek ahead, though work at first progressed effortlessly as the survey team passed through the rich Palouse grasslands. No obstacles blocked their path; the deep topsoil proved easy digging for setting survey markers. This would become some of the nation's richest agricultural country, America's most abundant wheat-producing land. Already in 1873, Reeves encountered scattered farms where families grew vegetables and grazed cattle. He would surely have noticed some of the early settlers in a place then called, for good reason, Paradise Valley. A few years later, a town named Moscow would arise here. The surveyors marked land near ground that would be occupied by the future University of Idaho.[12]

The party continued north, stretching their measuring chains, taking astronomical observations, leaving behind wooden boundary markers. About 50 miles north of Lewiston they sank markers along what became the western border of the Coeur d'Alene Indian Reservation, recently established by President Ulysses Grant. On September 2, they reached Spokane Bridge, a community of about three dozen people settled near a toll bridge over the town's namesake river.

From this point north, the going got trickier as the crew encountered timbered country. Rather than digging postholes in the rocky terrain, they often indicated the line by blazing marks in trees. They did find a soft spot to dig a post at mile 121 in "a beautiful natural pine park" near the Pend Oreille River. That peaceful setting belied the task before them. From here, Reeves and his party raced against a fast-approaching winter, through a "mountainous country of the roughest character." They did not yet know it, but operating in those severe conditions, they would not reach their 49th parallel goal. Indeed, they were fortunate to return alive to the bucolic setting where they placed milepost 121.

The party paused for three days on the south bank of the Pend Oreille River as they built log rafts to ferry across their provisions and equipment. The boundary here crossed two islands. On one, they surprised two trappers "who were astonished at the appearance" of the surveyors.

Reeves gathered what information he could about the northern land-scape from them—the only white men they would encounter during their remaining time in the field.

The farther they ventured, the more rugged the terrain. They con-fronted "fallen timber over the entire mile" between markers 171 and 172. The next mile took them across land strewn "with large bowlders and plenty of rock [causing]…the greatest labor of any since leaving Lewiston."

Things only got worse. The next mile, encountered on a cold, clear day, saw them plodding through "ground covered with snow." After blazing a mark on a tree at mile 174 they trudged on through "a steep, brushy hillside…the surface…covered with snow" that rendered their progress "slow and almost perilous."

On October 25, they staggered to mile 176. They had purchased their last mile at heavy cost. "Numerous logs, stumps, and large bowlders are crossed every few chains," Reeves recorded. "These, together with the abruptness of the grade, loose stones, thick underbrush, snow, cold, and general exhaustion, have rendered the establishment of the mile one of the most difficult, tedious, and painful of the entire boundary."

Reeves knew they were near the 49th parallel and sent a party to find it. He "confidently expected" his scouts would discover "a well-de-fined boundary between British Columbia and the United States." His instructions from the General Land Office had informed him that the border would be marked by a wide swath where "timber had been razed to the earth's surface." But, like his counterparts more than 20 years later surveying the Montana-Idaho line, after two days of a "vain search," Reeves's scouts found no evidence of a survey party ever hav-ing marked the international boundary at this jagged intersection with Idaho. "The party was greatly surprised…and puzzled to find no indi-cations whatever of any white man having ever been in the vicinity of this parallel," a nonplussed Reeves reported. He attributed it to "the belief among the engineers of the two governments that the land was too worthless to ever be settled by white men."

While the scouting party futilely searched for a boundary line, Reeves and the main crew pushed on, slashing through brush, crawl-ing over boulders, sliding on snow over country "of the very roughest character." They labored to gain a half mile, and there they set a post at mile 176 1/2. The weary crew called a halt to their effort to reach the international border. As it turned out, they were less than a mile from their destination. But it was stop here or perish in the attempt.

Five days and 15 miles earlier, they had left behind all their horses and packers at a meadow, "the last vestige of grass on the…route." At that point, their remaining rations consisted only of "several sacks of flour." Reeves had divided most of this among the crew that would forge north. With "blankets on their backs and their ration of flour," the field party had slogged its way toward Canada. As they set their final maker and received that discouraging news about the scouts' inability to locate the 49th parallel, the party found their provisions nearly exhausted. The cook gathered the remaining scraps of flour, baked a few small loaves of bread, and rationed them to the men. Even then—miserably cold and short on food—the survey party labored on. On Little Snowy Top, north of Priest Lake, "all hands now proceeded to cut down trees and otherwise clear the view" so their astronomer could "make final observations for latitude." He worked all night in ten-degree weather.

Then the bedraggled group retraced its route back to their horses. Too weak to tote their equipment, they left it behind, carried their remaining bread and blankets, and "after three days of unremitting toil" in an "almost famished condition," made it to their main camp. "By this time we were thoroughly convinced that to have remained only a day or two longer in endeavoring to push the work to its completion would have been fatal," Reeves reported. Fortunately, the packers they had left behind in the meadow had purchased some dried salmon from Indians and killed a moose. "Upon this diet," the party managed to make its way back to Spokane Bridge. There it purchased provisions, made the easy ride across the Palouse prairie, and disbanded at Lewiston. Though they had not reached their final goal, they had completed an astonishing feat of surveying under most demanding circumstances.

In 1908, Congress appropriated money for another survey crew to retrace the route, install permanent markers, and complete the survey to the 49th parallel. To head the team, the U.S. Geological Society contracted with one of its finest professionals. Samuel Gannett, a co-founder of the National Geographic Society, knew something about terrain. He understood the severe hardships Reeves experienced. As Gannett noted, "one can but marvel at the persistence and hardihood of that party of men who did not falter until actual lack of food compelled retreat." Gannett's team faced few of those difficulties.

By 1908, the country had filled in. The surveyors passed through comfortable towns, remarked on prosperous sawmills and farms, and noted the bustling University of Idaho campus—where Reeves had observed only prairie grass. When they got farther north, Priest Lake steamboats ferried their supplies. Even so, there were places that still required "practically continuous chopping" in order to clear paths for the chainmen. As snow and rain set in, the surveyors called it a season. They finally completed their task the next year, reaching the 49th parallel on August 29, 1909—a much preferred time of year to be in that vicinity than Reeves had experienced.

The 20th-century survey team found several of Reeves's wooden markers, though farmers had plowed many under. They replaced the wooden posts with wrought-iron tubes filled with concrete, and "wherever practicable" placed a six-foot granite monument every five miles, cementing bronze locational markers on top. At the international boundary, the crew dug a pit two-feet deep and three-feet square. They stacked rocks six-feet high, bonding them with mortar. They packed soil around the monument and sealed a bronze tablet on top. It read, "1909-Canada-United States-Washington-Idaho." Forty-six years after a preoccupied Civil War Congress had bowed to William Wallace's clever lobbying and established the boundary between Washington and Idaho, that border had finally been surveyed.

Samuel Gannett returned to the District of Columbia. If he paid close attention to the Washington newspaper on December 29, 1909, four months after his surveyors had set the bronze marker at the international boundary, he might have noticed a small story announcing the death in that city of 79-year-old John Mullan. Mullan had built a military wagon road that helped open up a vast territory in the Inland Empire. Nearly half a century later, Gannett's crew might have seen automobiles on Mullan's road as the surveyors crossed that highway east of Spokane. Many of the Idaho and Washington residents Gannett's team encountered in the rapidly growing region had traveled to their homes on the Mullan Road.[13]

Decades earlier, Mullan had lost his battle with William Wallace over Idaho's borders. Now, 46 years after that late-night congressional decision that would so influence Idaho history, the boundary between Washington and Idaho had been surveyed. When the 1909 team completed its work to the Canadian border, it had surveyed the last of Idaho's more than 1,800 miles of borders.

CHAPTER SIX

1864
The Northeastern Border:
Montana

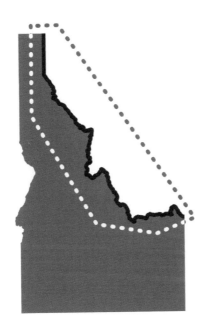

William Wallace knew the Lewiston of 1861. He had campaigned there to become territorial delegate to Congress—when Lewiston was part of Washington. It had been a swashbuckling town squatting on Nez Perce Indian land, many of its buildings sheathed in canvas, few constructed with any thought of permanency. Lewiston just grew, without plat or plan, a supply depot for mining camps to the east. Resting on a bank of the Snake River, the town received supplies from Portland whenever water ran high enough that steamers could negotiate the rapids. No one kept a strict accounting, but Lewiston probably boasted several thousand residents by 1862. As Idaho's new territorial governor, Wallace had that robust community in mind when, on his trip west, he proclaimed Lewiston the seat of territorial government. Of course, there was not much competition. Idaho boasted a land mass larger than Texas, virtually devoid of towns.

Governor Wallace arrived in the capital on July 10, 1863, and found a Lewiston little resembling its heyday. Much of Idaho's population had already streamed south to new diggings in the Boise Basin. Lewiston, only two years old, looked a bit long in the tooth. Wallace did find an oasis—a place of comparative elegance in the rickety town. He set up residence in the Hotel DeFrance, the center of Lewiston's social life, featuring hand-carved furniture and a glamorous French owner eager for the publicity her new occupant would provide. From these pampered quarters, Wallace oversaw the initial organization of Idaho's first territorial government.

Sidney Edgerton lived a more austere life, 400 miles to the east. An ardent abolitionist, Edgerton had served two terms in Congress, a colleague of his fellow Ohio Republican, James Ashley. Edgerton lost his reelection bid in 1862 and President Abraham Lincoln appointed him chief justice of the Idaho Territorial Supreme Court. On June 1, 1863, Edgerton departed for Idaho, along with his wife Mary, their four children, and a niece. The party traveled by train to St. Louis, riverboat to Omaha, and wagon to Idaho. Shortly after the family crossed the South Pass summit, a telegraph operator overtook them to relay word that Wallace had named Lewiston as Idaho's capital. The Edgertons journeyed on, planning to rest a few days at Bannack City before continuing to Lewiston. Though they arrived at Bannack in mid-September, snows already blanketed the mountains, so they decided to winter over in the raucous miners' camp. They purchased a log building and remodeled it into a home. The family made its own furniture: benches for the handmade table, bunks nailed to walls, mattresses stuffed with straw. "It was a poor excuse for a house," Edgerton's daughter later confided.[1]

Bannack had arisen quickly. The town's first inhabitants arrived barely a year ahead of the Edgertons, part of a rush to new gold diggings a couple miles east on Grasshopper Creek. By 1863, the makeshift community housed several hundred miners and shopkeepers. Bannack still had rough edges. A few months after the Edgertons arrived, vigilantes hanged the sheriff on gallows on the fringe of town. Sidney Edgerton could only aspire to William Wallace's relatively comfortable life at the Hotel DeFrance on the other side of the Bitterroot Mountains.

In the winter of 1863–64, people from these two disparate towns plotted divergent visions of Idaho's future. Residents of Bannack had a plan for Idaho's eastern border that defied the desires of Lewistonians. Because of Sidney Edgerton's skillful politicking, northern Idaho would shrink in size to a thin, bizarrely shaped panhandle. And Edgerton, the architect of that geographic perversion, became the first governor of a new western territory chiseled away at Idaho's expense. That place took the name Montana.

Notwithstanding his pleasant accommodations at the Hotel DeFrance, William Wallace grew restless in Lewiston. He longed again for Washington, DC. In October 1863, he won election as Idaho's first territorial congressional delegate and returned to the national capital. Despite his absence, the legislature would still meet, and Lewiston's residents giddily set about sprucing up their community in anticipation of the legislators' first session. They dressed up some of the town's few wooden structures. These would serve as official governmental offices and meeting places. They rolled boulders off streets, removed trash, and dismantled the abandoned frames of former canvas tents. They planned for an inaugural ball at the fashionable-by-Lewiston-standards Luna House Hotel. There they would wine and dine legislators when they gathered in December 1863—a tough time to travel in Idaho.[2]

Sidney Edgerton had thought it unwise to attempt a mountain crossing to Lewiston in September. Imagine that same landscape of ice-clogged rivers and snow-banked mountains in December. So treacherous was the travel that, come spring, legislators from Bannack chose not to retrace their initial route to Lewiston over the mountains. Instead they took a most circuitous trip, journeying by steamboat to Portland (portaging around rapids along the way); sailing on an ocean ship to San Francisco; hopping a stage to Salt Lake City; and finishing their trek on horseback to their homes.[3]

That first territorial legislature had a very busy schedule. It organized counties, adopted legal codes, created a revenue stream, and established public school policies. But the very first legislative action, deemed more important than all others, had nothing to do with any of that. William C. Rheem, one of those representatives who hazarded the mountains between Bannack and Lewiston, introduced Council Memorial One, praying "for a division of Territory." Within a couple of weeks, both houses of the legislature had approved the measure and sent it to Congress. The legislators explained that "the great extent of the territory, and its intersection by ranges of Mountains, the trails across, and through which are, in the Season when the legislative assembly should convene, obstructed by Snow, renders it in all cases difficult and hazardous, and in some, impossible for the members of that body to meet at any point on either side of the Mountains." The legislators proposed that Congress split off a new territory from the enormous Idaho. The border between Idaho and the new territory should be the continental divide, along the crest of the Rocky Mountains. Such a border would have followed long historical precedent, for that was the eastern boundary of the old Oregon Country, and had also served as the eastern border of Oregon Territory and later, Washington Territory. Legislators did not believe they needed to convince Congress of the logic of the continental divide border, since it had such durable antecedents.[4]

Acting Governor William Daniels sent a copy of the memorial to Idaho's new congressional delegate, William Wallace. Daniels included a note stating, "I think the whole people of this territory desire it to be divided, and expect you to labor to that end." With that work out of the way, legislators moved on with their crowded agenda. They paid no attention to the residents of faraway Bannack, who also agreed the territory should be divided, and were also busy that winter doing something about it. They had a very different concept about where Idaho's eastern border should lie.[5]

Congressman James Ashley, chair of the House of Representatives Committee on Territories, had fumed over Idaho's shape since the previous spring when Congress rejected his boundary proposal based on John Mullan's map. A few days before Rheem proposed his memorial to the Idaho legislature, Ashley introduced a bill in Congress to create some order out of the chaos of Idaho's boundaries. But he struggled trying to determine just how many territories should be created out of ungainly Idaho, and where their borders should be located. The previous Congress's rejection of Mullan's concept of an east-west orientation for Northwest territories complicated things for Ashley—and indeed for generations of politicians. They attempted to make political sense out of a north-south orientation for Idaho that defied logic, geography, and hundreds of years of Native American trade patterns. Ashley made no progress on his boundary conundrum until the residents of Bannack proposed a solution he thought made as much sense as possible out of a confusing situation.

Sidney Edgerton's isolation in Bannack created political opportunity. While William Rheem convinced the territorial legislature in Lewiston to shrink Idaho, his fellow Bannack residents raised money to send a delegation to lobby Congress about the location of the western border of the newly created territory. After collecting $2,000 in lobbying funds, they dispatched a small party headed by Edgerton to Washington, DC. Edgerton left behind his family, including his pregnant wife Mary, who gave birth to a daughter in his absence. Ironically, Mary named her Idaho. The baby, along with the rest of Bannack's residents, would soon be living in a place called Montana, thanks to the efforts of the infant's father.[6]

Bannack's residents chose well when selecting Edgerton. As a former member of Congress, he knew that body well. He had a good relationship with President Lincoln and visited him frequently. And he had a good rapport with his fellow Ohioan, James Ashley.

Edgerton carried a letter from Bannack's citizens to William Wallace. It did not exactly contradict the letter Idaho's acting governor

William Daniels had previously sent Idaho's congressional delegate. Daniels wrote that Idaho's citizens expected Wallace to encourage Congress to create a new territory. Bannack residents were more specific. Wallace should not only advocate the creation of a place they called Montana. He should also promote the border of their choice, which lay west of the continental divide. For reasons not exactly clear, Wallace agreed. So when Edgerton began lobbying in Washington, James Ashley proved willing to ignore the Idaho legislature's proposal seeking a border along the continental divide. After all, Idaho's delegate to Congress agreed with Ashley's friend Edgerton that the border should lay farther west.

Edgerton had political self-preservation in mind. If Congress approved the Idaho legislature's proposal for a Rocky Mountain border, Bannack would remain in Idaho, and Edgerton would reside in a community far removed from the territorial capital at Lewiston, providing little opportunity to advance his political ambitions. So, when Edgerton met with Ashley shortly after arriving in Washington, he proposed that the border between Idaho and Montana should indeed follow the Rocky Mountains—for part of the distance. However, instead of arcing north at the continental divide, Edgerton proposed the border continue west to the Bitterroots and then begin its northern ascent to Canada. This would leave Bannack as one of the largest communities in Montana. Edgerton had "a number of meetings with President Lincoln" and found the president "earnestly in favor" of his border concept. Edgerton also noted that Ashley was "a strong supporter." Ashley, though, probably had some qualms. Idaho would remain a strangely odd shape, offending his sense of patterned orderliness. But at least Montana would be roughly rectangular. Since both Idaho's congressional delegate and President Lincoln approved of the dividing line at the Bitterroots, Ashley concurred.[7]

Both Edgerton and Wallace appeared before Ashley's Committee on Territories. A border along the Rockies would do nothing to alleviate Bannack's isolation from Lewiston, they argued. The Bitterroots provided a more natural boundary. When no one spoke against the idea, the committee passed a Montana territorial bill with the border that Edgerton and Wallace requested. The full House of Representatives approved the measure. Then things bogged down.

Most members of Congress really did not anguish much about western territorial borders. Just as during the previous year when creating Idaho, they had more serious issues on their minds—a seemingly never-ending Civil War and the ongoing national discussion over African American rights. The issue of African Americans dominated debate about Montana in the Senate.

When the House bill reached the Senate, Morton Wilkinson of Minnesota introduced an amendment striking the word "white" from the section on voter qualifications. Some senators claimed the amendment irrelevant, believing erroneously that the future Montana had no Black residents. The Senate ultimately agreed on the amendment giving franchise to African Americans. The bill then went to a conference committee to resolve differences between the House and Senate, but the committee failed to reach a resolution. It appeared the Montana territorial bill might fail. Then a second conference committee proposed that Montana abide by the same provision Congress had established when creating Idaho in 1863. That bill restricted voting to white males. The House readily accepted the proposal with little discussion. Some senators balked, insisting the principle of Black suffrage should not suffer simply to hasten creation of a new territory. But Oregon Senator James Nesmith summarized the feelings of a majority of senators. "I have no particular sentimentality on this subject so far as the negro is concerned," he pronounced. "But I do take some interest in the white men who are there...who are entirely destitute and deprived of government by reason of the present condition...of the Territory." The Senate approved the conference committee proposal. On May 26, 1864, President Lincoln signed the act creating Montana Territory. He effectively disenfranchised the few Blacks living in Montana, just as he had done the previous year when signing the Idaho territorial bill. Not until 1867 did Congress pass the Territorial Suffrage Act that finally enfranchised Black men in American territories.[8]

As Congress debated the bill, Sidney Edgerton agonizingly observed from the galleries. Though an ardent abolitionist, he worried that a controversy over African American suffrage might derail the Montana bill. But he need not have fretted. The debate only delayed Edgerton's main cause—the western border location. No one in all that Senate debate over Montana so much as mentioned the Idaho legislature's request for a boundary at the continental divide. Edgerton and his ally William Wallace dominated that issue. The western line separating Idaho and Montana would be "along the crest of the Bitter Root mountains." It was a complete victory for Edgerton. He would soon be rewarded, for he made good use of his spare time while Congress haggled. He asked former congressional colleagues to support his appeal to Lincoln to appoint him Montana's first governor. His lobbying paid off. Once Lincoln signed the Montana bill, he named Edgerton governor. Edgerton in turn selected Bannack as the territory's first capital. The residents of Bannack had indeed done quite well when sending Sidney Edgerton to Washington.[9]

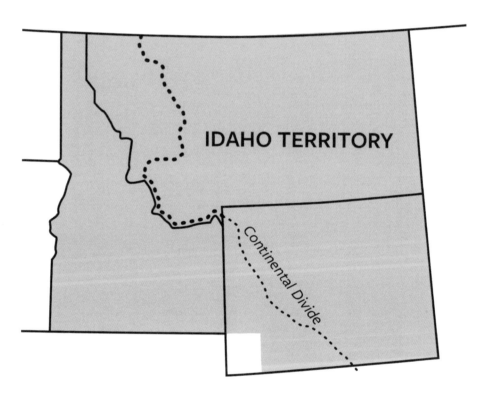

When establishing Montana Territory in 1864, Congress ignored the Idaho legislature's request that the continental divide form the border between the two territories. That action gave Idaho its narrow, isolated panhandle.

Meanwhile, out in Idaho, the territory's residents labored under the delusion that they might finally have some influence over the location of one of their borders. Their legislators, after all, had made a specific boundary request to Congress. Idahoans waited anxiously. "The all absorbing topic of interest with us at the present time is as to the division of the territory," wrote one to William Wallace, mistakenly believing Wallace was busy in the nation's capital working in Idaho's best interests. "Where are the boundary lines…[is the] question often asked but never answered."[10]

Wallace had long since abandoned the legislature's border request. When Edgerton and Wallace convinced Ashley to support the Bitterroot border, it sealed Idaho's fate, as no other member of Congress showed any interest in the border issue. About the only indication that Congress awoke at all during those discussions came when it set the last 70 miles of border from the point where the Bitterroot Mountains intersect the 39th degree of longitude. From there, the border would extend "northward to the boundary line of the British possessions." In other words, that part of the border would be a straight line to Canada. Below that, the Idaho-Montana boundary squiggles wildly following the Bitterroots and Rockies, the only western state boundary set along mountain ridges. But that northern 70 miles is as straight as can be. It helped satisfy the desires of those in Congress who appreciated the elegance of straight lines on a map.[11]

With that congressional decision on Montana's western boundary, northern Idaho shrank from a potential of 180 miles in width—had the continental divide formed the boundary—to 44 miles. As historian Herman Deutsch wrote, the outcome had the result of "squeezing the upper torso of the mother territory into a very small corset."[12]

Idahoans attempted for two years to persuade Congress to designate a more reasonable border, but the effort never gained traction. Throughout Idaho's territorial era, disgruntled northern Idahoans tried to redress their border grievances, either by seceding to Washington or establishing a new territory carved out of eastern Washington, northern Idaho, and western Montana. Indeed, well into the 20th century, advocates for a new state in that region, one that reflected the reality of an east-west rather than a north-south orientation, continued to make that case, though their efforts always had only the longest of long shots for success.

Since those congressional actions in 1863 establishing the boundary with Washington and 1864 creating the border with Montana, Idahoans have lived with the consequences of men meeting in Congress, distracted by the Civil War. The vast majority of them had no knowledge of the Northwest and virtually none gave any serious thought to the consequences of boundaries in that far-distant, little-populated region. Yet much of the political and economic history of Idaho since that time has been one of attempting—usually without great success—to find ways to connect north and south Idaho. Idaho's narrow panhandle remains largely isolated from the rest of the state, its residents much more tied to Spokane, Washington, than Boise, Idaho—a place many northern Idahoans contentedly go lifetimes without visiting. Northern Idaho would have been much better served had Congress adhered to the border request of the first Idaho territorial legislature, rather than to Sidney Edgerton. Of course, Montanans have a different perspective.

Sometimes history just gets in the way of good stories. This is what Congress specifically decreed in 1864 about Montana's border with Idaho. It would follow "the crest of the Rocky Mountains northward till its intersection with the Bitter Root mountains; thence northward along the crest of said Bitter Root mountains to its intersection with the thirty-ninth degree of longitude west from Washington; thence along said thirty-ninth degree of longitude to the boundary line of the British possessions." That is very precise—and boring. No wonder alternative stories arose as to how Idaho got its squiggly boundary with Montana. The line is so eccentric, people are convinced there must be a dramatic reason. It simply could not be that a bunch of politicians in Congress merely chose that peculiar form.

First and foremost among the legends—one of the most enduring of Idaho myths—holds that Idaho owes its northeastern border to a group of inebriated surveyors. They trudged their bulky equipment along mountain crests for more than 600 miles in a drunken stupor before miraculously sobering up in time to finish with that last 70 miles of perfectly executed straight-line surveying. There are variations on this theme. Sometimes the surveyors are sober—but lost. Sometimes they are neither intoxicated nor lost but saddled with defective equipment. Other times the surveyors start dutifully enough but become so distracted by the potential of discovering gold that they pay scant attention to their work. Some Idahoans, ever unforgiving of Sidney Edgerton and his accomplices, insist unscrupulous Montanans bribed the crew. In any event, the end result is always the same: The surveyors made a colossal error, and as a result Idaho lost a lot of land, not to mention future communities like Missoula and Hamilton.[13]

The problem with the legend—other than the inconvenient fact that congressional language clearly spelled out the course the crews were to take—is that surveyors did not mark the boundary until nearly half a century after Congress established Montana. When they did, they started in the north and surveyed a straight line south until they reached the Bitterroots. Even if the party occasionally tipped a few drinks, it would have been impossible for it to confuse those mountains with the Rockies, for the crew would have never encountered the Rockies by heading due south. And, of course, there is also this: Idaho and Montana got along just fine with no controversy over the border in the decades before the surveyors undertook their work. Idahoans did not admire the boundary. But they never questioned that members of Congress had set it just where they meant it to lay.

Assured that President Lincoln would appoint him Montana's first governor, Sidney Edgerton made his way west. He received the official word of his appointment at Salt Lake City, continued on to Bannack, and immediately began making political enemies.

Edgerton, uncompromising in his anti-slavery convictions, never tempered his views. Many southern Democrats, escaping Civil War turmoil, resided in Montana in 1864. Campaigning for Republicans in legislative elections shortly after he returned to Montana, Edgerton fanned flames of division rather than reconciliation.

Edgerton had other problems. For more than a year after his appointment, Montana went without a territorial secretary. With no secretary, Edgerton could not legally spend federal money. He personally funded many of Montana's expenses. His austere Bannack house became a center of legislative and lobbying activities. But he was not wealthy. Running out of money and facing increasing political opposition, Edgerton returned to Washington, DC, to seek relief. He found the new president, Tennessean Andrew Johnson, unsympathetic to his Radical Republican ideals. Few Montanans came to Edgerton's defense. Johnson fired him and appointed a new territorial governor.

Edgerton never returned to Montana. He limped back to Ohio and continued his law practice. Largely ignored politically for the remainder of his life, in 1900 he finally received an official invitation to attend a Republican national convention. Edgerton, then 81, declined, stating he labored "under great infirmities of body." He died one month later.[14]

Although Edgerton spent only two years in the West, he had profound influence over the histories of two states. Had Edgerton been a less skilled lobbyist, one could well imagine that the border between Montana and Idaho would today run along the continental divide. Montana owes its great size to the abolitionist from Ohio. He served his adopted territory's interests well. Idahoans, on the other hand should recognize that their illogical panhandle confirms that there are times when a single individual can influence the course of history, not always for the better.

Sidney Edgerton had journeyed west in 1863 hoping to burnish his languishing political career. He exited two years later and never again held political office. William Wallace suffered similar political misfortune.

Many Idahoans seethed when their delegate to Congress connived with Edgerton on the border issue. Edgerton later wrote that Wallace's border stance "caused his defeat at the next election." That exaggerates matters. Wallace had "won" election in 1863 as Idaho's congressional delegate under suspicious circumstances. Wallace's colleagues had somehow fabricated 479 Republican votes out of a precinct with fewer than 100 people. Those ballots proved critical, as Wallace won the election by only 367 votes. Little wonder that a shroud of fraud accompanied him. And like Edgerton, Wallace represented a territory roiled by Civil War politics, filled with ever more southern-leaning Democrats. Wallace did not even receive his party's 1864 nomination to return to Congress. If he had, he would have no doubt lost the election, for Idaho had by then emerged "as a strongly southern territory."[15]

William Wallace completed his term as territorial delegate and assisted in planning President Lincoln's second inauguration. He was one of the last people to visit Lincoln in the White House before the president's assassination, and in his last official congressional act, rode in the president's funeral train.

Wallace's brand of moderate Republicanism suited Lincoln's successor, Andrew Johnson, who, in 1865, hoped to reappoint him as Idaho's governor. But political infighting killed that assignment. Wallace never returned to Idaho. Following Johnson's aborted effort to appoint him governor, he made his way back to Puget Sound. There he resumed his law practice, served as a probate judge, and became the first mayor of Steilacoom. He died in 1879.

Wallace could have been in the audience in September 1865 when James Ashley, chair of the House of Representatives Committee on Territories, gave an "eloquent speech" in the nearby town of Olympia, Washington's capital. If so, Wallace must have smugly smiled. Still simmering after being outmaneuvered by Wallace in 1863, when Congress established the border between Washington and Idaho, Ashley journeyed west to convince Washingtonians it would be in their best interests to extend their "boundary to the east" so it included north Idaho, as he and John Mullan had originally proposed. But he found few allies. Olympians still fretted—as they had in 1863 when Wallace helped to set the border—that a more conveniently located Walla Walla might abscond with the capital if Washington's territorial boundary lay farther east. Further, with the region still embroiled in Civil War-era animosities, Olympians had no desire to absorb "the rebel element so rife" in Idaho.[16]

Unable to convince Olympians to rally around a different border, Ashley returned to Washington, DC. He had been the first congressman to call for a constitutional amendment outlawing slavery. His concept formed the basis of the Thirteenth Amendment, and Ashley had acted as House floor manager for that constitutional reform. Ashley assailed President Johnson for his anti-civil rights behavior and initiated the proceedings that led to Johnson becoming the first impeached president. A leader of the Radical Republicans, Ashley's positions on race did not endear him to Ohio voters, and he lost his reelection campaign in 1868.[17]

Ashley remained fascinated with the Northwest, the region that had occupied so much of his congressional time. In 1869, President Ulysses Grant reluctantly appointed him territorial governor of Montana. Grant preferred another candidate but yielded to Ashley's allies who flooded the White House with letters of support.[18]

Ashley "proved to be very nearly the worst possible choice" as Montana's governor. The territory's southern-leaning, Democratic majority did not take kindly to his appointment. Helena's newspaper called him "a broken down political hack," and Ashley did nothing to endear himself to locals. He appointed Republicans to all key territorial offices, appointments the Democratic legislature refused to approve. Government ground to a gridlocked halt. In 1870, Grant abruptly removed the man he considered a "mischief maker" and "worthless fellow." Ashley called it "the hardest blow I ever received." He rallied friends to intercede, but Grant proved unyielding.[19]

Ashley returned to Ohio, twice ran unsuccessfully for Congress, and then served as a very capable president of the Ann Arbor Railroad. He died of heart failure on a fishing trip in 1896. James Ashley had a vision for the Northwest—one that would have retained an east-west orientation for northern Idaho. He did not get the borders he hoped. Idaho would have been better off if he had.

And what of Bannack, the city whose residents sent Sidney Edgerton east? At one time, Bannack boasted hotels, bakeries, meat markets, saloons—and of course, those gallows on the outskirts of town. Bannack's residents reveled in their capital city status—briefly. In 1865, the capital moved to Virginia City, and eventually to Helena. Bannack went on a long downward slide. Most people left town, and the few remaining did nothing much to spruce up the place. But that neglect worked out well for those interested in historic preservation. In the 1950s, Bannack became a state park, one of the best-preserved communities left over from the boom-day mining West. Today, visitors traipse through streets that still harken to that time in the 1860s when the residents of this town sent Sidney Edgerton to Washington, and forever changed the histories of Idaho and Montana.

Border Story

BIG HOLE

It would be difficult to encounter the Big Hole Battlefield and not weep. Here, at dawn on August 9, 1877, ambushing soldiers deliberately shot low into the tipis of sleeping Nez Perce in a surprise assault. They intended to slaughter as many Indians as possible, and were quite effective. Approximately 90 men, women, children, and infants died here that day. This is now hallowed ground. But had the Nez Perce better understood the concept of borders, it might today be merely another bucolic meadow of little historical significance.

On May 24, 1855, more than 500 Nez Perce mounted warriors made a grand entrance to the treaty council Isaac Stevens called in Walla Walla. Stevens, in the midst of signing a profusion of treaties in the Pacific Northwest, had never seen such an Indian show of force. The Nez Perce arrived resplendently painted and decorated, "with plumes and feathers…fluttering in the sunshine." They fired guns, beat drums, and encircled the Stevens party. Stevens realized he would be negotiating with a powerful tribe, one that had been cordial to whites since it had befriended Lewis and Clark 50 years earlier when the emaciated members of the Corps of Discovery staggered out of the Bitterroot Mountains onto the Weippe Prairie.[1]

After a week of tough bargaining, the Nez Perce agreed to cede more than five million acres to the United States. In return, the tribe retained exclusive rights to seven-and-a-half million acres, an area slightly smaller than Maryland. Their reservation covered large swaths of the future states of Idaho, Oregon, and Washington. The government agreed to survey the reservation, mark its boundaries, and enforce a policy prohibiting "any white man" from residing "upon the said reservation without permission of the tribe."[2]

Reservation boundary markers never appeared. It did not take long for the Nez Perce to realize that the United States government did not intend to restrain whites from such a valuable piece of property. "The barrier of an unseen reservation line could not protect the Nez Perce," observed historian Alvin Josephy. Once Elias Pierce discovered gold in 1860, floodgates opened. Thousands of whites indiscriminately trespassed on Nez Perce lands. Rather than enforce the 1855 treaty terms, the government opted instead to compel the tribe to sign another treaty relinquishing even more land. The only way to "protect" the Nez Perce, claimed the government, was to concentrate them on a much smaller reserve.[3]

Idaho had been a territory only two months when, on May 10, 1863, Indian agents Calvin Hale, Charles Hutchins, and Samuel Howe rode into Lapwai bent on negotiating a new treaty with the Nez Perce. They found the Indians decidedly unenthusiastic. Indeed, the agents waited nearly two weeks for any Nez Perce to show up.

When they finally arrived, the agents found a sharply divided tribe. Some Nez Perce had converted to Christianity; others retained traditionalism. Some had willingly signed the 1855 treaty; others only reluctantly agreed to those treaty terms. Most significantly, the Nez Perce were not a monolithic tribe with one "headman" as whites like Isaac Stevens contended. They were a group of independent bands with homes scattered over a wide region, often far distant from one another.

The federal government tasked Hale, Hutchins, and Howe with shrinking the reservation—the one the government had granted just a few years earlier. The agents did not know just what shape the new reservation would take or where it would be located, but they soon settled on land along the Clearwater River. That worked well for some Nez Perce who already lived there, particularly Lawyer, a Christian whom Stevens had designated as the tribe's "headman" during the 1855 treaty council. After days of long, mostly acrimonious negotiating in Lapwai in 1863, the Indian agents convinced Lawyer and 51 other Nez Perce to endorse the new treaty. All signers lived inside the new reservation boundaries; they would relinquish no land. The leaders of all the bands living outside that area, including White Bird and Old Chief Joseph, refused to sign, as did Looking Glass, despite residing inside the new reservation.

Many Nez Perce later referred to the 1863 document as the "Steal Treaty," and it is hard to dispute that description. It reduced the size of the Nez Perce reservation by 90 percent. Imagine a map of the continental United States. Draw a line from Mexico to Canada that cuts through Idaho. Should the United States cede 90 percent of its continental nation, it would give up everything east of that line, all of America from Idaho to the Atlantic Ocean. No wonder the Nez Perce felt betrayed. The agents gave those bands living outside the new reservation boundaries one year to move inside—to a land they knew only as visitors.

Though many Nez Perce angrily left the council, agent Calvin Hale, who headed the negotiations, celebrated. The Nez Perce had surrendered to future white exploitation "country...exceedingly valuable." That is certainly true. It is also true that Hale, Howe, and Hutchins had lit a powder keg. That spark would smolder for 14 years before exploding into America's last major Indian war.

The Nez Perce had learned considerable about white ways in the decades since they met, fed, and assisted Lewis and Clark. They had known missionaries and miners, trappers and traders, shopkeepers and soldiers. Old Chief Joseph even understood something about the concept of borders. Disgusted with the Steal Treaty and anxious to retain hold of his Wallowa homeland in northeast Oregon, Joseph established a perimeter boundary around Nez Perce lands. He marked it with tall poles set in stone cairns—similar to markers he had seen surveyors use to define borders. He determined to keep whites outside, and he successfully did until 1871, the year he died. He left these last words to his son, the younger Chief Joseph: "A few years more, and white men will be all around you. They have their eyes on this land. My son, never forget my dying words. This country holds your father's body. Never sell the bones of your father and your mother."[4]

Although the Nez Perce grasped the concept of borders as fences, they misunderstood the more nuanced legal ramifications of boundaries—especially ones not marked by fences. Three years after Old Chief

Joseph died, some Nez Perce living near Lapwai asked the reservation Indian agent to assist them when whites killed a tribal member. The event occurred in Washington Territory, outside the reservation boundary. At first, the agent agreed to intercede, asserting the federal government's authority over Nez Perce matters even if events transpired off the reservation. But when local whites claimed jurisdiction, things got messy. Finally, the agent retreated amidst a maze of bewilderment over borders and jurisdictions. How could the Nez Perce comprehend the subtleties of a legal system with varied lines of authority and invisible borders? That confusion contributed to the tragic events at Big Hole three years later.[5]

For a time, it appeared Joseph's band of Nez Perce might remain in the Wallowa Country. President Ulysses Grant said they could, signing an executive order in 1873 declaring whites be "withheld from entry and settlement." He proposed establishing a separate Wallowa reservation. That sentiment lasted just two years before the concept of state borders intervened to wreck Grant's good intentions. Oregon officials demanded the Nez Perce leave the confines of their state. Grant quickly retreated before this political pressure, revoked his executive order, and reopened Nez Perce lands to whites.[6]

Things spiraled downhill from there. Settlers moved in. They demanded the Nez Perce leave. The federal government argued the only way it could protect the Wallowa band would be to relocate them onto the Clearwater reservation. Local Oregon residents, trying to speed up both the tribe's removal and white settlement of former Nez Perce lands, constructed a road over the boundary markers Old Chief Joseph had so carefully erected.

The Army informed other Nez Perce bands outside the reservation that they, too, needed to move inside its boundaries. General Oliver Howard, commander of the Army's Department of the Columbia, called a council to meet with those Nez Perce still outside the reservation. Again, the concept of borders confused and angered the Nez Perce. "You white people get together, measure the earth and then divide it," observed Toohoolhoolzote, spiritual leader of a band of Nez Perce living along the Salmon River. You "pretend to divide the land and put me on it." General Howard, not interested in debating, had Toohoolhoolzote arrested for being "surly." There could be no compromise on borders—or on which side of certain borders Nez Perce should live. Howard gave the Nez Perce an ultimatum: Move inside the confines of the reservation willingly, or the Army would force them.[7]

Reluctantly, young Chief Joseph prepared to move. Adhering to his father's wishes, he did not sell his land. But he realized he had no choice but to leave it for the Clearwater reservation. In June 1877, other bands, including those of White Bird and Toohoolhoolzote, also made plans to relocate. On their way to the reservation, they congregated at an ancient Nez Perce summer gathering spot, a small pond today called Tolo Lake, on the Camas Prairie near Grangeville. Looking Glass joined them. Although his people lived within the confines of the reservation, Looking Glass had found reasons not to sign the 1863 treaty. This would be the Nez Perce's last meeting in freedom before moving onto the reservation, and emotions ran hot as people reminisced about years of injustices. Not too surprisingly, young warriors set out on a retaliatory raid of nearby white settlers. Over the course of a few days, they burned houses, destroyed crops, stole cattle—and killed 18 people.

Looking Glass, recognizing the situation's severity, led his people back to the reservation. Joseph and his brother Ollokot guided their band to White Bird's village on the Salmon River. Frightened whites sent couriers to Fort Lapwai to report the bloodshed.[8]

The Army dispatched two companies from the fort to restore order. Volunteers joined the troops, creating a combined force of 115 men. They arrived at the top of the hill overlooking White Bird's camp early on the morning of June 17, exhausted after trudging all night through mud and rain. Nez Perce approached them with a truce flag, but a volunteer inexplicably opened fire. A battle ensued. It became a complete rout. The Nez Perce killed 34 soldiers in a very brief encounter while suffering no fatalities.

The Nez Perce escaped following the White Bird Battle. General Oliver Howard gathered an overwhelming force of soldiers from throughout the West to give chase, but throughout that summer he proceeded languidly, bogged down with massive supplies and heavy equipment. "General Howard's actions of dilatoriness…caused great bitterness among the people," recorded one chronicler of the events. The majority of the Nez Perce were women, children, and old men. They had to transport their lodges and belongings while herding hundreds of horses. Even so, they moved with a fluidity the bulky Army troops could not match. The Nez Perce easily eluded Howard.[9]

As Howard ineffectively attempted to corral the Nez Perce, he grew suspicious of Looking Glass. After violence erupted on the Camas Prairie, Looking Glass, a renowned warrior respected for his bravery, sought to avoid the fighting. Howard, skeptical of Looking Glass's neutrality, issued an order to arrest him. On July 1, a force of 87 soldiers and volunteers arrived at Looking Glass's camp on the Clearwater River. They looked out on a pastoral scene. Here the Nez Perce farmed fields and raised dairy cattle. Looking Glass sent a message to the troops reiterating he did "not want war." Shortly after that, the peaceful scene disintegrated as an unprovoked soldier fired a shot. Then a fusillade ripped into the village. The Nez Perce scrambled into the surrounding hills and forests. Three died, two by drowning trying to cross the river. The troops descended on the camp, burning lodges, destroying farm fields, killing horses, and stealing cattle. They never came close to accomplishing their mission of arresting Looking Glass. But they did successfully incite him. "We thus stirred up a hornet's nest," admitted Howard. Looking Glass soon joined the other Nez Perce, increasing the number of warriors by about 40.[10]

On July 11 and 12, Howard's full command finally intercepted the retreating Nez Perce near the present-day Idaho community of Stites. At the Battle of the Clearwater, vastly outnumbered Nez Perce warriors killed 13 soldiers while suffering four casualties. Howard destroyed food, tipis, and supplies, a critical loss for the Indians, who escaped to the Weippe Prairie to contemplate their next steps. On this prairie, the Nez Perce had warmly welcomed the Lewis and Clark expedition 72 years earlier. As the tribe gathered now, it included an elderly man, his daughter, and grandchild. The elderly head of the family was the son William Clark had left behind. This peaceful tribe, for so long the friends of whites, now protected the family of that most famous of whites who, long ago, had sought their aid. Here on the prairie, tribal leaders contemplated their next moves, not just for the couple hundred warriors in their number, but more critically how to protect several hundred non-combatants, like the Clark kin, people of all ages and health. Their theory of borders played a crucial role in their decision-making.

Leaders at Weippe disagreed on future actions. Joseph and Ollokot favored returning to their homelands. But most realized that would provide only a temporary reprieve, until the Army arrived to capture them. White Bird advocated going to Canada. The Nez Perce had heard that Sitting Bull had led his people to safety there following the Sioux's destruction of George Custer's force the previous summer. They understood enough about borders to realize the international boundary would protect them from the pursuing Army. They believed Sitting Bull would welcome them. But escaping to Canada would take them far from home.

Looking Glass proposed an alternative involving a much closer border he thought would provide equal protection. There were several reasons Looking Glass suggested the Nez Perce travel the Lolo Trail to Montana. The tribe knew that country. They knew whites there, who had always been friendly. They thought they could find safety with the Crow, who had welcomed them when they crossed to the Plains to hunt buffalo. But Looking Glass also thought he understood the white concept of borders. Their enemies were in Idaho. Once the tribe crossed into Montana, he believed the Army would cease its pursuit. It was an understandable—but ultimately fatal—miscalculation.

The Nez Perce agreed to follow Looking Glass, and now recognized him as their battle leader, should they need to do battle. Seven hundred and fifty people and 2,000 horses strung out in lines miles long as they forged their way over the rugged mountain trail, carrying all their worldly possessions. They descended into Montana and camped near Lolo Hot Springs. They heard that the Army had hurriedly built a fort just to their east. Looking Glass met with the temporary outpost's commander, Captain Charles Rawn. Looking Glass said his people wanted to pass peaceably; Rawn said he had been ordered to block their way. Rawn attempted to explain to Looking Glass that the territorial boundary the Nez Perce had just crossed made no difference to the Army. Both Idaho and Montana were part of one nation, with one Army. "The soldiers of the west side and those of the east side" were brothers, he explained, "all under one great chief, and when [Indians] fought with one they had to fight with the other."[11]

The warning failed to impress Looking Glass, and Rawn's meager makeshift fort certainly did not frighten him. The Nez Perce simply took to the mountains and bypassed the paltry fortress, which local white residents justifiably nicknamed Fort Fizzle. This encounter in Montana might have surprised the Nez Perce, who thought they had left the Army behind, but it did not dissuade them from continuing. The token military resistance had done nothing to prevent their entrée to Montana, and Rawn did not pursue them. It seemed they were indeed safe. Looking Glass thought so, and led his people on a leisurely jaunt through the Bitterroot Valley, seeing no reason to rush, now that they had crossed the border.

"From the Nez Perce perspective, finding safety and peace simply by crossing Lolo Pass was perfectly sensible," reasoned historian Elliott West. "In fact…that thinking was calamitously flawed. Crossing the Lolo divide, they passed as well the boundary of their understanding into a new reality they could no more have comprehended than they could have imagined subways."[12]

Unconcerned about Army pursuit, Looking Glass led the Nez Perce to beautiful, flat grassland along the Big Hole River. Here they would stop, rest, and graze their horses. They would play games, collect poles for their lodges, race their ponies. Some tribal members grew wary about the relaxed pace since leaving Fort Fizzle. They questioned an extended stay in this idyllic spot. But Looking Glass insisted his people need not worry.

Looking Glass could not have known that, as he led his people through the Bitterroot Valley, William T. Sherman, commanding general of the Army, was just to the east, preparing to visit Yellowstone, America's first national park. Looking Glass also could not have understood the powerful, instantaneous reach of the telegraph. When Sherman heard the Nez Perce had crossed into Montana, he wired General Irvin McDowell, commander of the Army's Division of the Pacific in San Francisco, providing instructions that General Howard be permitted to ignore the administrative boundaries of his Department of the Columbia—which ended at the Idaho border—cross that line, and track the Indians. Sherman traveled with another former Civil War officer, General Philip Sheridan, then commander of the Division of the Missouri, which included Montana. Sheridan did some telegraphy himself, which would lead to a bloody conclusion to the Nez Perce's peaceful encampment at Big Hole.[13]

Sheridan wired Colonel John Gibbon, commander at Fort Shaw in western Montana, ordering him to intercept the Nez Perce. Gibbon left the fort with 166 men and marched to Missoula. Augmented there with additional troops and volunteers, Gibbon continued quickly through the Bitterroot Valley, rapidly gaining on the slow-paced Nez Perce. When he found them on August 8, Gibbon ordered a stealthy overnight march toward their camp. His troops encountered no Indian scouts or guards; Looking Glass did not believe them necessary. At 2:00 a.m., Gibbon's men halted on a forested hillside across the river from the Nez Perce. They formed a battle line and awaited the dawn.

At 4:00 a.m., Gibbon ordered his men to charge the camp. His troops fired furiously, aiming low into the tipis to better slaughter the sleeping Nez Perce. "Bullets were like hail on the camp," recalled one Nez Perce survivor. "The noise was like Gatling guns, as I have since heard them....I heard bullets ripping the teepee walls." As troops forged the river and reached the camp, they entered tents, shooting and bludgeoning victims, crushing skulls, and burning lodges.[14]

Warriors rushed to save their families. Others formed a defensive line. Sharpshooters took to trees for better line of sight. They were effective. Lieutenant James Bradley, the first white to come upon the carnage of Custer's annihilated troops the previous summer, became the first white killed at Big Hole, leaving his command leaderless and drifting. The Nez Perce took advantage of increasing confusion among Gibbon's men. Realizing he might soon be flanked, Gibbon retreated to a wooded enclosure back across the river. He had to hastily select a spot on which to make a stand, and in his rush did not pick the best. Advancing Nez Perce, gathering rifles from dead and retreating soldiers as they pushed ahead, pinned down Gibbon's men. Gibbon lost his horses. He had no medical supplies and little water. All day, warriors kept up their salvos as gun-shot soldiers moaned in agony.

Things were no better at the Nez Perce camp, filled with "women and children lying dead and wounded," recalled one warrior. "Wounded children screaming with pain. Women and men crying, wailing for their scattered dead."[15]

As the Nez Perce confined Gibbon's men, Joseph hastily organized his people into a retreat. They buried their dead in shallow graves, packed belongings, and lifted their seriously wounded onto travois. As they headed southeast, they left behind as many as 90 dead men, women, and children. Gibbon lost 31 men, with another 38 wounded. "The Indians kicked the hell out of us," recalled one civilian volunteer.[16]

Looking Glass's reputation crashed. He lost his position as war chief. Joseph, never a war leader, gained authority. The national press, which began viewing the war as a David and Goliath conflict, embellished his reputation, anointing Joseph as the tribe's undisputed leader. Some began calling the conflict Chief Joseph's War. "A man of intelligence and character," gushed *Harper's Weekly*. "A shrewd and active fighter."[17]

The Nez Perce made their sorrowful way to Yellowstone, losing along the way people who died or could not keep up. There, Crow scouts engaged by the Army stalked them, ending any illusion the Nez Perce held about finding safe haven among that tribe. The Nez Perce now realized what White Bird had expressed at the Weippe council—they would only find safety across the international boundary in Canada. The Tribe pushed north on the most direct route it could.

Remarkably, despite traveling with wounded and with families, with belongings and a huge horse herd, the Nez Perce kept well ahead of General Howard, who was increasingly mocked by the same press that raised Joseph to heroic eminence. But again, unbeknownst to the Nez Perce, the telegraph was critically affecting the war's trajectory. Howard wired ahead, and Colonel Nelson Miles, with more than 500 men, rode west across Montana to intercept the Nez Perce.

Surprisingly, Looking Glass had by then regained his stature as the major war chief. And again, he felt uncompelled to hurry, understanding how far behind the Indians had left Howard. It proved another fateful mistake. Miles caught the Nez Perce at the Bear Paw Mountains, drove off most their horses, and laid siege to the weakened, poorly provisioned people.

The Nez Perce fought bravely—indeed, they easily outmaneuvered the Army in the initial battle. But they were unprepared for a siege. Six days after the initial attack, Joseph walked to Miles's headquarters, where Howard had finally arrived. There he gave his heartbreaking surrender speech, the one that sealed his reputation as one of America's most eloquent Indian leaders:

> I am tired of fighting. Our chiefs are killed....The old men are all dead....It is cold, and we have no blankets. The little children are freezing to death. My people...have no food....I am tired. My heart is sick and sad. From where the sun now stands I will fight no more forever.[18]

There, just 40 miles south of the international boundary, the Nez Perce War ended.

The Nez Perce experience was unique in western wars. The tribe chose neither to remain in place and fight insurmountable odds, nor to capitulate and surrender. Instead, it engaged in a four-month-long running battle. The Nez Perce left Idaho with about 750 people of all ages and health, along with all their personal belongings and a huge horse herd. At peak strength they might have had 250 warriors, but fought most battles with far fewer. They traveled 1,700 miles, engaged in four major battles and numerous skirmishes, engaging 2,000 military regulars and volunteers. They lost about 120 people, while killing 180 white combatants. They had proven themselves superior to the United States Army as a fighting force. But by war's end, they were destitute, having lost their horses, possessions, cattle, and homes.

Toohoolhoolzote and Ollokot died on the first day of fighting at Bear Paw. The Nez Perce called a council on October 5, the last day of the siege. Joseph explained that he had chosen to surrender. White Bird and Looking Glass refused, deciding instead to attempt an escape to Canada. The ill-fated Looking Glass never got that opportunity. Shortly after the council adjourned, one of Nelson Miles's Indian scouts shot him—the last casualty of the Nez Perce War. Though a controversial war leader, no one ever questioned his courage.

Joseph surrendered at 2:00 p.m. the day Looking Glass died. The press had followed this war closely as it inconceivably raged on through the summer and into the fall. Joseph became a national icon. Following his surrender, the government sent Joseph and 430 Nez Perce to Fort Leavenworth, and later to Indian Territory—Oklahoma, where harsh weather and miserable living conditions extracted a grievous toll. Among those making the horrific trek were William Clark's son, granddaughter, and great-grandchild.

Joseph took advantage of his national reputation to lobby on behalf of his people. He traveled to Washington, DC, and met with the president, the Interior secretary, and other officials. Finally, in 1885, the United States allowed the Nez Perce to return to the Northwest. About 120 moved to the Lapwai reservation. But Idaho residents clearly did not want Joseph inside the borders of their territory. His group of 150 went to the Colville Reservation in eastern Washington.

Joseph then began another long, but unsuccessful campaign to allow his people to return to the Wallowas. Again he met with the president and other high officials. Twice, Joseph got to briefly visit his beloved homeland, but whites there did not want him back as a permanent resident. He died on the Colville Reservation in 1904. The agency physician reported the cause as a broken heart.

White Bird achieved the goal he believed the Nez Perce should have sought from the beginning. He, along with some 200 others, escaped across the 49th parallel to Canada. Sitting Bull welcomed the weary survivors. Over the ensuing years, many homesick Nez Perce made their ways back to Lapwai. White Bird chose to remain in Canada. He moved his people west to the edge of the Piegan Reservation in Alberta. In 1892, another Nez Perce killed him, believing White Bird, known as a shaman, had hexed his family.

On a warm August day in 1968, an elderly Nez Perce man slipped into the passenger seat of a car in Lapwai. He watched the scenery glide by as the driver headed east. They traveled the recently completed Lewis and Clark Highway, paralleling the Lolo Trail that the Nez Perce had journeyed on their flight out of Idaho 91 years earlier. They crossed into Montana at Lolo Pass and continued past Lolo Hot Springs, where the Nez Perce had camped, and Fort Fizzle, which they had easily avoided. Through the Bitterroot Valley past Stevensville, where tribal members had purchased supplies. Up Lost Trail Pass and on to the site of the Big Hole Battle, where the car stopped. It was the first return to this sacred ground for 96-year-old Josiah Red Wolf. He had come reluctantly. This place of sadness held painful memories.

He was five years old and asleep here inside his family's tipi in 1877. He awakened suddenly as bullets tore through the camp. "My mother gathered up [my] little sister and, taking me by the…hand started to run," Red Wolf recalled. "A single shot passed through the baby and her. She dropped down." Both died instantly.

His father hid him under a blanket while he fought the Army invaders. Josiah Red Wolf lived, and with the rest of the Big Hole survivors made his way on that perilous journey that ended at Bear Paw. There, his family surrendered along with Joseph.

Red Wolf moved back to Lapwai from Indian Territory in 1885. Later, he attended the Carlisle Indian Industrial School in Pennsylvania where he learned shoe repair. He returned to Lapwai as a cobbler. A talented musician, he also performed at local weekend dances.

In 1968, the National Park Service invited him to attend dedication ceremonies for the new visitors center at Big Hole National Battlefield. Red Wolf had not been back since the death of his mother and sister, and he hesitated about returning now. But he reluctantly agreed, and on that summer day 91 years after his family's tragedy, he cut the ribbon opening the new facility. He refused to speak at the event. A Park Service employee remembered it as "a moment that [was] a profound but awkward testimony to the lasting personal scars of the Nez Perce War and to the challenge of effective communication between two cultures." Following the dedication, Red Wolf returned home, across the border to his beloved Idaho.[19]

On April 5, 1971, *Time* announced the death of Josiah Red Wolf. He was, the magazine noted, the last survivor of the Nez Perce War. He had, along with his people, undertaken that long, deadly march in the summer of 1877 in the expectation that borders would protect them.

CHAPTER SEVEN

1868
The Southeastern Border:
Wyoming

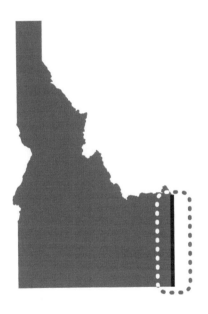

In 1868, Idahoans could have finally had a say in the establishment of one of their borders. But they chose to remain silent.

Things had not worked out in the northern West as James Ashley, chair of the House Committee on Territories, had planned. William Wallace had outmaneuvered him in 1863, setting a boundary between Washington and Idaho far different than the one Ashley desired. When Sidney Edgerton arrived in the nation's capital the following year, seeking territorial status for Montana, Ashley acquiesced to Edgerton's desire for a Montana-Idaho border that left Idaho with its scrawny panhandle. Ashley had traveled west in 1865 to make amends. He hoped to convince Washingtonians to support moving their border farther east, appending the Idaho panhandle to Washington. But he found that territory's residents remarkably indifferent, and the boundary remained unmoved. So, he resolved to do a better job of creating rectangles east of Washington territory.

Ashley looked at a map of the northern West and saw the annihilation of his vision for neat, orderly, rectangular territories. Montana, while mostly rectangular, sprawled 550 miles wide. Idaho just looked strange. It had at least shrunk to a more reasonable size than when it first became a territory. In 1864, Congress not only sliced Montana out of Idaho, but also gave most of today's Wyoming to Dakota Territory. But to Ashley, Dakota now seemed an ungainly abomination, consisting of the future states of North and South Dakota, as well as Wyoming. The territory looked something like a chair, with the Dakotas as the back and the future Wyoming jutting out as the seat.

In 1865, Ashley attempted to carve Dakota into smaller, neater parcels, in the process advocating the creation of a territory he called Wyoming. His bill went nowhere. No one much cared about Wyoming, because few whites lived there. Then, on July 4, 1867, Grenville Dodge, chief engineer of the Union Pacific Railroad, made his way to the future Wyoming and, standing on the bank of Crow Creek, proclaimed that spot a future headquarters for the Union Pacific, then rapidly building west. The next day, railroad surveyors platted a town. People soon called it Cheyenne. By the time the tracks reached that burgeoning town in November, Cheyenne boasted a few thousand residents who patronized hotels, restaurants, saloons, brothels, gambling halls, and a couple newspapers. It had become the "Magic City of the Plains."[1]

As the Union Pacific laid rails farther west, other communities arose: Laramie, Green River, Evanston. In a familiar refrain, those towns' residents complained about lack of governmental responsiveness, with their territorial capital located hundreds of miles away in Yankton. Just as the residents of Bannack had done four years earlier, in 1868 residents of Cheyenne sent a lobbyist to Washington, DC, to convince Congress to create a new territory. They chose Hiram Latham, an Army surgeon, as their "Agent for the People of Wyoming Territory." Latham distributed brochures to members of Congress that optimistically claimed Wyoming already had 35,000 residents and would soon boast "60,000 white people." Those citizens, he lamented, suffered in a region "practically without government and without law" and "earnestly desire[d]" that Congress establish "a territorial government for them."[2]

Latham faced no opposition from politicians in Yankton. They proved remarkably eager to jettison Wyoming. Dakota's territorial governor, Andrew Jackson Faulk, believed Latham greatly exaggerated Wyoming's population. He saw no reason for hanging onto the place. The territorial legislature agreed, urging Congress to create Wyoming. Legislators saw little future in maintaining jurisdiction over a "broad extent of wild Indian country."[3]

Latham enjoyed immediate success in the Senate. Richard Yates, chair of the Committee on Territories, introduced a bill to create the new territory. Senators boisterously debated it, but those deliberations had nothing to do with the shape of the place—only what to call it. The fact that residents of the territory seemed very content with Wyoming did not deter senators from suggesting other options—Cheyenne, Shoshone, and Lincoln proving particularly popular. Senators finally deferred, some grudgingly, to Wyoming. While the name debate raged on and on, discussion about the new territory's borders lasted only a few minutes. In essence, senators agreed to take the bulk of the territory from Dakota, add a little bit from both Idaho and Utah, give the place a rectangular shape with straight-line boundaries—and call it a day. The bill passed the Senate with no dissenting votes.[4]

Despite James Ashley's previous support of a new territory of Wyoming—and even despite Wyoming's proposed neat rectangular shape—Latham could now gain no traction with him or the House of Representatives. Ashley had had a complete turnaround since 1865. Now his committee refused to draft a Wyoming bill of its own, and Ashley attempted to kill the Senate version, chastising his upper house colleagues. "They have not examined this matter as carefully as I have," he fumed, "being a member of the committee [on territories] for ten years, and having twice passed through this proposed Territory...I understand what I am talking about, and I say...no greater folly could be perpetuated than to erect this Territory at this time."[5]

Like Dakota's governor, Ashley alleged Wyoming had only a sliver of the population Latham claimed. Its communities were mere "paper cities," not actual towns. The proposed borders created a Wyoming "almost as boundless as the desert of Sahara, and for the most part as worthless." But that was all subterfuge. In an earlier time, Ashley would have eagerly supported a new, rectangular territory. But now he raged about the sitting president, Andrew Johnson, a former slave owner. Ashley, the ardent abolitionist, abhorred him. A new territory in the West would allow Johnson to appoint handpicked officials of like politics. The Senate might have suggested a neat and orderly rectangle for a new territory, but Ashley now had good reason to oppose its creation.[6]

Dakota's territorial delegate to Congress blasted Ashley's inaction. He had repeatedly requested that Ashley's committee take up the matter so Dakota could be rid of Wyoming. "Week after week passed away, and there was no action," he thundered. "It soon became apparent that the chairman, for reasons best known to himself, would not act in the matter at all."[7]

The House overrode Ashley's objections and passed the Senate's Wyoming bill. On July 25, 1868, President Andrew Johnson signed it into law, creating yet another new territory in the West.

Idaho went virtually unmentioned in all the congressional debate over Wyoming. Idaho would forfeit a chunk of land to the new territory. But unlike the angst over losing property to Montana in 1864, no one in Idaho seemed bothered.

At the time of the congressional debate, the Union Pacific had not yet reached the part of Wyoming that then still belonged to Idaho. Precious few, if any, whites lived there. The only mention of Idaho in the Senate debate came when Senator Yates informed his colleagues that his bill "proposed to transfer an irregularly-shaped strip of territory

nearly a degree in width, and something over two degrees in length...
now attached to Idaho." He continued, "The committee are told that
there is not a single inhabitant in that portion of Idaho transferred by
this bill, therefore no opposition can come from that quarter." He, of
course, left out Indians. But he was very clear why Congress should
take this land from Idaho. It all had to do with forming a more perfect rectangle. "This was deemed proper by the committee in order to
attain symmetry in the geographical boundaries of the new Territory."[8]

No one in Congress questioned the wisdom of carving out a part
of Idaho to create a rectangle. And so, with President Johnson's signature, Idaho received its last border, a perfectly straight line separating
it from Wyoming—the last of its six boundaries. And just as with the
previous five, Idahoans had virtually no say in the matter, though in
the case of the Wyoming border, Idahoans hardly cared. Wyoming was
welcome to that strip of worthless property.

But borders have consequences. Idahoans would one day have reason to regret that they so nonchalantly relinquished that 50-mile-wide
piece of landscape.

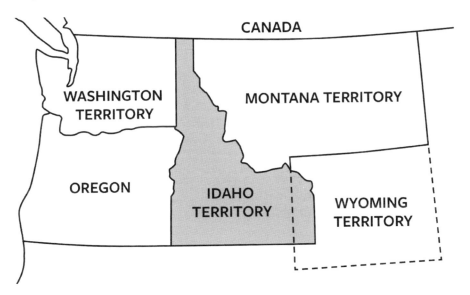

No one protested when Congress granted a narrow strip of Idaho to Wyoming
to create a tidy, rectangular new territory. This 1868 action had consequences. It
gave Idaho its final shape—and granted to Wyoming the Grand Tetons, Jackson
Hole, and much of the future Yellowstone National Park.

◆ ◆ ◆

The land Idaho surrendered ran in a straight line north from the 41st parallel until in intersected the continental divide. It then snaked along the Rocky Mountains to the Montana boundary. Not too many whites had traversed that country. Still, by 1868 many Idahoans would have heard tales about it. They would have been familiar with the risky trek Astorians had taken across southern Idaho in 1811. Employees of John Jacob Astor's American Fur Company were headed to the mouth of the Columbia River to establish a trading post they called Fort Astoria. Along the way, they spent some time in a picturesque valley and did a little trapping. By the 1820s, other trappers regularly traversed the place. In 1829, it finally got a name, honoring one of those trappers, David Jackson. It would from then on be known as Jackson Hole.

The hole—or valley—lay at the base of a majestic mountain range that became a landmark to western adventurers. Over the years, different fur traders gave those mountains different names. Some called them the Pilot Knobs; others the Three Paps. But by 1837, they were appearing on maps as the Tetons.

Just north of those imposing mountains lay an area that, by 1868, had already acquired a reputation as a fanciful land of wonder. In 1824, British fur trader Alexander Ross wrote of encountering "Boiling Fountains" there. Three years later, American trapper Daniel Potts sent a letter to a Philadelphia newspaper describing "hot and boiling springs" that threw "particles to the immense height of from twenty to thirty feet" while the earth nearby experienced "a tremendous trembling." By the 1860s, prospectors crisscrossed the region, searching for gold. They found little, but their descriptions of a hellish—yet wondrous—landscape added to its fame. Four years after Congress created Wyoming, this place called Yellowstone became the nation's first national park.[9]

And so it was in 1868 that Congress set the permanent border between Idaho and Wyoming. And, although Idahoans knew about that country, they considered it worthless. Without dissent, they amiably agreed to give Wyoming Jackson Hole, the Grand Tetons, and about a fourth of Yellowstone National Park, in the process forfeiting millions of dollars of future tourism revenue. It is true that Idahoans in 1868 could hardly be expected to have understood the powerful economic engine those places would one day drive. But it is also true that borders have repercussions, and the creation of Idaho's last border, carving off a narrow band of Idaho's eastern fringe, land that had seemed so inconsequential at the time, deprived Idaho of "an area that could today be pumping tourist…dollars into the Gem State's treasury instead of Wyoming's."[10]

In 1868, Idaho acquired its final configuration. It is a shape that has baffled Americans since that time. It squiggles along mountain crests on its east and curves with the Snake River on its west. And yet for all its whimsical lack of symmetry, Idaho's borders consist of a lot of straight lines. The southern and northern boundaries, forged through international diplomacy, run straight along parallel lines of latitude. The southwest border with Oregon, the northwest with Washington, the northernmost 70 miles of border with Montana, and the boundary with Wyoming are all perfectly straight lines.

There would be many efforts in future years to change Idaho's borders. Indeed, at one point the curiously shaped and consequently difficult-to-govern Idaho almost ceased to exist, a near casualty of its configuration. But through all that, Idaho retained its form, its contours determined through international and domestic politics in a 50-year period between 1819 and 1868. It is a shape created virtually devoid of input by Idahoans, but one they have learned to accept—not always easily—since Congress set that last boundary with Wyoming three years after the end of the Civil War.

Border Story

LAWLESS

If a person wanted to escape the law, a good place to consider would be eastern Idaho, along the border with Wyoming. At least bestselling author C. J. Box thought so. He sent Joe Pickett there in his 2007 novel *Free Fire*. In his long career as the central figure of Box novels, Pickett, a lean, quiet, Wyoming game warden, confronted terrorists, animal mutilators, cowboy hitmen, and corrupt bureaucrats. In *Free Fire*, he investigates a cold-blooded mass slaying in a remote stretch of land where, it appears, a person can legally get away with murder—an eastern Idaho "Zone of Death."

As it turns out, Joe Pickett was far from the first to encounter legal peculiarities on the Idaho-Wyoming border.

It is not unusual for borders to generate quirks and confusion. The residents of Strevell paid Idaho taxes and voted in Idaho elections for the duration of their town's existence. Not until the last resident exited in the 1970s did people discover the community had been located in Utah all along. The citizens of northern Idaho and western Montana lived with what they believed to be their border for decades before surveyors finally marked the official line in 1899. That delay cost the taxpayers of Kootenai County, Idaho. County commissioners approved spending "a considerable sum of money" grading a road from the mining town of Leonia to another mining community at Sylvanite. Once surveyors completed their boundary work, the commissioners realized their Idaho tax dollars had actually paid for road improvements in Montana. About the same time that Kootenai County commissioners spent money in their neighboring state, the residents of Moyie, British Columbia, faced a different border imbroglio. They understood they lived north of the 49th parallel. But most of the town's residents were Americans, and as July approached, they considered whether Moyie should celebrate Dominion Day on July 1 or Independence Day on July 4. Town residents equivocated. They held their community celebration on July 4, 1898, but featured two speakers, "one for the Canadians and one…for the Americans."[1]

Border concerns had more serious connotations along the Idaho-Wyoming line. For members of the Church of Jesus Christ of Latter-day Saints, freedom could depend upon which side of the border one settled. "Nowhere else in the United States did the Mormon and non-Mormon populations divide as sharply as they did in Idaho," commented historian Carlos Schwantes. As the Mormon Church sent increasing numbers of colonists north from Utah, resentment in Idaho grew.[2]

Mormons called themselves a "peculiar people," and many non-Mormons agreed. Latter-day Saints tended to live in close-knit communities not always welcoming to non-Mormons. They had some unusual dietary restrictions. Idahoans could have abided all that. Two other issues turned the territory into a virulent anti-Mormon hotbed. Mormons overwhelmingly voted as a block for Democrats, angering Republicans. And Mormons sanctioned polygamy. Republicans used the latter as rationale for disenfranchising people of another political party, and they were ruthlessly effective. Proclaiming righteous indignation against plural marriage, Republicans, in a very short time period, managed to turn a territory trending Democratic into a Republican bastion. With few short-term exceptions, Idaho has remained Republican since. That party can thank Fred Dubois for its ascendency.

In 1882, Congress passed the Edmunds Act prohibiting polygamists from voting or holding office in federal territories—like Idaho. For Dubois, this measure did not go far enough. Only a tiny fraction of Idaho's Mormons practiced polygamy, so the Edmunds Act disenfranchised few Idaho Mormons. To ensure electoral victories, Republicans needed to more effectively suppress Mormons' voting rights.

Fred Dubois grew up in Springfield, Illinois, and knew Abraham Lincoln's family. That connection came in handy after Fred followed his brother—hired as physician at the Fort Hall Indian Agency—to Idaho. Fred tried cowboying for a while, but soon capitalized on his family connections, asking Secretary of War Robert Lincoln to help him find a more secure position. Not surprisingly, in 1882, at Lincoln's urging, President Chester Arthur appointed Dubois U.S. Marshal for the Territory of Idaho. It made no difference that Dubois had no experience for the job.[3]

Dubois held higher political aspirations, viewing the marshal position as a stepping-stone to future opportunity. A marshal gains prominence by fighting crime, and Dubois knew just where to find it. Passage of the Edmunds Act, in his opinion, made "every member of the Mormon Church...a criminal either actually in practice or as an accessory." He set about arresting as many as he could.[4]

Arresting Mormons helped burnish his reputation, but to win higher office demanded that the Republican Dubois also curtail the voting rights of Democratic Mormons. In 1881, he joined the Oneida County Independent Anti-Mormon Party and recruited allies to his anti-Mormon campaign. The movement gained power and influence, and in 1885 steamrolled through the territorial legislature the Idaho Test Oath. It went much further to suppress Mormon voters than the Edmunds Act. The Test Oath prohibited anyone belonging to an organization that sanctioned polygamy from voting, holding office, or serving on juries. The Edmunds Act disenfranchised Idaho's few polygamists. The Test Oath invalidated the voting rights of all members of the LDS Church. Overnight, Republicans in Idaho became a supermajority. To ensure Mormons did not creep back to the ballot box, delegates to the 1889 Idaho constitutional convention—none of whom was Mormon—wrote a disenfranchisement clause into the state Constitution. No Mormon—or "idiot, criminal, Chinese or persons of Mongolian descent, or non-taxed Indian," for that matter—could vote in the new state. Although Idaho voters did not repeal the Mormon disenfranchisement clause of their state Constitution until 1982, in 1892 the legislature rescinded the Idaho Test Oath. Idaho officials ceased enforcing the constitutional clause after the LDS Church relaxed its bloc-voting tactics. Most Idaho Mormons switched parties. Republicans no longer felt threatened by Mormon Democrats.[5]

While he worked to pass anti-Mormon legislation, Dubois continued to polish his anti-LDS bona fides as a law officer. With a legion of U.S. Marshal deputies whom he paid for each arrest, Dubois ransacked southeast Idaho, imprisoning Mormons. "Mr. Dubois was relentless in his war upon the Latter-day Saint people," lamented one church member. "He hired many deputies who would prowl around at all hours of the night in order to catch a victim."[6]

It was a tough time to be a Mormon in Idaho. But some folks found freedom by settling in a town appropriately named Freedom.

In the late 1870s—before the Edmonds Act—LDS families began settling the Star Valley, spanning Idaho and Wyoming. They were part of a Latter-day Saint migration colonizing the region north of Utah, pioneers seeking a place to live, farm, and practice their religion. In the 1880s, the region became a magnet for bigamists fleeing enforcement of anti-polygamy laws. Most Mormons seeking escape moved directly to Wyoming, for reasons clarified by a visitor to the valley in 1891. "Wyoming has always treated our people fairly and justly," he wrote, "while her neighbor, Idaho, has exhibited a hatred and vindictiveness towards some of her best citizens that would be more in keeping with the spirit of the middle ages than that of the nineteenth century."[7]

Still, some Mormons chose to settle in Idaho. A few established Freedom, a town directly on the border. The community grew on both sides of the line, part in Idaho and part in Wyoming. That proved handy when Dubois's marshals came arresting. The town residents had merely to walk a few feet to freedom in Wyoming—hence the town's name. Dubois held no authority on that side of the street. Of course, people could move in the opposite direction should a Wyoming marshal decide to enforce federal anti-polygamist laws. A local poet commemorated the unique Freedom lifestyle:

> Now some had many wives and secluded lives.
> Made it nice for them when there would be polygamist drives.
> If the Idaho sheriff came, you could go to Wyo
> And if you saw a Wyoming badge you could flee to Idaho.
>
> Everyone is happy now and things are going fine.
> There's no controversy on location of the line.
> And if you think another state would make your joy complete,
> Brother, all you have to do is move across the street.[8]

Fifty miles north of Freedom, another group of Mormons escaping prosecution settled a different border community. Their town did not split the boundary, but they experienced a convoluted existence trying to decide whether they wanted to be Idahoans or Wyomingites.

Latter-day Saint families began settling the Teton Valley in the late 1880s. Like the Mormon residents of Star Valley, they came to make a living and practice their religion in an isolated region removed from those who disdained them. The earliest colonizers settled in Idaho, primarily around Driggs. As their numbers grew, they moved up the valley and built homes around a community eventually called Alta, hugging the state border. People knew they had crossed into Wyoming but welcomed living near Idaho. "Here they could have a family on both sides of the state line and hopefully avoid the law," wrote historian Brooks Green.[9]

Save for a bureaucratic mistake 40 years earlier, those first residents to Alta would have been Idahoans. In 1850, Congress passed an act establishing the Washington meridian for all astronomical purposes, such as locating territorial and state boundaries. The meridian passed through the newly constructed Naval Observatory in Washington, DC. While the United States continued to calculate nautical measurements based on the international Greenwich, or prime meridian, for more than half a century, American surveyors in the West relied on the Washington meridian as their base. Not until 1912 did Congress rescind the act, establishing Greenwich as America's legal prime meridian.[10]

This would all be just topographers' technical chatter if not for a slight problem. When surveyors set the meridian through the Naval Observatory, they miscalculated. A. V. Richards, when surveying the border between Wyoming and Idaho in 1873 naturally pegged his calculations to the Washington meridian, as instructed. As a result, he inadvertently gave a swath about two-and-a-half miles wide and 160 miles long to Wyoming—including the place that came to be called

Alta. When Idaho and Wyoming became the 43rd and 44th states in 1890, Congress made no provision to resurvey the boundary between them. Richards's inaccurate line became the official state border.

In a correctly surveyed world, Alta would today be in Idaho. That would have made sense. As roads developed, the only way in and out of Alta, save trekking through mountainous wilds, ran through Idaho. Alta lay deeply isolated from any Wyoming community.

So, in 1897, when residents of Alta requested that the State of Idaho annex their region, the legislature petitioned Congress to append about ten square miles of Wyoming to Idaho. "There are over twenty-five families residing on said area," the legislators wrote. "The Teton range of mountains, forming the eastern boundary…is an impossible barrier.…The present situation imposes many annoyances and unnecessary hardships upon said residents without in any manner benefiting the State of Wyoming." Further, according to the petitioners, "the said residents are all in favor of annexation." Wyoming politicians saw things differently. Senator Francis Warren claimed to understand why Idahoans would "ask for a portion of some good and fertile State [like Wyoming] to add to that somewhat dry and barren" Idaho, but could not support the proposition of a border change. Neither could Congress, which rejected the overture.[11]

The United States Constitution allows for border changes, but it is an arduous process. The legislatures of all states involved, as well as Congress, must approve. Changes to state borders are rare. Moving the border to allow Idaho to annex Alta would have been unusual. Still, at one time it could have happened—save for a change of heart by Alta's residents.

In 1903, Idahoans finally became aware of the Washington meridian surveying error that had set the Idaho-Wyoming border too far west. Now Idaho legislators no longer viewed annexation as taking country from Wyoming. Parts of western Wyoming rightfully belonged to Idaho, and legislators sought to rectify the situation. In that year, they sent another petition to Congress, seeking annexation of part of the Teton Forest Preserve. When Congress established that preserve in 1897, it set its western border on the state line. However, as "the boundary line between the States of Idaho and Wyoming is not correctly defined, and…the present boundaries of the Teton Forest

Preserve are improperly extended…more than 2 miles beyond the true line," the legislature petitioned Congress to resurvey the boundary. Congress provided funding to better mark the existing line to eliminate confusion. But it refused to change the border.[12]

In the 1930s, though, it appeared a border change might actually transpire. In 1931, Congress recognized the inconvenience of Alta residents essentially living as Idahoans inside Wyoming. Those citizens had to "travel great distances or undergo great hardships to reach their natural markets, railroads, and county seats," members of Congress observed. "The transaction of private and public business would be benefitted by a change in the boundary line."[13]

Remarkably, Congress granted permission to Idaho and Wyoming to "negotiate…the boundary line." Congress established a three-person commission, including one representative from each state, to investigate the matter. The commission held hearings in Alta over the course of three days in 1931. Seventy-four people attended and gave a collective "never mind" to the long-contemplated concept of transferring Alta to Idaho. They unanimously disapproved altering the border. After years of brooding over their isolated position in Wyoming, they decided they wanted to remain Wyomingites after all. "It was the conclusion of the commission" following its reception in Alta "that the situation did not justify any change in the existing boundary."[14]

Alta, Wyoming, stayed Alta, Wyoming. Yet it remained an unconventional place. By the 21st century, Teton County, Wyoming, provided law enforcement to the unincorporated community. Teton County, Idaho, supplied ambulance and fire services. After completing grade school, families had equal opportunity to send their children to secondary schools in either state. Alta residents voted several times after 1931 on whether Idaho should annex the community and rejected the concept each time. Though the days of Fred Dubois hunting polygamists had ended, Alta's residents showed no desire to become Idahoans.[15]

Suppose you were not simply attempting to escape ambitious marshals like Fred Dubois. Suppose you wanted to commit a serious crime. Say, for example, you wanted to murder someone. For that, you might want to journey to another part of the Idaho-Wyoming borderland.

Had you wanted to commit a crime between 1868 and 1873, you might have made your way to a tiny, triangular piece of land about a third the size of Manhattan. It borders Idaho, Wyoming, and Montana. To the few who have heard of it, it has taken the name Lost Dakota.

When established in 1861, Dakota Territory spanned much of the American northern West, including most of today's Montana and Wyoming. Dakota shrank as Congress created new territories. When establishing borders for Idaho, Wyoming, and Montana, Congress inexplicably left a small patch of Dakota outside the borders of each— isolated by hundreds of miles from the rest of Dakota. Sharp-eyed Senator Thomas Hendricks of Ohio questioned the accuracy of the border description in 1868 debates over the Idaho-Wyoming bound-

Due to a mapping error, between 1868 and 1873 a small, isolated piece of land inadvertently remained part of Dakota Territory. In the latter year, Congress— recognizing the mistake—assigned "Lost Dakota" to Montana.

ary. He believed some land lay unaccounted for within the proposed borders and thought the Senate should delay establishing Wyoming until Congress gained assurance of the boundary's accuracy. Senator Richard Yates of Illinois, chairman of the Senate Committee on Territories, assured him the problem lay in Hendricks's reliance on an outdated map. He brought into the chamber a large, newer map. "Senators gathered in a group around it," and satisfied themselves "the description in the bill is right." Hendricks withdrew his opposition. Congress approved the borders for the new Territory of Wyoming.[16]

The senators would have been better advised to have listened to Hendricks, for it had indeed "lost" part of Dakota in the proceedings. In 1873, Congress recognized it had a problem with its border descriptions. It assigned that tiny leftover bit of Dakota to Montana. Prior to that, the property rested many days' travel from governmental authority in Dakota Territory. "In retrospect, it would have been a great place for outlaws to hide out since there were no lawmen around," quipped author Michael Trinklein.[17]

It is doubtful any 19th century criminal considered that option. Indeed, it is doubtful any 19th century crook even knew about the short-lived, secret life of Lost Dakota. But a 21st-century person with criminal intent might take a more serious look at a strip of Idaho just south of Lost Dakota.

Idahoans frequently complain that, with the exception of Nez Perce Historical Park, there are no national parks within the boundaries of their beautiful state. But that is not entirely accurate.

Members of Congress established the nation's first national park at Yellowstone in 1872. They set park boundaries before surveyors marked any of the borders between Idaho, Wyoming, and Montana. The park came into existence nearly two decades before those territories became states. When they did, Congress did not shrink the park's boundaries to fit it all within Wyoming—nor did it expand Wyoming's borders to encompass the entire park. As a result, slivers of Yellowstone National Park spill over into Montana and Idaho. About a 50-square-mile, narrow strip of Yellowstone rests in Idaho. In the 21st century, many on the internet took to calling it the "Zone of Death."

When Congress admitted Montana, Idaho, and Wyoming to the union, it retained exclusive federal authority over Yellowstone, and placed the park entirely under the jurisdiction of the Wyoming U.S. District Court. That ensured the federal government's ability to prosecute people committing crimes within the vast majority of the

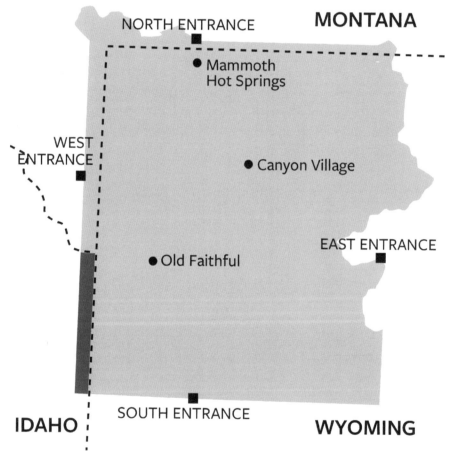

The small parcel of Yellowstone National Park within Idaho took on the 21st century name "Zone of Death." Existing outside the jurisdiction of the Wyoming U.S. District Court, some speculated that lawbreakers could evade prosecution if they committed crimes within this area.

park that lies within Wyoming. Arrest them, prosecute them, try them before a jury of their peers.

But a jury of peers requires that there be peers who can be called to jury duty. The total population of humans living within the Idaho section of Yellowstone National Park is precisely zero.

In 2005, law professor Brian Kalt wrote about the resulting conundrum in "The Perfect Crime," an article in the *Georgetown Law Journal.* "Say that you are in the Idaho portion of Yellowstone, and you decide to spice up your vacation by going on a crime spree," Kalt wrote. "You make some moonshine, you poach some wildlife, you strangle some people and steal their picnic baskets. You are arrested, arraigned in the park, and bound over for trial in Cheyenne, Wyoming, before a jury drawn from the Cheyenne area."[18]

So far, it seems like standard criminal case operating procedure. But then a thing called the United States Constitution gums up the works. Article III, Section 2 states that trials of all crimes shall be by jury, held in the state where the crimes were committed. Logically, the prosecutor would move the trial to Idaho, the state where the strangler committed murder. But the Constitution's Sixth Amendment states that trials must be held not just in the state in which a crime was committed, but also within the district—in this case, the jurisdictional territory of the Wyoming U.S. District Court. Put those two constitutional provisions together, and prosecutors would need to draw their jury from those residents of Idaho who lived inside that narrow parcel of land within the bounds of the Wyoming District Court. And no one lives there. Unless a witless criminal consented to a trial in Cheyenne, "the Yellowstone State-Line Strangler...should go free," Kalt maintained. And just in case some feisty prosecutor thought of convincing Congress to redefine district court boundaries after the heinous crime, allowing prosecutors to transfer the trial to Idaho, the Sixth Amendment has an answer for that as well: Trials shall be held in districts that "have been previously ascertained by law." In other words, Congress cannot redefine court boundaries after the crime.[19]

It did not take long for a talented, bestselling author of criminal suspense novels to latch onto the potential of this legal complexity. After reading Kalt's article, C. J. Box had Clay McCann, the criminal in *Free Fire*, walk into a backwoods ranger station, turn over "his still-warm weapons," and confess to the gruesome murder of four campers in the Idaho section of the park. McCann, a lawyer familiar with his Constitution, then challenged the startled ranger to do anything about it. Authorities did arrest McCann. But when he demanded to be tried by a jury from the state and district where he had committed murder, they had to release him.[20]

Box then sends intrepid game warden Joe Pickett to investigate. But he cannot get past the legal loophole. "The only thing they can legitimately get him on is possessing firearms in a national park," Pickett laments, "and they booked him for that and he was tried and convicted of it. But that's just a Class B misdemeanor, no more than six months or a fine."[21]

Joe Pickett, who does a lot of meandering through Yellowstone, discovers the motive for McCann's crime spree. The park is home to unique organisms that criminals are illegally mining to generate profits from energy development. Pickett soon realizes McCann killed the campers to hide the conspiracy to exploit those rare Yellowstone species.

Justice ends up being served, but not in a way that would inspire those who seek legal remedies. Let's just say the solution thwarting future McCann mayhem came not from condemnation by a jury of his peers, but rather from a sudden introduction to the excruciatingly hot springs that make Yellowstone famous. Pickett did not get his man; nature got his man for him.

Once Kalt and Box exposed this legal riddle, chronicles about Idaho's "Zone of Death" took a life of their own. Filmmaker Julian Pinder produced "Population Zero" about a lone gunman randomly killing people there. Journalists wrote about the topic. The Zone of Death even got its own Wikipedia entry. Visitation increased to the previously obscure strip of Idaho park land.

Wyoming Senator Mike Enzi made a lackluster effort to convince the Department of Justice to close the legal loophole, and in 2022, Idaho legislators encouraged Congress to take action. The solution could be simple: change district lines so the Idaho portion of the park falls under the jurisdiction of the United States District Court for Idaho. Of course, even the simplest bureaucratic options move slowly, and since no abhorrent crimes had ever occurred in the Zone of Death, neither Congress nor the Justice Department took any action.[22]

Kalt did not advocate a crime spree in Yellowstone National Park, Idaho. "Most of the clickbait stories about the Zone overstate it," he noted sixteen years after publication of his provocative article. "They make it sound like it is a settled matter of law." Like every good hypothesis, it is open to interpretation. For example, courts might choose not to take "a hyper-realistic view of the Sixth Amendment" and allow a case to be tried in Wyoming District Court. A real-life crime actually did occur in the "lawless" section of Yellowstone Park lying in Montana when a Montana poacher illegally shot an elk there in 2005. His lawyer invoked the Kalt defense. The federal judge found it interesting—before he dismissed the argument and ruled the trial could proceed in Wyoming. The poacher took a plea deal. The legal issue remained unresolved.[23]

Joe Pickett proceeded on to other novelistic adventures, but the Idaho Yellowstone legal conundrum remained. Barring bureaucratic progress in closing the loophole, C. J. Box might someday send the crime-fighting game warden back to the "free fire" zone for a sequel.

Fred Dubois also moved on after his crime-fighting days along the Idaho-Wyoming border. He parlayed his Mormon-hunting credibility into a long political career. In 1886, Dubois won election as Idaho's territorial delegate to Congress—an election in which Mormons could not vote, thanks to the Idaho Test Oath. He served two terms, and proved an effective voice in Washington, helping prepare the way for Idaho statehood in 1890. In 1891, he became a United States senator.

There have been precious few times when Democrats have gained control of the Idaho legislature following Dubois's highly effective purge of the 1880s. One came during the economic turmoil of the 1890s. At the time, legislators selected United States senators. After Idaho Democratic legislators gained control in 1896, they defeated Dubois's bid for a second term. He returned to his ranch in Blackfoot. His political career appeared to be over. But Dubois could detect changing political trends as well as anyone in Idaho history. He left the Republican Party, and in 1900 the Democratic legislature sent him back to the Senate. As soon as he arrived in Washington, DC, he became a Democrat, a remarkable transformation from the man who had done more than anyone to marginalize that party in Idaho. The state's natural political order restored itself in the early 1900s. Republicans again gained control of the legislature. In 1907, that body replaced Dubois in the Senate with Republican William Borah.[24]

After leaving Congress, Dubois spent the rest of his life in Washington, DC. The man who once patrolled the territorial border between Idaho and Wyoming served on the International Joint Commission, a group formed to resolve disputes along the Canadian-United States boundary. And today, the man sometimes frustrated by the clever efforts of Mormons to escape his reach by adroitly manipulating Idaho's border with Wyoming has towns in both states named for him.

CHAPTER EIGHT

Connections

Idahoans have long struggled to unite their eccentrically shaped state. Its unwieldly borders proved more than an inconvenience. Indeed, the graceless boundaries nearly led to Idaho's demise before it even had a chance to become a state. Twenty-two years after imposing the gaunt panhandle on Idaho, some members of Congress recognized their mistake, William McKendree Springer, representative from Illinois, among them. In 1886, he recommended Washington Territory annex northern Idaho. He reasoned his proposal "simply the adoption of a natural boundary as against an artificial one. The northern part of Idaho…is [isolated by] an almost impassable mountain barrier.…The people in the Pan Handle desire to be annexed to Washington."[1]

Springer found many allies. The House Committee on Territories had previously unanimously recommended the move. And in that winter, the entire house voted in favor of the annexation plan, as did the Senate.[2]

Former Senator William Stewart of Nevada cheerfully observed those proceedings. He was in Washington and would shortly take office once again representing Nevada. Congress had prematurely admitted that state to the union during exuberance over its mineral riches, when it seemed the world rushed to Nevada. It operated under a territorial government only three years before becoming a state. But by 1880, mining activity in the Comstock Lode had plummeted. The world withdrew as quickly as it had rushed in, leaving the Silver State's finances a mess, with precious few taxpayers left to bankroll government. So many abandoned the place that governmental officials began contemplating a first in American history: revoking statehood.

Stewart foresaw a solution. Just across the 42nd parallel, Idaho thrived. Annex southern Idaho to Nevada, and his state would gain people, tax revenue, and rich agricultural land. He planned to support Washington's annexation of the north, thus weakening Idaho, and then snatch the south for Nevada. The awkwardly shaped Idaho would cease to exist. Only the reluctance of President Grover Cleveland provided Idahoans with time to straighten out their internal affairs—and enabled Idaho to survive into statehood.

Idaho's inaugural territorial legislature met in Lewiston in 1863. As their first order of business, legislators petitioned Congress to shrink their unmanageable territory. Congress obliged by carving out Montana. As one of their next orders of business, legislators from southern Idaho proposed moving the capital to Boise. Their effort failed, but they quickly took up the task again when they met in Lewiston the following year. That time, over the vehement objections of north Idaho lawmakers, the measure passed. It caught Idaho's new governor, Caleb Lyon, in a bind. If he endorsed the bill to move the capital, he would placate most legislators, but incur the considerable wrath of Lewistonians. Lyon did what any self-respecting politician would do in such a dilemma. He signed the bill, then quickly snuck out of town to escape furious Lewiston residents. He professed to be going duck hunting. It turned out to be quite a safari. He did not return to Idaho for nearly a year. Lewistonians fumed at his "obnoxious" actions and alleged, quite accurately, he had "clandestinely and degradingly left the Territory under false pretenses," guided by "fear, caprice or bribery."[3]

Northern Idaho legislators filed suit, claiming the action illegal. A probate judge agreed, declaring the legislative bill and Lyon's signature unlawful. He ordered the official territorial papers locked up and posted an armed guard to protect them. Abraham Lincoln had recently appointed Clinton DeWitt Smith as territorial secretary. In Caleb Lyon's absence, Smith assumed the duties of governor. He arrived in Lewiston in the spring of 1865 and ordered troops from nearby Fort Lapwai to seize the records. The soldiers easily overpowered the local guards, and Smith rode off to Boise with the territorial seal and official papers. A U.S. Marshal pursued to arrest Smith, but Army troops kept him at bay. Smith arrived in Boise on April 14, 1865, the day of Lincoln's assassination, though Idahoans had not yet received the news. He gave a speech to an ecstatic crowd from the balcony of Boise's Overland Hotel. Smith in essence had brought the seat of government to Boise, where it has remained. Boiseans welcomed him as a hero. Northern Idahoans seethed, and debates over whether

Boise stole the capital or merely accepted what was legally theirs have engaged generations of Idahoans.

While people debate the legality of the move, there is unambiguous consensus about the cause of the transfer of power. It is taken as uncontested truth professed by generations of historians. One of the very best of them, Leonard Arrington, succinctly laid out the argument. As the gold diggings of the Clearwater region played out, miners moved south. Lewiston's population plummeted while the new city of Boise grew exponentially. "Consequently," Arrington wrote, "the second...legislature voted on December 7, 1864, to remove the capital to Boise City."[4]

There is certainly some truth in that theory. But a shrinking population does not preordain a capital move to a larger city. Idaho's neighbors—Washington, Oregon, Nevada, and California—all retained their small capital cities long after people had concentrated in larger centers. The move of Idaho's capital had much more to do with Idaho's strange shape and rugged terrain than with population shifts.

The capital's move created a bountiful trove of quotes for future historians, as editors of their respective town newspapers defamed one another. The editor of Boise's *Idaho Tri-Weekly Statesman* called the editor of Lewiston's *Golden Age* the "flea-brained king of the flea patch." The Lewistonian returned the volley, proclaiming the Boise editor "so lazy he never worked but once—and that was when he mistook castor oil for bourbon." On it went as the two defended their communities in the ongoing clash over the capital's rightful home.[5]

The editorial jousting provided levity, but the issues underlying the move had more serious consequences. Lewiston—indeed, all of northern Idaho—had a westward orientation. Nearly all those miners and camp followers who created a boomtown on the Nez Perce Reservation had arrived from the west—overland from Walla Walla, or by river steamer from Portland. When miners moved south, they elected legislators who had to grapple with a north-south orientation just to get to work. It proved unpleasant—and sometimes dangerous— as southern Idaho legislators careened north in hazardous conditions to get to Lewiston for winter legislative sessions—or took the safer, but much longer, detour through Oregon and Washington to reach that destination. They can be excused for desiring to relocate the meeting place.

Of course, that move just traded one inconvenience for another. Southern Idaho legislators could now more easily access the capital, but northern Idaho legislators faced the unpleasant task of journeying south to Boise. Idaho is just not laid out for north-south travel. It did not take north Idaho residents long to conclude that John Mullan had been correct. When he drew his map for proposed new Western territories for Congressman James Ashley in 1863, he recognized the historical east-west orientation of what became northern Idaho. There would today be no isolated Idaho panhandle had Mullan won the day.

Immediately after Governor Lyon signed the capital removal bill, Lewiston residents dispatched emissaries to Walla Walla to propose an alliance, suggesting both communities petition Congress to create a new Territory of Columbia that reflected the east-west reality. The concept proved enticing to both cities. Walla Walla had been unable to wrest Washington's capital from Olympia. A new territory offered an opportunity to sever ties with the "half dead carcase of Puget Sound." Northern Idahoans saw value in aligning themselves with the booming Walla Walla region. But the alliance soon collapsed amidst intercity rivalries. A Columbia Territory, after all, could have only one capital, and either Lewiston or Walla Walla was destined for disappointment.[6]

Although its collaboration with Walla Walla failed, north Idaho's acrimony continued unabated. For the next two decades, citizens from that part of the territory continued their efforts to break away from the thieves of south Idaho. For some time, northerners focused on a new Territory of Columbia. Once Congress had established Montana, northern Idahoans generally agreed the new territory should consist of eastern Washington, northern Idaho, and western Montana. They believed Columbia would appeal to Congress's desire for rectangular territories. It would eliminate the "giant jigsaw puzzle with its jagged pieces overlapping both political and geographic metes and bounds" by creating neater, rectangular shapes for Idaho and the new Columbia. The concept would also whittle Montana down to a more manageable rectangular size. And Washington would retain its boxlike shape, albeit as a diminished rectangle.[7]

Southern Idaho legislators proved very amenable to jettisoning the miscreants of north Idaho. "There is no community of interest between the two sections...divided by a high Mountain Range," the legislators affirmed. In 1866, they eagerly sent a memorial to Congress commending creation of the new territory. But Montanans did not look quite so favorably upon the "robbery" of their land. Montana Governor Thomas Meagher argued passionately against Columbia: "I trust that all attempts against [Montana's] rich and rare domain, as Idaho has undertaken…will be…effectively resisted." Confronted by Meagher's ardent opposition, Congress refused to act on the Columbia Territory issue in 1866.[8]

Undeterred, Lewistonians pressed on. If Montana chose not to join, Columbia could function effectively with territory carved out of northern Idaho and eastern Washington. Again, the Idaho territorial legislature proved amenable to allowing north Idaho to secede. When legislators next gathered in Boise, they sent another memorial to Congress encouraging north Idaho secession and the creation of a smaller Columbia. Even residents of Walla Walla returned to the cause, having grown as frustrated with Puget Sound as northern Idahoans were with Boise. Not surprisingly, western Washington legislators proved less ecstatic about shrinking the size of their territory, and the Washington legislature convinced Congress to reject the concept.

For a time, northern Idahoans harbored thoughts of going it alone, encouraging Congress to carve a new territory just from Idaho, north of the Salmon River. But they soon recognized the region lacked the population to prosper as a territory. So, in 1867, the north Idaho secession movement took a new tact. Rather than create a new territory, northern residents now endorsed annexation to Washington.[9]

Legislators from Washington for a time fought annexation. But as fear of Walla Walla possibly seizing the capital from Olympia subsided, they looked more favorably upon that additional space. In 1868, 1873, and 1875, the Washington legislature sent memorials to Congress advocating the annexation of north Idaho. Meanwhile, the Idaho legislature continued to find no reason to dissent. It repeatedly memorialized Congress in favor of granting north Idaho to Washington. In 1878, 96 percent of northern Idaho voters approved a measure that would have united them with Washington. In an 1880 referendum, northern Idahoans cast 1,208 votes in favor of annexation—while two voters preferred remaining in Idaho.[10]

By the early 1880s, Washington's annexation of north Idaho enjoyed nearly universal political support in Idaho. Both Republican and Democratic parties recommended annexation. That led to those

1886 bills in Congress supporting the concept. But the Senate and House bills differed, and Congress proved unable to reconcile those dissimilarities in 1886. In 1887, however, it appeared all the stars had finally aligned. Congress was ready to act. North Idaho would soon become eastern Washington.[11]

There is today a panhandle in Idaho—and a university in Moscow—thanks largely to overreach by Nevadans. Southern Idahoans had remarkably few qualms about abandoning north Idaho—until they discerned the eagerness of Nevadans to gobble up southern Idaho. The high-handed efforts of Senator Stewart and other Nevada politicians succeeded when nothing else could. Their attempted power grab finally unified a majority of influential Idaho politicians to oppose north Idaho secession in order to save south Idaho.

Congress adjourned in the spring of 1886 with the House and Senate annexation bills unreconciled. Had it acted quickly on the issue when it reconvened in December 1886, it is likely that today north Idaho would be eastern Washington. But Congress had multiple momentous issues before it, including the Interstate Commerce Act, Indian Allotment Act, and a provision for improved counting of electoral votes following the disputed election of 1876. William Stewart sensed opportunity slipping away. He had no personal interest in northern Idaho. But north Idaho secession would weaken Idaho, easing the path for Nevada to annex the remainder of the territory. In late February 1887, Stewart appeared before the Senate Committee on Territories. He gave an impassioned plea for north Idaho annexation. The committee resurrected the House annexation bill of the previous session.

Finally, on March 1, the Senate passed the annexation bill the House had supported in 1886. The next day, the House easily approved the Senate's minor changes. On March 3, 1887, the last day of Congress, only the signature of President Cleveland remained for northern Idaho to become part of Washington. The north would be freed at last from the "cold-hearted, avaricious, scheming leeches" of southern Idaho, as one northern resident ecstatically proclaimed. But Cleveland refused to sign, pocket vetoing the legislation. That pause gave Idaho annexation opponents a chance to rally.[12]

In 1887, both houses of the U.S. Congress passed a bill allowing northern Idaho to secede to Washington. Only President Grover Cleveland's pocket veto preserved the panhandle in Idaho.

It is good to let these events sink in. Both houses of the United States Congress easily passed a bill providing for Washington to annex northern Idaho. The bill sat on President Cleveland's desk awaiting his signature. Once north Idaho vanished, Nevada Senator Stewart would pounce on a weakened southern Idaho. Idaho came that close to disappearing. A brother's dispute with his elder sibling helped it survive.

The "scheming leeches" of southern Idaho finally had a change of heart. And Senator Stewart found a resolute adversary in Idaho Governor Edward Stevenson, who adamantly opposed both north Idaho secession and Nevada expansion. "Confronted with annexation on the north by a sister Territory very anxious for a slice of our area," he wrote, "we are attacked again by a hungry neighbor to the south, Nevada by name, who is willing to gobble up the remaining part of Idaho."[13]

William Stewart, raised in New York, moved to California with the gold rush and became a politician. He followed mining to Nevada and became a United States senator. In the 1880s, he found a powerful ally in his effort to annex southern Idaho in Nevada Governor Charles Stevenson. But Charles's brother Edward caused Stewart all sorts of problems.

The careers of William Stewart and Edward Stevenson ran on remarkably parallel courses. Like Stewart, Stevenson grew up in western New York, followed the gold rush to California, and became a politician. He served in the California state legislature when Stewart was the state's attorney general. Like Stewart, Stevenson moved inland to follow the gold diggings, but chose Idaho over Nevada. He served multiple terms in the Idaho legislature before President Grover Cleveland appointed him territorial governor.[14]

While Stewart persuaded Congress to pass the north Idaho annexation legislation, Governor Charles Stevenson lobbied the Nevada legislature, which easily approved a bill recommending the annexation of south Idaho to Nevada. Despite his younger brother's determined opposition, Charles Stevenson happily signed the act to enlarge Nevada.

Just as Stewart had Governor Charles Stevenson back home promoting south Idaho annexation, Governor Edward Stevenson had an ally in Washington, DC, supporting his cause—Fred Dubois, Idaho's new territorial delegate to Congress. Dubois had narrowly won election in 1886. A Republican, he broke with most members of his party and ran on a platform opposed to Washington's annexation of the panhandle. He won in large part due to the surprising support of Moscow power broker Willis Sweet, whose political machine turned out Dubois supporters. Sweet was one of the few north Idaho politicians opposed to the panhandle's annexation. Though Dubois would not take office until March 4, 1887, like Stewart he arrived in DC early, and as an incoming congressional delegate helped persuade Cleveland to pocket veto the annexation legislation.[15]

Willis Sweet's endorsement of Dubois shocked many of his northern colleagues. But Sweet knew if Dubois won, he could call in political favors. Sweet later reminisced that southeast Idaho "was grateful for the support given Mr. Dubois....For one thing, the 'southeast' was...in favor of anything within reason that north Idaho asked for....North Idaho had come into her own; and all we had to do was ask for what we wanted."[16]

Sweet knew just what to request: a university for his hometown. When Idaho's territorial legislature convened in 1888, Representative Sweet arrived early, bent on shepherding through a bill creating a university at Moscow. The measure passed easily, and Governor Edward Stevenson gladly signed it. Noted one legislator when endorsing the bill, "It would be recognized as an olive branch in the interest of peace and good-will extended by one section of the Territory to another, between which there has been long and bitter contention." When Governor Stevenson called a constitutional convention in 1889, delegates gathered in Boise. Moscow representatives were wary of southern Idahoans' recently acquired affection for the north. They recalled the disappearance of the capital to Boise a quarter century earlier. They determined to write the location of the university into the state constitution. The only way future southern Idahoans could expropriate the university would be via constitutional amendment. The convention delegates approved the provision making Moscow the permanent home for the University of Idaho—a rare example of constitutional protection for the location of a state university. That provision came in handy many times in future years as Idaho politicians attempted to move all or part of the university. Only the Idaho State Constitution blocked their efforts.[17]

Washington became a state in 1889 and Idaho in 1890. It seemed the issue of Idaho retaining its peculiar panhandle had been settled. But the concept of separating north and south Idaho had one more serious run. More than a quarter century after statehood, old sectional antagonisms flared again. The culprit: the supposedly secure location of the University of Idaho in Moscow.

The Idaho Constitution confirmed the location of the university. But it seemed to many northerners that the "scheming leeches" of southern Idaho had reappeared when legislators attempted to nibble away at the constitutional language. First, they argued that document did not require that "all" the university's schools and departments be in one location. In nearly every legislative session, southern Idaho legislators introduced bills to move the College of Agriculture to the south. A bill to transfer all federal land-grant funds to the Idaho Technical College (later Idaho State University) came within one vote of Senate passage. Other legislators suggested moving the School of Mines. University supporters successfully battled efforts to dismember the university piecemeal. They were unprepared for a more audacious move in 1917, when some legislators decided just to ignore the state constitution altogether.

In January 1917, the education committees of the House and Senate proposed moving the university to the south. Immediately, north Idaho legislators renewed the old call for northern secession. They had grown weary of defending the state constitution and its provision for the university's location. Their bold move forced the legislature to postpone plans to remove the school; southern legislators believed this would halt the secession movement. Instead, the effort grew stronger. Northerners perceived the legislative action as merely temporary appeasement. The issue of the university's location would surely flare again. In addition, many issues divided north and south, not just the university's placement. Northern legislators wanted a new state. The former Idaho panhandle should become the State of Lincoln.[18]

In 1907, residents of Spokane had advocated the merger of eastern Washington, northern Idaho, and northeast Oregon into a State of Lincoln, a re-envisioning of various 19th-century concepts that had recognized the region's east-west orientation in a diversity of proposals for a new territory. But the Spokane effort would require the unlikely approval of three state legislatures, in addition to the U.S. Congress. In 1917, Idahoans sought to reduce the requisite number of bureaucratic maneuvers. A new state carved entirely out of Idaho required the blessing of only one state legislature. That process seemed eminently achievable when, in February 1917, the Idaho House of Representatives twice voted overwhelmingly to memorialize Congress in support of the secession of the northern ten counties, allowing them to establish a new state. Large rallies in north Idaho endorsed the concept. A call went out for a constitutional convention to meet in Moscow in June. People even began writing the new state's constitution. It noted that geographic barriers prohibited uniting the economically and culturally disparate sections of Idaho. A poll of state senators showed a majority approved the establishment of the new state. Idaho once again sat on the cusp of separation.

Then, on the last day of the legislative session, senators had a change of heart, voting 32–10 to table a resolution to Congress supporting the formation of Lincoln. Only the ten senators from north of the Salmon River opposed the measure.

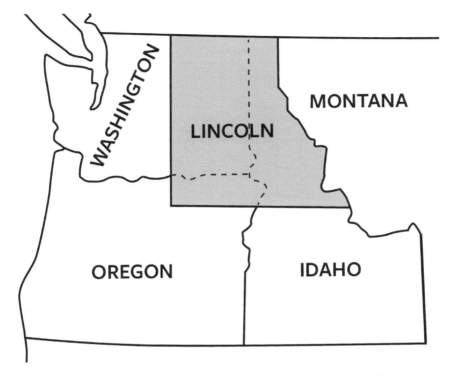

For more than 150 years, some northern Idahoans advocated seceding from Idaho and establishing a new state. They usually wanted to name the place Lincoln or Columbia, and contemplated carving it from Idaho and neighboring states. This map is a 21st-century iteration of the concept.

Idaho had dodged the last serious effort to separate north from south. Over the years, various proposals arose—most lighthearted and all ineffective—to create a new State of Lincoln (or Columbia) in the Inland Empire. By the late 20th century, the old secession movement had morphed into a bumper-sticker slogan that promoted North Idaho as a "State of Mind," with North always capitalized. While serious secession efforts subsided after 1917, the underlying complications of connecting two discordant parts of western America's most peculiarly shaped state remained.

Packer John Welch understood the transportation challenges that would confront generations of Idahoans. In 1862, before Idaho existed, he set out from Lewiston with a load of supplies for Boise Basin miners. Welch soon learned just how difficult it would be to connect north and south Idaho as he struggled through rugged mountains and rapidly accumulating snow. Realizing he would never reach the basin that year, he and his men holed up at Little Salmon Meadows in a makeshift cabin. There they endured the winter before continuing their trek. Packer John's cabin became a prominent way station for those brave enough to travel the road—actually more of a trail—between Lewiston and Boise. It also turned into a significant halfway meeting place for Idaho politicians. Both Republicans and Democrats held party conventions at the tiny hut. Though rustic, it proved much easier for groups to meet at this juncture than for northerners to travel all the way south, or vice-versa.[19]

Lewistonians believed they had the perfect solution to the virtually impassable road Packer John had encountered: get to Boise by boat. In the 1860s, Lewiston residents dispatched a scouting expedition to determine the Snake River's navigability south of their town. The community's newspaper enthusiastically reported the result: "They found nothing in the river to impede navigation whatever....A new route will now be opened for steam, the results of which cannot now be foretold. We shall penetrate Nevada and Utah Territories by steam."[20]

In fact, between Lewiston and Boise there were 135 miles of river, dozens of rapids—and Hells Canyon. Still, that failed to deter Lewistonians. In 1865, they sent captain Thomas Stump on the steamer *Colonel Wright*, to prove their case about navigability. Stump managed to wrench his way 80 miles upstream before destroying his boat. Five years later, determined adventurers constructed the steamer *Shoshone* and attempted to reach Lewiston by navigating downstream from Parma. The boat made it—but in a "badly demolished condition." The middle Snake would never be navigable.[21]

It proved as impossible to connect north and south Idaho by rail as it had by boat. In the early 1900s, entrepreneurs built a railroad to reach copper mines in the Seven Devils Mountains of north-central Idaho. The Pacific & Idaho Northern Railway made it about as far north as Packer John's cabin, constructing a depot a few miles away in the recently founded town of New Meadows. About the same time as the P&IN laid tracks north, the Camas Prairie Railroad built south out of Lewiston, trestle-bridging canyons so spectacularly high and otherwise impassable it became famed as the "Railroad on Stilts." That line terminated in Grangeville. No railroad would ever make it through the brutal 80 miles between New Meadows and Grangeville to complete a rail connection between north and south. People or material traveling by train between north and south Idaho had to navigate through neighboring states before reaching Idaho destinations.[22]

That left a highway as the only viable option to link the regions—a damnably difficult alternative. As part of the conciliation that granted the University of Idaho to Moscow, the legislature also approved $50,000 in bonds to build a wagon road connecting the Little Salmon Meadows—the location of Packer John's cabin—with the Camas Prairie near Grangeville. Nothing happened. Ten years later, the legislature approved another measure for a road connecting north and south, with much the same result. Recollected one man who braved the trails that then sufficed for a highway, "The first time I went over that road I led my saddle horse. It looked safer that way."[23]

As early as the mid-1860s, other regions in Idaho had been connected by major roads. The Oregon Trail ran through the south, the Mullan Road connected Washington and Montana with the Idaho panhandle, and the Montana Trail out of Salt Lake City navigated the east. With some alterations, these well-traveled routes became, respectively, Interstates 84/86, 90, and 15. But the challenge of a north-south highway running the length of Idaho, connecting the panhandle with the south, remained a vexing problem.

By 1913, when automobiles began appearing, the north-south road had been a topic of discussion for decades. A highway of sorts did exist, but only in the flatlands in the southern part of the route. In the north, the road became nothing more than a trail that proved "hardly passable through the rugged mountains" as geographer Benjamin Thomas noted. "In some places the grades were more than 30 per cent. Along streams much of the road was submerged during high water. Wooden bridges… were washed out regularly.…Snowslides, floods, and falling rocks intermittently covered or destroyed parts of the narrow roadbed."[24]

Connecting Idaho would be no easy task. By the early 20th century, residents of Sandpoint had two options if they wanted to journey south. They could row a boat across the outlet of Lake Pend Oreille. Or they could walk across the nearly two-mile-long railroad trestle, "a hike that required nimble feet and a good knowledge of train schedules." In 1910, the city celebrated completion of a wooden bridge across the lake. It rested upon 1,540 pilings. Locals touted it as the longest wooden bridge in the world. It marked one small step in the generations-long effort to link Idahoans with one another.[25]

One hundred and fifty miles south, engineer C. C. Van Arsdol completed an elegant piece of the connectivity puzzle. Van Arsdol, well-known in the Lewiston Valley, had partnered with Charles Francis Adams Jr. in the plan to irrigate farmland around the community of Clarkston, Washington. Residents of Lewiston hired him for a different task. Lewiston had suffered since its inception not only with transportation hazards to the south, but also to the north. The city lies more than 2,000 feet below the rich Palouse Prairie agricultural lands north of it. A tortuous wagon route connected the two areas, but only for the adventurous. Travelers sometimes tied logs behind their wagons to slow their descent. "It wasn't a trip one wished to make often," understated historian Margaret Day Allen. The nearly impassable wagon road proved so burdensome that residents of northern Nez Perce County could scarcely make it to Lewiston to conduct business. So, in 1888, Congress did something unique. It created Latah County. Moscow became the county seat. It is the only county in America established by an act of Congress. That served the residents of the new Latah County well in terms of transacting governmental business. But the precarious route that prevented them from journeying south for other reasons remained.[26]

Van Arsdol began his task of engineering one of the country's most spectacular roads in 1916. A year later, he completed the Spiral Highway connecting Lewiston with the Palouse. With its 64 sweeping curves, it quickly earned a well-deserved reputation as a model of highway design.[27]

E. A. White, the man responsible for hiring Van Arsdol, later described the Spiral Highway as "the spark that kindled a deep interest in highway development in this entire section of northern Idaho." As Van Arsdol worked on the road to the Palouse Prairie, 80 people met in Lewiston's Elks Club and formed the North and South Highway Association, with a goal of connecting the northernmost communities of the panhandle with Boise and the south. "If ever a State or community had occasion to stress the importance of a highway from a social or economic standpoint, Idaho has," noted a writer in *Western Highways*

Builder. "The northern and southern portions of the State [are] as separated as if an ocean divided them." Crossing an ocean might have been easier. "Along the western boundary from the Canadian line to Ada [County] runs virtually a continuous mountain range," observed the same author. The new highway association faced a daunting task.[28]

In 1916, Congress established the Federal Aid Road Act to provide financial assistance for road building. The North-South Highway became the first in Idaho—and one of the earliest nationally—to qualify for money under the act. With federal financing, the highway made dramatic progress, and by 1920, Idaho claimed another engineering feat. That year saw completion of an eight-mile system of switchbacks that allowed automobiles—albeit slow-moving and often overheated—to negotiate the White Bird grade south of Grangeville. Cars crawling along the road gave the "impression of a confused snake." Still, it stood as another marvel of highway construction.[29]

In good weather, utilizing the new White Bird highway, motorists could now travel from Boise as far north as Grangeville in 18 hours. Covering that ground continued to prove a challenge, for the route included "many a rough and rugged road." Still, a booster writing in *Western Highways Builder* reassured drivers. "The careful pilot will experience no serious difficulties," he pledged, "provided he is accustomed to shifting gears on short notice, and provided, also, that he is not averse to twisting around grades that tower several hundred feet above a tortuous rock-studded river."[30]

In 1925, after spending more than six million dollars on improvements, the road received designation as U.S. Highway 95. Idahoans declared the elusive passage between regions completed. "The two states of North and South Idaho are now united," gushed a writer in *Good Roads* magazine. That assessment proved a bit premature.[31]

As late as the 1970s, the quickest route from northern Idaho to Boise still ran through Washington and Oregon. Idaho Governor Cecil Andrus gave Highway 95 a lasting nickname: The Goat Trail. As a reporter for the *Lewiston Morning Tribune* clarified, "A goat trail isn't exactly the path of economic prosperity, unless you're in the business of making cheese."[32]

New routes over the White Bird and Lewiston grades dramatically shortened travel times in the 1970s. Sandpoint got a new bridge in 1981, its fourth iteration at that location. Yet as late as 1988, the

Idaho Transportation Department classified 210 miles of the 540-mile, north-south road as "substandard." Throughout the late 20th century and into the 21st, the department spent millions of dollars to widen and realign the "outmoded, dangerous highway." Indeed, the department spent more on Highway 95 improvements than any other road in the state. Highway 95 typically gobbled up as much as 40 percent of all state road funding. Gradually, it became a beautiful highway through spectacular country. It truly was "one of the most picturesque scenic routes in the West" for those patient enough to enjoy its treasures. For those in a hurry, in the 21st century just as in the 19th, it remained the slowest of Idaho's major arterials.[33]

It is impossible to comprehend Idaho history without understanding the long struggle to connect north and south Idaho. It is a continuous narrative thread tying Idaho's present and future with its past. If Idahoans of the 21st century are curious about why it is that so much has been expended—in money, in political strife, in frustration—attempting to link the panhandle with the rest of the state, all they need do is review those congressional decisions of 1863 and 1864 that gave their state its unwieldy shape. During the most perilous time in the nation's history, members of Congress, distracted by a grisly, protracted Civil War, decided Idaho's fate. Those men created Idaho's spindly, isolated panhandle. "We considered the formation of the Panhandle a blunder, if not a crime," lamented the Wallace newspaper nearly 30 years after those congressional actions. The 1860s decisions by a group of men who understood little about Northwest geography forever complicated life for those who would call Idaho home.[34]

EPILOGUE

Walking Idaho's Borders

You can hike around the borders of Idaho. If you average 25 miles a day, it will take you about 100 days to travel some 2,500 miles. You will clamber uphill some 317,000 feet—similar to climbing from sea level to the tip of Mount Everest 11 times. You will scramble downhill the same distance. You will need to tote a tent, sleeping bag, compass, maps, water bottles, water filter, duct tape, sewing kit, first aid kit, and enough food to sustain you until you reach the next store or restaurant. You should take very dependable GPS equipment, because you will encounter many places where there is "no trace of a trail." And you will need to be capable of hiking 30-mile days through southern Idaho's parched desert terrain. On the other hand, you should plan on July snow in northern Idaho, strong winds, "mosquitoes...in Arctic numbers," and icy stream crossings. But there will be rewards. You will meet wonderful people and enjoy some of the most magnificent of American vistas.[1]

It would also be advisable to take along Mike O'Brien's *Idaho Boundary Trail Hiker's Guide*. In 2012, O'Brien "wanted to do a long walk." So, he circumnavigated the state. He repeated the trek two years later. "It is a challenging and scenic walk," he noted in his understated way.

O'Brien and his hiking companion, Jim Fulmis, who was unable to finish for health reasons, began their excursions at the confluence of the Snake and Clearwater Rivers in May and headed south to encircle Idaho counterclockwise. Following their schedule gets you through the desert before searing summer heat, into the mountains "late enough for most of the snow...to melt," and back into your own bed by autumn. That is, if you can average 25 miles a day.

O'Brien's trail does not strictly adhere to boundary lines. In seeking the most favorable route while traversing public rights-of-way, he zigged and zagged across the border into Washington, Oregon, Nevada, Utah, Wyoming, and Montana. Even at that, his course is challenging enough. O'Brien has a healthy respect for those surveyors who lacked the luxury of deviating off track in search of a more amenable path. At a point on the craggy Idaho-Montana border, he detoured around, rather than going over, some intimidating mountains. "Even then it was difficult terrain," he recalled. "The slopes extremely steep, clothed in thick brush and downed trees. I tripped several times, once flipping completely head over heels....I can hardly imagine how they were able to survey and mark those mountain tops."

Now, as then, a journey along Idaho's borders is not for the timid.

So, how does it appear from ground level in the 21st century, this implausible boundary forged by faraway 19th-century diplomats and politicians? Mike O'Brien has a perspective not shared by any of the people who actually conceived Idaho's borders. He knows the lay of the land. Even the survey teams that marked the borderlines knew only sections of the boundary. O'Brien was almost certainly the first person to walk around the entire state.

Like O'Brien, Rollin Reeves began his journey at the confluence of the Snake and Clearwater Rivers. Hired to survey the Washington-Idaho border, Reeves spent two weeks in 1873 in a frustrating attempt to ascertain "the middle channel of the Snake River opposite the mouth of [the] Clearwater." Unable to find the precise spot from which to begin his survey, Reeves estimated the best he could, then proceeded north laying the line.[2]

Similarities between O'Brien's walk and Reeves's survey mostly ended at their mutual starting point. O'Brien lodged in a hotel the night before his departure and enjoyed a restaurant dinner a stone's throw from the riverbank where Reeves launched buoys into the river in a futile effort to determine the middle channel. O'Brien had other advantages. He began his walk two months earlier than Reeves, providing a cushion of better weather before winter's onset. While Reeves marched north, nearly meeting catastrophe in winter snows near the Canadian border, O'Brien headed south. He, too, confronted snow when he got to northern Idaho, but came upon it in a better season.

O'Brien and Reeves did share a common experience—the bewildered reactions of people they encountered. Rollin Reeves happened upon two trappers "who were astonished at the appearance" of a survey party traipsing through their seemingly isolated wilderness. Three days into his 2014 walk, on highlands above Hells Canyon, O'Brien flabbergasted a rancher out tracking cows. When O'Brien explained his purpose, she could only manage, "You must like walking!"[3]

O'Brien also experienced the topographical and climate challenges that confronted various survey parties. His journal entries of Hells Canyon reflect its jagged contours: "Up, down, from drainage to drainage, down a road that ended, bushwhacking." They also provide cautionary comment on Idaho weather, no matter the season. On his 2014 walk, O'Brien camped above the canyon in a rain and windstorm. The next day he trudged five miles through snow, his feet sinking 18 inches each step before settling on firm ground. He made it through, but only after a "hard-won" battle.

As O'Brien exited Hells Canyon, he encountered the first of the straight-line sections of Idaho's boundary, the southern part of its border with Oregon. For the first part of that stretch, he traveled in Oregon, then crossed into Idaho. His trip took him through irrigated farms of potatoes, beets, and onions; into range country; and then to desert scablands. Sheriffs in both states cautioned him about strolling into Idaho's blistering and desolate sagebrush-steppe highlands. The sheriffs, perhaps, knew their history.

In 1811, Wilson Price Hunt led the first party of whites through southern Idaho's desert. A partner in John Jacob Astor's Pacific Fur Company, Hunt led 62 men and one woman—Marie Dorion, and her two young sons—on an overland expedition to establish Fort Astoria, a fur post at the mouth of the Columbia River. Things did not go well in Idaho. Some famished members of his party resorted to gnawing on their moccasins. Others drank their own urine in a desperate effort to relieve thirst. Several members of the party died, and Hunt left others, too weak to continue, with Shoshone Indians. Reduced to a group of 32, Hunt finally staggered into Astoria. But the accomplishment proved bittersweet when Astorians lost their post to the British in the War of 1812. The grand Astor venture had failed.[4]

As discouraged Astorians made their way back home, a small group led by Robert Stuart traversed a gap in the Rockies, making the first recorded crossing of South Pass. It would become one of the most significant landmarks of the Oregon Trail, the highway that brought thousands of emigrants through southern Idaho—all hoping to exit as quickly as possible to less-harsh landscapes. Idaho was not a place to linger. Oregon Trail journals are rife with bleak descriptions of the country O'Brien was soon to enter.[5]

Undeterred, Mike O'Brien thanked the sheriffs for their concern, and continued into the desert. Sometimes he followed trails, sometimes he bushwhacked, sometimes he took roads—though the interpretation of "road" challenged conventional wisdom. "The road became even more vague," he noted one time. "I doubt it had seen a wheel in decades." It was proving a tough go through a land of little water. But O'Brien persevered, navigating his way to the 42nd parallel, Idaho's southern border.

As he did, he skirted the Duck Valley Reservation, an uncommon place. The United States has more than 300 Indian reservations. Indian ancestral lands paid no heed to what eventually became state boundaries. Yet the same federal bureaucracy that designed state borderlines, often ignoring geography, also prescribed that spots reserved for Indians should fit within the confines of those artificial state boundaries. About two dozen reservations nationwide extend across state lines. Duck Valley is one, with about half its land in southwestern Idaho and the other in northwestern Nevada.[6]

That there even is a Duck Valley Reservation is largely attributable to tribal resolve. In 1873, John Wesley Powell—one-armed Civil War hero, western explorer extraordinaire, director of both the U.S. Geological Society and the Smithsonian Institution's Bureau of Ethnology—met with Western Shoshone leaders. On this occasion, he also bore the title "Special Commissioner of Indian Affairs" and had traveled west to investigate the "conditions and wants" of Native Americans in the Great Basin. Generally progressive in his approach to western tribes, Powell did the Western Shoshone no favors this time, recommending they move to the distant Fort Hall Reservation in southeast Idaho. Tribal leaders protested, insisting the Western Shoshone deserved a reservation of their own, on their traditional ancestral lands.[7]

In 1877, President Rutherford B. Hayes acquiesced to Western Shoshone tenacity and established two reservations in close proximity, one at Duck Valley. In typical federal Indian-policy fashion, the government soon reneged. Two years later, Hayes acceded to white settlers' demands that agricultural lands within one of the reservations be opened. He rescinded his previous executive order and eliminated one of the reservations, leaving many Western Shoshone landless once again. But Hayes's 1877 order authorizing the Duck Valley Reservation held. It carved out of public lands in Idaho and Nevada a reserve for Western Shoshone people.

Soon, Paiutes would join Shoshones at Duck Valley. Some Northern Paiutes had allied with Bannocks and other tribes in the 1878 Bannock War. As punishment for engaging in that conflict, the government confined more than 500 Nevada and Oregon Northern Paiutes onto the Yakama Indian Reservation in Washington. In 1886, the United States set aside additional land for the Duck Valley Reservation, a rare example of an Indian reservation enlarging, and moved the Northern Paiutes onto the reserve. Today, Shoshone and Paiutes jointly occupy Duck Valley.[8]

For years, Shoshone and Paiute people resisted ongoing efforts to open Duck Valley's rich farmlands to white settlement, and rather remarkably triumphed. Indeed, in 1910, President William Taft took the rare step of enlarging the reservation once again. By the 21st century, the Duck Valley Reservation encompassed 450 square miles, home to about 1,700 Shoshone-Paiute people. A near perfect rectangle, it shares with many western states the United States government's predilection for straight-line boundaries.

Mike O'Brien resupplied on the eastern edge of the reservation and began his long march eastward along Idaho's oldest border, the 42nd parallel. In 1819, American John Quincy Adams and Spaniard Luis de Onís drew this straight-line boundary on a blank map—a stroke on paper separating western empires. Neither of those 19th-century diplomats had any concept of the diverse landscape their international boundary transected. But as O'Brien learned, it courses through some geographically disparate country. He hiked into desert sage and exited in Douglas fir forests; encountered antelope, coyotes, and beaver, as well as cows and sheep; scaled up—and scrambled down—more than 41,000 feet in elevation, always "up, down, up, down," as he wrote.

In 1871, Daniel George Major, sent by the General Land Office to survey the southern Idaho boundary, found it considerably more difficult running a straight path than it had been for Adams and Onís to scribe their mark on a map. Modern cartographers now understand that Major's borderline occasionally meandered as he labored to follow the parallel, leaving parts of the country that rightfully belonged to Utah within Idaho, and vice versa. O'Brien could commiserate with Major's struggle. He had the advantage of modern maps and 21st-century navigational equipment, but even so strained adhering to a course. "I walk down the road to where our track turns up," he wrote, "to find no road; no trails; washed away." He diverted to another route that forced him to needlessly climb 8,000 feet of craggy terrain. Frustrated, he at times just ignored the GPS and trusted his instincts: "I follow the real trail and leave the virtual trail behind."

Making his way east, O'Brien encountered Mormon families who provided food, water, a place to pitch a tent, companionship, and advice on best routes. Some of them descended from families Brigham Young had sent to settle northern Utah, years before Major had surveyed the boundary. Major's work disclosed that some of those Mormon emigrants had in fact crossed the border into Idaho. There, many of their descendants remain. When asked to recount the best-liked part of his long journey around the state, O'Brien highlighted the 42nd parallel. That place of 19th-century confusion was, for O'Brien, the "favorite part of the hike because of the friendly Mormons I met."

From Death Canyon Shelf, a place not as "scary as it sounds," O'Brien gazed upon the Grand Tetons, a "spectacular" view. He was nearing the end of his traverse of the Idaho-Wyoming border. Both the shelf and the mountains stood in Wyoming. Had he traveled here a century-and-a-half earlier, both would have been Idaho landmarks. In 1868, Congress created Wyoming, in the process granting Idaho's Tetons to the new territory. No Idahoans protested, oblivious to the potential of future tourism revenue. But O'Brien—like other Idahoans since 1868—might have paused to contemplate what could have been. How different Idaho would be had Congress not transferred the Tetons, Jackson Hole, and a large swath of what became Yellowstone National Park to Wyoming in order to create that perfectly rectangular new territory.

O'Brien often rhapsodized on the beauty of this Wyoming border country. Clambering up Idaho's Snowdrift Mountain—a place that can "live up to its name" even in July—O'Brien reached "a long undulating ridge which forces clouds of rain and fog to blow over, creating one of the most beautiful sights I've ever seen."

Yet the rugged beauty of this boundary exacts its toll on those who walk it. "It was a long, long stiff climb up to the pass at about 9,700 feet," O'Brien recorded on one ascent, "there to meet a very sketchy trail through another pass to a bowl full of snowbanks. Descending... was a jumble of avalanche debris, branches, trees, boulders littering the trail." On another segment he "struggled from the start, making perhaps a hundred feet at a time, gasping from the shade of one tree to the next shady goal for a reward of a gulp of water." Throughout this endeavor, O'Brien had company—mosquitoes. "I had to put on the headnet and mittens, and even then they were maddening."

The Wyoming border is one of the state's most challenging. But as O'Brien made his way to Montana, he knew he would soon enough face the Bitterroots—"an intimidating range."

"The border with Montana is a mystery to me," O'Brien wrote. "The southern part is the continental divide, but I often wondered how the northern portion of the Montana border was determined." O'Brien could thank Sidney Edgerton and his effective 1864 congressional lobbying for that intimidating border along the Bitterroot crest, which left Idaho with its awkwardly narrow panhandle.

On July 19, 2012, not far out of Lima, Montana, O'Brien reached the halfway point of his initial journey, having traveled 1,328 miles in two months. He would spend another month traversing 687 miles along the Idaho-Montana boundary.

Though O'Brien was the first to hike around Idaho, he shared experiences with others who had preceded him along sections of that voyage. On July 23, he had one of those inspiring occurrences that can result when one encounters a memorable historic site, a place where one can palpably feel history. Those moments usually occur in times of quiet solitude, and O'Brien's came at a summit on the Idaho-Montana border.

On August 12, 1805, Meriwether Lewis, leading a small reconnaissance party of the Corps of Discovery, came upon a spring just on the Montana side of the continental divide. Lewis considered it the source of the "heretofore deemed endless" Missouri River, which the Corps had traveled for 3,000 miles. Here he allayed his thirst with its "pure and ice cold water." O'Brien did the same, and the historical symmetry moved him: "Meriwether Lewis stood here, drank from this very stream!" Like Lewis, O'Brien "proceeded to the top of the dividing range," a place we know as Lemhi Pass.[9]

The best-known book about the Lewis and Clark Expedition is Stephen Ambrose's *Undaunted Courage*, and it is true Meriwether Lewis's courage seldom waivered. But the view from Lemhi Pass distressed him. As he crested the divide, he gazed west into his destiny, the object "on which my mind has been unalterably fixed for many years." He thought that from this long-sought vantage point he might see the Columbia River, shimmering close by, a stream that could provide a relatively effortless route to his destination, the Pacific Ocean. Perhaps, as President Thomas Jefferson believed, Lewis would gaze onto a gentle prairie that the explorers could easily cross to the Columbia's banks. Whatever he viewed, Lewis knew he would soon be leaving the confines of the Louisiana Purchase, recently acquired by the United States, and making his way west, staking a claim for his young nation on the Pacific Northwest, a contested region likewise claimed by England, Spain, and Russia.

What Lewis saw when he reached the summit proved to be one of the most tormenting disappointments in the annals of exploration. On that day, Meriwether Lewis became the first white person to confront Idaho's unforgiving landscape. There would be no gentle walk to the Columbia, no easy paddle to the Pacific. Instead, Lewis found "immence ranges of high mountains to the west of us with their tops partially covered with snow." A hard slog awaited. Mike O'Brien stood in the same spot 207 years later, peering into the Lemhi Range, the Lost River Range, and the jumble of mountains beyond in central Idaho. He understood Lewis's predicament: "He looked to the west, saw range upon range of mountains, and his heart sank; his trip to the Pacific would not be easy."

Lewis and O'Brien could have commiserated had they both reached this point on the same day. Lewis, too, was an inveterate walker, having hiked nearly the entire trip to this spot while Corps members strained to move boats up the Missouri. Like Lewis and Clark, O'Brien by now was well aware of Idaho's challenges. But O'Brien and those early explorers also recognized its sheer beauty. A month beyond Lemhi Pass, having trudged through Idaho's "immence mountains,"

a famished William Clark recorded the Corps of Discovery's progress. Lewis and Clark are this nation's epitome of outdoor adventurers,
but Idaho presented severe adversity even for them. Clark reported
being as "wet and cold in every part as I ever was in my life." Yet as
the Corps staggered through "terrible mountains," Clark also recorded
his pleasure traveling "through a butifull Countrey." When you are
malnourished, exhausted, and your fate is uncertain, it takes a special
landscape to induce a journalist to pause and admire. Clark took that
time, and Mike O'Brien could identify with his impulse. A few days
removed from Lemhi Pass himself, he recorded how "I could hardly
keep my camera in my pocket, there were so many beautiful scenes."[10]

Having crossed Lemhi Pass, O'Brien made his way north on Idaho's
longest border—its boundary with Montana. He would next confront
its shortest, the international border at the 49th parallel. His journal
entries mirror those of people who passed that way before.

In 1860, topographer Henry Custer found the going so rugged
that he conducted his "survey" of the 49th parallel by speculating its
location from a mountaintop observation point. Thirteen years later,
surveyor Rollin Reeves and his party nearly starved near this point in
their effort to mark the Idaho-Washington line. Suffering from "cold
and exhaustions," unable to slash their way through to the international boundary, they turned back short of their goal.[11]

Mike O'Brien recorded of that same country in late August 2012:
"There are big rocks, as big as cars....I feel like an ant on a pile of sugar
cubes, and I am climbing very slowly and carefully since some of the
rocks are still icy." The next day he noted, "where this trail follows the
shore of Upper Priest Lake I found nearly continuous down trees, so
bad it took me two hours to go one-half mile."

Having paralleled Idaho's 44-mile boundary with Canada, O'Brien
was ready to head south, tracing Idaho's boundary with Washington.
He resupplied in Ione, Washington—mile point 2,141—a place with
"3 motels...a medium size grocery, a pizza parlor, and a couple of
bar/grills." As he had all along his journey, O'Brien would crisscross
the boundary in search of the most accessible route. In times before

surveys, there were no artificial boundaries. Native Americans paid no attention to the confines whites subsequently marked on maps. Since time immemorial, they had traveled across those later-imposed borders in search of food and shelter.

As O'Brien left Ione, he walked on the ancestral lands of the Coeur d'Alenes, which had once stretched from the Palouse grasslands of eastern Washington to the Bitterroot Mountains of Montana, from the Clearwater River of north-central Idaho to the northern reaches of the Idaho panhandle. O'Brien would traverse that homeland for the remainder of his odyssey. Yet, in 2012, he barely touched tribal holdings, just skirting the eastern edge of their reservation. Even when he traveled within the confines of the reservation, most of the property he walked past belonged to whites. How did this happen? In the long history of American dispossession of tribal lands, the story of the Coeur d'Alenes is particularly convoluted.

As seen on a highway map, the land set aside as the Coeur d'Alene Reservation is roughly triangular, bounded mostly by straight lines. Indeed, its western border is just as straight and inattentive to geographical features as the boundary between Idaho and Washington—because it is the same line. When William Wallace won the Idaho Territorial boundary dispute over John Mullan in 1863, he not only set the demarcation between two future states, but also unknowingly provided the "logic" for a future reservation border.

As O'Brien proceeded south, he walked for miles on ground that President Ulysses Grant had initially set aside for the tribe in 1873. Unsurprisingly, the Coeur d'Alene Reservation had shrunk since then. At one point, as O'Brien edged along the eastern fringe of the reservation, he came upon a maze of logging roads. He had hit upon the reason for the reservation's downsizing in the 19th century—increasing white incursion onto lands originally reserved for the Coeur d'Alenes.

At the time Grant established the reservation, few whites cared about the remote property set aside for the Coeur d'Alenes. But soon miners, farmers, and loggers trespassed onto the reserve, crisscrossing it with roads and trails. By the time O'Brien trekked through, non-native residents far outnumbered Indian inhabitants on the "reserved" lands, and the Coeur d'Alenes controlled only a fraction of the land within their own reservation boundaries.[12]

This story actually begins before Grant's 1873 executive order. The United States imposed its first reservation upon the Coeur d'Alenes without even consulting them. Territorial Governor David Ballard proposed a reservation for the tribe within the confines of Idaho Territory, its western border resting along "the boundary line of Washington and Idaho Territories." At Ballard's request, President Andrew Johnson in 1867 issued an executive order creating the initial Coeur d'Alene Reservation. Not only did no one consult the Coeur d'Alenes about the layout, no one even informed them that they had been granted a reserve. Yet in all the future iterations of the reservation, that western borderline would hold—the artificial straight line Congress had imposed between Idaho and Washington in 1863 when establishing Idaho Territory.[13]

In 1873, government commissioners finally met with the Coeur d'Alenes and learned, unsurprisingly, that the tribe claimed a much larger territory than Ballard had suggested. The commission prepared new reservation boundaries, more than doubling the original concept, and Grant agreed to that configuration in his executive order that year. It proved an easy concession, since whites had not yet discovered much of appeal within the reserve's confines. That soon changed.

The discovery of gold along the Coeur d'Alene River ushered a "widespread assault on the [reservation] boundaries," as miners and entrepreneurs flooded the northern reaches of the reserve. At the same time, farmers increasingly coveted the rich agricultural lands in the southern part. In the opinion of these white intruders, earmarking such profitable land for a few hundred Indians made no sense. It was time to shrink the newly minted reservation.[14]

In 1889, Congress set new reservation boundaries, seizing the northern two-thirds of Lake Coeur d'Alene and opening 289 square miles of land to white settlement. That action set the reservation boundaries as seen on modern highway maps. The reservation encompasses the lower third of Lake Coeur d'Alene along with several small towns. It is still a large and beautiful piece of property. But the Coeur d'Alene Tribe controls only a small portion of it.

In 1887, Congress passed the Dawes Act, aimed at assimilating Indians by turning them into farmers, providing heads of households with "allotments" of land. The government would sell the remaining "surplus" Indian reservation land to non-native United States citizens.

Nationwide, the government stripped more than 90 million acres from Native Americans.

In 1906, Congress authorized the secretary of the interior to allot small parcels of land to Coeur d'Alene tribal members. In 1910, more than 100,000 non-Indians registered in a lottery to acquire the remaining reservation property. This "opening" of the reservation created a strange checkerboard pattern of land ownership, with tribal members controlling only about one-fourth of the reservation. It created an Indian reservation whose majority population is non-native. For anyone traveling through the reservation today—like Mike O'Brien—it is difficult to know if one is on tribal or non-tribal land.

But this disheartening story of governmental chicanery has a happier ending than most tales of Indian-white relations. In 2001, the Supreme Court confirmed that the United States still held in trust for the tribe the lower third of Lake Coeur d'Alene, even though whites had acquired most of the land adjoining the lake. This gave the tribe administrative control over part of one of the world's most beautiful lakes. For more than a century, tons of mine wastes had been dumped into streams that feed the lake. As a result of the Supreme Court ruling, the tribe now has jurisdiction over those sacred waters and has begun to clean up the mine waste, working with federal and state agencies in ongoing monitoring efforts. At the same time, with the success of its casino and hotel, the Coeur d'Alene Tribe has vigorously purchased lands within the reservation. In the 21st century, the amount of land under tribal control has grown.

Mike O'Brien's route took him south from the reservation into the sinuous, rolling hills of the Palouse Country. In 1873—the same year President Grant established the Coeur d'Alene Reservation—Rollin Reeves had zipped through this undulating prairie, planting his boundary survey markers with ease in the deep topsoil, before reaching those nearly impenetrable forests farther north. The Palouse—once Coeur d'Alene ancestral lands and now the nation's greatest wheat producer—proved equally unchallenging to O'Brien. By now a trail-hardened hiker, O'Brien enjoyed some of his easiest walking on the final days of his trips.

In mid-September, O'Brien reached his final destination—and original starting point—at the confluence of the Snake and Clearwater Rivers. He had spent 120 days and walked 2,496 miles in 2012;

115 days and 2,568 miles in 2014. "It's a long walk," he summarized.

Mike O'Brien became the first person to circumnavigate Idaho's peculiar borders. It was not only a "long walk," but a difficult one. Congress did Idahoans no favors, packaging a land of breathtaking diversity and stunning beauty into a state with the nation's most convoluted boundary. But Idahoans adapted and persevered. In the process, a distinct Idaho character emerged. For while it is true that Idaho is a "geographic monstrosity" with "the most counterintuitive boundaries in the country," it is also true that Idaho would not be Idaho without its curious borders—and the challenges they created.[15]

ACKNOWLEDGMENTS

In 2007, Janet Gallimore, executive director of the Idaho State Historical Society, and the Society's Board of Trustees, appointed me Idaho State Historian. How do you say thank you for that? What an honor and privilege.

As I met with people around the state in that position, I found myself asked one question repeatedly: How did Idaho get its unusual shape? I had heard the stories about drunken surveyors, and about Idaho being the part of the West left over after all the neighboring states had taken the land they wanted. I figured there must be more to the story.

I started taking a few notes, but never had time to pursue the topic in depth. As I prepared to retire in 2015, my wife Mary Reed gently suggested that if I was going to be hanging around the house full time, I should have something to do. So, the Idaho borders project found new life.

The Idaho Humanities Council awarded me a fellowship to research the topic. The IHC board and staff do invaluable work providing access to the humanities for all Idahoans. I am indebted to the council for its support of this and many other projects over many years.

I have traveled the paths of Idaho history for nearly half a century. During much of that time, I was affiliated in one way or another with the Idaho State Historical Society. My colleagues always proved helpful and supportive. I would particularly like to thank the talented people over those many years at the Idaho State Archives. You cannot dig very far into Idaho historical research without the assistance of ISA professionals, who provide access to vast troves of Idaho historical treasure. For this project, I would especially like to thank former ISA archivist Danielle Grundel. Equally significant for Idaho historians, particularly for those interested in north Idaho history, are the outstanding resources at the University of Idaho Library's Special Collections and Archives. My thanks to former head of Special Collections Erin Passehl-Stoddart, and most particularly to archivist Amy Thompson, who graciously fielded and answered my many queries. Thanks also to Evan Herbison at Washington State University Libraries. I came to the writing phase of this project during the time of COVID-19, with libraries and archives mostly closed. Evan proved ever willing to retrieve books from the stacks and have them waiting for me at the door.

I have worked with Melissa Rockwood of R*design* in Moscow on many projects. She is always innovative, hardworking, and fun. Thanks to her for taking my quaint scribbles and turning them into informative maps. Carole Simon-Smolinski graciously shared her deep knowledge of the Lewiston-Clarkston Valley and Adams family history. Mike O'Brien patiently answered all my questions about walking around Idaho and provided me with access to his journals. He proved inspirational; I have found myself upping my daily walking mileage. Still, I don't see a hike around Idaho's borders in my future.

Linda Bathgate, assistant director and editor-in-chief at Washington State University Press, shepherded this project through the Press's review process and into publication. I thank her for her enthusiasm, patience, and encouragement. It is a better book because of her. I have had the privilege of working with the press on other books in the past and have always enjoyed the experience. I would also like to recognize the support of current WSU Press staff members Caryn Lawton, Kerry Darnall, and Ed Sala. Former staffers Robert Clark and Beth DeWeese provided encouragement in the early stages as I contemplated a book about Idaho's boundaries Beth also edited the manuscript, demonstrating the equal parts of good humor and firm resolve that are hallmarks of all talented editors.

It has proven immensely beneficial to my professional career to be married to a gifted historian. Mary Reed, a native Idahoan, is a part of every book I write. Over our many years together, we have traveled to every corner of Idaho. Her curiosity has inspired many delves into Idaho's past. A colleague, sounding board, thought provoker, editor, and inspirational encourager, I can't imagine undertaking a project without her advice and support. Thank you. Again.

ENDNOTES

PROLOGUE

1. Norman Maclean, "USFS 1919: The Ranger, the Cook, and a Hole in the Sky," in *A River Runs Through it and Other Stories* (Chicago: University of Chicago Press, 2001), 125, 131.

2. Moscow *Daily Star-Mirror*, December 22, 1922.

3. For the first quote, Moscow *Daily Star-Mirror*, December 19, 1922. The "milk train" quote is a reminiscence by former student Martha Rigby about her 1945 Student Special trip, in Joann Jones, "Do You Remember a Train Called the Student Special?", *Latah Legacy: The Annual Journal of the Latah County Historical Society* 36:1 (2008), 4.

4. For the first quote, Benjamin E. Thomas, "Boundaries and Internal Problems of Idaho," *Geographical Review* 39:1 (January 1949), 109; for the second, Moscow *Daily Star-Mirror*, July 31, 1923; for the third, Jones, "Remember the Student Special," 10.

CHAPTER 1

1. For good summaries of the role of Jefferson, see Andro Linklater, *The Fabric of America: How Our Borders and Boundaries Shaped the Country and Forged Our National Identity* (New York: Walker & Company, 2007), esp. 44–52; and Derek R. Everett, *Creating the American West: Boundaries and Borderlands* (Norman: University of Oklahoma Press, 2014), esp. 30–57.

2. The 1786 congressional report is quoted in William D. Pattison, *Beginnings of the American Rectangular Land Survey System, 1784–1800*, University of Chicago Department of Geography Research Paper No. 50, 1957, 32.

3. Herman J. Deutsch, "The Evolution of the International Boundary in the Inland Empire of the Pacific Northwest," *Pacific Northwest Quarterly* 51:2 (April 1960), 64.

4. Quote in Everett, *Creating the American West*, 10–11.

5. August Heckscher, *The Politics of Woodrow Wilson: Selections from His Speeches and Writings* (New York: Harper & Brothers, 1956), 38.

6. Vardis Fisher, *The Idaho Encyclopedia* (Caldwell, ID: Caxton Printers, 1938), 15; Michael J. Trinklein, *Lost States: True Stories of Texlahoma, Transylvania, and Other States that Never Made It* (Philadelphia: Quirk Books, 2010), 63; Laura Woodworth-Ney and Tara Rowe, "Defying Boundaries: Women in Idaho History," in Adam M. Sowards, ed., *Idaho's Place: A New History of the Gem State* (Seattle: University of Washington Press, 2014), 148; Carlos Arnaldo Schwantes, *So Incredibly Idaho: Seven Landscapes that Define the Gem State* (Moscow: University of Idaho Press, 1996), 47; Merle Wells, "Idaho's Centennial: How Idaho was Created in 1863," *Idaho Yesterdays* 7:1 (Spring 1963), 46.

CHAPTER 2

1. For a description of Washington in 1819 see Adam Hodgson, *Letters from North America Written During a Tour in the United States and Canada* (London: Hurst, Robinson & Co., 1824), Vol. I, 10. For details on the meeting and the house, Allan Nevins, ed., *The Diary of John Quincy Adams, 1794–1845* (New York: Longmans, Green and Co., 1928), 211–12; Paul C. Nagel, *John Quincy Adams: A Public Life, a Private Life* (New York: Alfred A. Knopf, 1997), 242; and Fred Kaplan, *John Quincy Adams: American Visionary* (New York: Harper, 2014), 341–42.

2. The quote is in Hudson Parsons, *John Quincy Adams* (Madison, WI: Madison House, 1998), 144.

3. For the quotes, respectively, *Alexandria Gazette & Daily Advertiser*, February 24, 1819; Marie B. Hecht, *John Quincy Adams: A Personal History of an Independent Man* (New York: The Macmillan Co., 1972), 299; and Samuel Flagg Bemis, *John Quincy Adams and the Foundations of American Foreign Policy* (New York: Alfred A. Knopf, 1949), 340.

4. Warren L. Cook, *Flood Tide of Empire: Spain and the Pacific Northwest, 1543–1819* (New Haven: Yale University Press, 1973) is the best source for Spain in the Northwest. See pp. 460–83 for efforts to pursue Lewis and Clark.

5. For Onís see "Luis de Onís to Thomas Jefferson, 17 Oct. 1809," National Archives, Founders Online, founders.archives.gov/documents/Jefferson/03-01-02-0475. Also Nancy Bergeson, "History of the Forty-Second Parallel as a Political Boundary between Utah and Idaho," MA Thesis, Utah State University, 1983, 2–3; and Philip Coolidge Brooks, *Diplomacy and the Borderlands: The Adams-Onís Treaty of 1819* (Berkeley: University of California Publications in History, 1939), 13–14, 88–89.

6. Parsons, *Adams*, 133.

7. Nagel, *Adams*, 244; Kaplan, *Adams*, 311.

8. Hecht, *Adams*, 223; Parsons, *Adams*, 134–35; Kaplan, *Adams*, 326.

9. For the quote, Cook, *Flood Tide*, 515.

10. For the quote, Andro Linklater, *The Fabric of America: How Our Borders and Boundaries Shaped the Country and Forged Our National Identity* (New York: Walker & Company, 2007), 185.

11. *The Debates and Proceedings in the Congress of the United States*, 15th Cong., 2nd Sess, 1908. For Adams's surprise proposal, pp. 1903–04. Onís first became aware of Adams's aspirations for a border to the Pacific in July 1818. But Adams seemed to raise it only as a hypothetical at that time. His hypothetical turned into a demand in October. See Bemis, *Adams*, 318–19.

12. Cook, *Flood Tide*, 518–20.

13. For the quote, Hecht, *Adams*, 297.

14. For the quote, Brooks, *Diplomacy and Borderlands*, 157.

15. For the quote, Cook, *Flood Tide*, 521.

16. Final ratification of the Adams-Onís Treaty occurred in 1821 and remained in effect for only half a year, when Mexico gained its independence. Later, the United States and Mexico signed agreements that recognized the line defined by the Adams-Onís Treaty as the border between the two countries. For the quote, Brooks, *Diplomacy and Borderlands*, 170.

17. Frank Freidel and Hugh Sidey, "John Quincy Adams," in *The Presidents of the United States of America* (Washington: White House Historical Association, 2006), at whitehouse.gov/about-the-white-house/presidents/john-quincy-adams.

18. For the Adams family in Clarkston and Lewiston, Carole Simon-Smolinski, *Just Add Water: From Barren Jawbone Flat to Bountiful Clarkston, Washington, 1890–1940* (Lewiston, ID: Northwest Historical Consultants, 2019), esp. i–iii, 1–10.

Border Story: Franklin

1. Walter W. Ristow, "John Melish and His Map of the United States," *Library of Congress Quarterly Journal of Current Acquisitions* 19:4 (September 1962), 159–78. For the Melish quote, Carl I. Wheat, *Mapping the Transmississippi West, 1540–1861* (San Francisco: The Institute of Historical Cartography, 1958), Vol. II, 62.

2. Nancy Bergeson, "History of the Forty-Second Parallel as a Political Boundary between Utah and Idaho," MA Thesis, Utah State University, 1983, 36–7.

3. Glen M. Leonard, "The Mormon Boundary Question in the 1849–50 Statehood Debates," *Journal of Mormon History* 18:1 (Spring 1992), 114–36. Fremont's map deserved a better reception in Congress. Carl Wheat, the outstanding scholar of 19th-century maps of the West, declared Fremont's map "a highly creditable production" and found Fremont "a careful cartographer [who] allowed no imaginary geography to encumber his excellent maps." Still, much of the West remained unexplored, so the decision of Congress to adhere to the long-established 42nd parallel was reasonable. Wheat, *Mapping Transmississippi West*, Vol. II, 181–82.

4. Joel Edward Ricks, *The Beginnings of Settlement in Cache Valley*, Utah State Agricultural College, Faculty Research Lecture No. 12, 1953, at digitalcommons.usu.edu.

5. Bergeson, "History of the Forty-Second Parallel," 82–3; A. J. Simmonds, "Southeast Idaho as a Pioneer Mormon Safety Valve," *Idaho Yesterdays* 23:4 (Winter 1980), 29–30.

6. Bergeson, "History of the Forty-Second Parallel," 85–6.

7. *Ibid.*, 86. "Council Memorial No. 10," January 5, 1867, Idaho Territorial Council and House Bills, AR 1, Box 1, Idaho State Archives, Idaho State Historical Society.

8. Bergeson, "History of the Forty-Second Parallel," 87.

9. *Ibid.*, 89; Simmonds, "Southeast Idaho as Mormon Safety Valve," 30.

10. "Treaty of Amity, Settlement, and Limits Between the United States of America and His Catholic Majesty, 1819," Avalon.law.yale.edu/19th_century/sp1819.asp.

11. For the "capacity and faithfulness" quote and the best biographical account of Major, see Paul S. Pace, "Brothers: Daniel and John Major in the Trans-Mississippi West," *The Nevada Traverse: Journal of the Professional Land Surveyors of Nevada* 45:3 (September 2018), p. 5*ff* (quote 25), and 45:4 (December 2018), p. 5*ff*. Also see "Daniel George

Major" in Jerry Olson, *Short Biographies of All of the Surveyors Associated with the General Land Office in Washington, 1851–1910*, at olsoneng.com/sites/default/files/surveying-history/files/glosurveyorspublishmr.pdf. The sunken post quote is in Clyde A. Bridger, "The State Boundaries of Idaho," Typescript, 1936, p. 8, MG 5188, University of Idaho Library Special Collections. Reference to the glazed earthen bottle is on a historical marker at the site. Also see Franklin K. Van Zandt, *Boundaries of the United States and the Several States*, Geological Survey Professional Paper 909 (Washington: Government Printing Office, 1976), 159–60; and Bergeson, "History of the Forty-Second Parallel," 92.

12. For the first quote, "City of Rocks and Granite Pass," *Idaho State Historical Society Reference Series No. 126*, 1993; for the second, Pace, "Brothers," Part II, 38. For the threatened lawsuit, *Los Angeles Times*, May 19, 1985.

13. The same topographers concluded that Franklin "would also move perilously close to the Utah border" should the line be re-surveyed but surmised it "would likely still remain" in Idaho. *Deseret News*, July 26, 1998. Also gatheringgardiners.blogspot.com/2014/04/strevell-idaho.

14. "The Grave of Hugh Moon," Oneida.idgenweb.org/cemeteries/thegraveofhughmoon. There are various reasons given for why Moon wanted to be buried in Utah. One claims he actually despised Brigham Young and wanted burial in Utah to spite him. Buried on that hillside near Moon is Jane Copeland Howell who died in 1869 and also apparently desired a Utah burial—but missed the mark. Utahspresenthistory.blogspot.com/2011/04/burial-spot-of-brigham-youngs-bodyguard.

15. Simmonds, "Southeast Idaho as Mormon Safety Valve," 30. Quote in Bergeson, "History of Forty-Second Parallel," 95.

16. *Annual Report of the Commissioner of the General Land Office* (Washington: General Land Office, 1872), 18; Bergeson, "History of the Forty-Second Parallel," 92.

CHAPTER 3

1. For Rush and Lewis, see E.G. Chuinard, *Only One Man Died: The Medical Aspects of the Lewis and Clark Expedition* (Glendale, CA: The Arthur H. Clark Company, 1980), 121–55; and David J. Peck, *Or Perish in the Attempt: Wilderness Medicine in the Lewis & Clark Expedition* (Helena: Farcountry Press, 2012), 38–51.

2. Richard Rush, *Memoranda of a Residence at the Court of London* (Philadelphia: Carey, Lea & Blanchard, 1833). For details on the trip across the Atlantic, 21–27; quote on 32.

3. *Ibid.*, 47, 298.

4. *Ibid.*, 335–37.

5. *Ibid.*, 345–47.

6. *Ibid.*, 372.

7. The Russo-American treaty negotiations were completed in April 1824 and ratified in January 1825. Adams, while not directly involved in the negotiations, oversaw and approved them. He had previously served as America's Minister to Russia and had long sought to clear Russian claims to the Oregon Country.

8. For the quote, Rush, *Memoranda of a Residence*, 377. The two countries had agreed to ten years of joint occupation when they signed the original treaty in 1818. In 1827, they renewed the treaty with the provision that either country could withdraw with a one-year notification.

9. For the quote, Robert C. Carriker, *Father Peter John DeSmet: Jesuit in the West* (Norman: University of Oklahoma Press, 1995), 44. For the 1841 emigration see Doyce Nunis, *The Bidwell-Bartleson Party: 1841 California Emigrant Adventure* (Santa Cruz, CA: Western Tanager Press, 1991), and John Bidwell, *A Journey to California, 1841: The First Emigrant Party to California by Wagon Train* (Berkeley: Friends of the Bancroft Library, 1964). While on the St. Joe River, the mission was known as St. Joseph.

10. For the quote, Michael Golay, *The Tide of Empire: America's March to the Pacific* (Hoboken, NJ: John Wiley & Sons, 2003), 286. For a synopsis of the treaty, "Webster-Asburton Treaty, 1842," history.state.gov/milestones/1830-1860/webster-treaty.

11. For the quote, Sam W. Haynes, *James K. Polk and the Expansionist Impulse* (New York: Pearson Longman, 2006), 19.

12. Polk, after winning the election, would reward Bancroft by naming him Secretary of the Navy, and Bancroft would establish the U.S. Naval Academy at Annapolis.

13. For the Clay quote, Walter R. Borneman, *Polk: The Man Who Transformed the Presidency and America* (New York: Random House, 2009), 108.

14. "The American Presidency Project: 1844 Democratic Party Platform," presidency. ucsb.edu/documents/1844-democratic-party-platform. For Clay quote, Robert W. Merry, *A Country of Vast Designs: James K. Polk, the Mexican War, and the Conquest of the American Frontier* (New York: Simon & Schuster, 2009), 63. "Inaugural Address of James Knox Polk," avalon.law.yale.edu/19th_century/polk.asp.

15. E. A. Miles, "'Fifty-Four Forty or Fight'—An American Political Legend," *Mississippi Valley Historical Review* 44:2 (September 1957), 291–301.

16. Polk, a lifetime slave owner, bought and sold enslaved people throughout his presidency. Though he called slavery "a common evil," he made no effort to ban it. John Seigenthaler, *James K. Polk* (New York: Henry Holt and Company, 2003), 85–87.

17. Merry, *Country of Vast Designs*, 170–75; quote 174.

18. *The Diary of James K. Polk During His Presidency, 1845–1849* (Chicago: A. C. McClurg & Co., 1910), August 26, 1845, 4.

19. For the first two quotes, *Diary of Polk*, 2–4. For the latter two quotes, Borneman, *Polk*, 219.

20. For the annual address, "James K. Polk Presidency, December 2, 1845: First Annual Message," millercenter.org/the-presidency/presidential-speeches/December-2-1845-first-annual-message. For Adams quote, Thomas M. Leonard, *James K. Polk: A Clear and Unquestionable Destiny* (Wilmington, DE: Scholarly Resources, Inc., 2001), 111.

21. The first quote is from Senator William Archer of Virginia; the second from Senator Edward Hannegan of Indiana. Merry, *Country of Vast Designs*, 209, 213.

22. *Diary of Polk*, June 3, 1846, 445.

23. "Treaty with Great Britain with Regards to Limits Westward of the Rocky Mountains," avalon.law.yale.edu/19th_century/br-1846.asp. For background on the final weeks of negotiations, see Merry, *Country of Vast Designs*, 263–67.

Border Story: War

1. For the first quote, R. Ignatius Burns, "A Jesuit at the Hell Gate Treaty of 1855," *Mid-Century: An Historical Quarterly* 34 (1952), archive.org.stream/midamericahistor34unse. For Stevens, see Kent D. Richards, *Isaac I. Stevens: Young Man in a Hurry* (Pullman: Washington State University Press, 1993).

2. Burns, "Jesuit at Hell Gate."

3. The consequences of the band being separated in different countries is explored in Karen Ashton Young, "Kootenai Sustenance Rights: In Fact and In Law," MA Thesis, University of Idaho, 1994.

4. For the quote, Cynthia J. Manning, "An Ethnohistory of the Kootenai Indians," MA Thesis, University of Montana, 1984, 60. For a very approachable biography of David Thompson, see Jack Nisbet, *Sources of the River: Tracking David Thompson across Western North America* (Seattle: Sasquatch Books, 1994).

5. For the first quote, Ian Chambers, "The Kootenai War of '74," *American Indian Quarterly* 42:1 (Winter 2018), 46. For the second, "Treaty of Hellgate 164 Years Old Today," *Char-Koosta News* (Flathead Reservation), July 18, 2019, charkoosta.com/news/blast-from-the-past-treaty-of-hellgate-164-years-old-today/article.

6. Certainly Michelle, a reluctant observer to the council, would have disagreed that he spoke for all Kootenai bands. And there is some speculation that his "X" might have been forged. See Chambers, "Kootenai War," 46-7. The quote is from "Treaty with the Flatheads, etc. 1855," fws.gov/pacific/ea/tribal/treaties/flatheads_1855.

7. Kootenai Tribe of Idaho, "History," kootenai.org/history. For Michelle's move to Canada, see Leonard Corwin Brant, *Kootenai Indians of the Columbia Plateau: A Gathering of History, Ethnography, and Sources* (Rathdrum, ID: Northwest Research and Publications, 2013), 94–5.

8. The American survey crew, which worked simultaneously with English teams, started the international survey in 1857, working from west to east, arriving in the Kootenai country in 1860. Unfortunately, most of the records of the boundary survey simply disappeared and were no doubt destroyed. In 1900, cartographer Marcus Baker pieced together the history of the survey as best he could from the documentary evidence he could find. Marcus Baker, *Survey of the Northwestern Boundary of the United States, 1857–1861* (Washington: Government Printing Office, 1900). For the Kootenai ferrying surveyors across the river, see Brant, *Kootenai Indians*, 47, 101. "Journal of the Survey of the 49th Parallel, 1857–1861," George Clinton Gardner Papers, Bancroft Library, University of California Berkeley contains descriptions of the rugged terrain and difficult work.

9. For the first quote, Young, "Kootenai Sustenance Rights," iv. For the second, Chambers, "Kootenai War," 48–9. For international perspectives on treaties see Alexandra Harmon, ed., *The Power of Promise: Rethinking Indian Treaties in the Pacific Northwest* (Seattle: University of Washington Press, 2008).

10. Chambers, "Kootenai War," 47–8.

11. Young, "Kootenai Sustenance Rights," 120–21.

12. *Ibid.*, 49–50; Brant, *Kootenai Indians*, 156–57. In the 1960s, through the efforts of Idaho Senator Frank Church, the federal government provided $425,000 to Bonners Ferry Kootenai as compensation for the cession of 1,160,000 acres in the Hellgate Treaty.

13. Chambers, "Kootenai War," 60.

14. The Resolution is Appendix 6 of "The Kootenai Indian Village," prepared by Charles P. Mathes, Bureau of Indian Affairs, Northern Idaho Agency, 1974, in Norman E. Ross Files, Box 9, Folder "Kootenai Nation," Gerald R. Ford Presidential Library, fordlibrarymuseum.gov/library/document/0009/18544528.

15. For the quote, Chambers, "Kootenai War," 67.

16. This is a very brief summary of the short—but complex—war of 1974. Sonya Rosario's 2008 documentary, "Idaho's Forgotten War" provides a good summary of events, including serious tensions that threatened to break out in violence.

17. restoringthekootenai.org.

18. kootenairiverinn.com/dual-currency-gaming.

CHAPTER 4

1. For the quote in the *Columbian* newspaper, Derek R. Everett, *Creating the American West: Boundaries and Borderlands* (Norman: University of Oklahoma Press, 2014), 128.

2. "Crafting the Oregon Constitution: Framework for a New State," sos.oregon.gov/archives/exhibits/constitution/Pages/during-process.aspx.

3. *Ibid.*

4. Constitutional convention details from Charles Henry Carey, *The Oregon Constitution and Proceedings and Debates of the Constitutional Convention* (Salem: State Printing Department, 1927) and *Journal of the Constitutional Convention of the State of Oregon* (Salem: W. H. Byars, 1882). William J. McConnell was president of the Senate at the time the legislature approved printing 1,000 copies of the latter document. He would later become the State of Idaho's third governor—and father-in-law of longtime U.S. Senator from Idaho, William Borah. For a summary of Oregon border discussions and debates at the constitutional convention see Lewis A. McArthur, "The Oregon State Boundary," *Oregon Historical Quarterly* 37:4 (December 1936), 301–07.

5. For the quote, "Biographical Sketch of Charles Meigs," sos.oregon.gov/archives/exhibits/constitution/Pages/during-about-meigs.

6. Carey, *Oregon Constitution*, 16–17.

7. *Congressional Globe*, 34th Cong., 1st Sess., June 24, 1856, 1454.

8. *Ibid.*

9. *Congressional Globe*, 34th Cong., 3rd Sess., January 31, 1857, 520–21 and February 18, 1857, 821. Carey, *Oregon Constitution*, 25.

10. Herman J. Deutsch, "The Evolution of Territorial and State Boundaries in the Inland Empire of the Pacific Northwest," *Pacific Northwest Quarterly* 51:3 (July 1960), 124.

11. Carey, *Oregon Constitution*, 155.

12. *Ibid.*, 157–58.

13. *Ibid.*, 157–72, 363.

14. *Ibid.*, 149–52.

15. For the quotes, *Ibid.*, 161, 363; Everett, *Creating the American West*, 137.

16. Everett, *Creating the American West*, 11.

Border Story: Greater Idaho

1. Charles Henry Carey, *The Oregon Constitution and Proceedings and Debates of the Constitutional Convention of 1857* (Salem: State Publishing Department, 1927), 151.

2. For the quote, Carey, *Oregon Constitution*, 15. For background on the movement for a new territory, Charles Henry Carey, "The Creation of Oregon as a State," *Quarterly Journal of the Oregon Historical Society* 26:4 (December 1925), 290-94.

3. For a summary of Oregon's exclusion laws, see Greg Nokes, "Black Exclusion Laws in Oregon," *The Oregon Encyclopedia*, oregonencyclopedia.org/articles/exclusion_laws. For a more in-depth analysis of race issues in Oregon, see the special issue devoted to "White Supremacy and Resistance," *Oregon Historical Quarterly* 120:4 (Winter 2019).

4. Carey, "Creation of Oregon," 294.

5. Marple, originally from Virginia, might not have been the best person to make the case for Jackson. He was a man "much disliked" by his fellow convention delegates. "Biographical Sketch of Perry B. Marple," sos.oregon.gov/archives/exhibits/constitution/Pages/during-about-marple.

6. "The State of Jefferson Secession Movement of 1941," web.archive.org/web/20070921220849/http://sisnet.ssku.k12.ca.us/~msusdftp/jones/ian/historypg1.html.

7. For State of Jefferson Declaration of Independence and more on the 21st-century secession movement, soj51.org. For an analysis of the frustrations fueling the separatist movement, Tay Wiles, "A Separatist State of Mind: In the Era of Trump, Rural Discontent Settles in the State of Jefferson," *High Country News*, January 22, 2018, hcn.org/issues/50.1/communities-rural-discontent-finds-a-home-in-the-state-of-jefferson.

8. The Greater Idaho concept came on the heels of a 2015 movement led by Oregon farmer Ken Parsons, who called for both eastern Oregon and Washington to join Idaho, dividing Oregon and Washington along the crest of the Cascades, as Meigs had originally proposed for Oregon. It was one in a long line of movements by disgruntled Northwest residents to separate rural parts of states from urban. Simultaneously with Parsons, Washington State Republican Representative Matt Shea and others promoted an independent State of Liberty for eastern Washington. Liberty, "founded in truth" even adopted a State Gun—the AR15. Liberty proponents left little doubt their movement sprang from cultural wars and did little to hide racial overtones. Eastern Washingtonians, they claimed,

"deserve a government that is more protective of individual rights and that better reflects their values, traditions, culture and heritage." Unlike the Liberty advocates, Parsons anticipated the virtual impossibility of establishing a new state and proposed instead a merger with Idaho, a tactic that directly influenced the later Greater Idaho efforts. Quotes from Liberty State website, libertystate.org.

9. "Some Oregonians Want to Leave and Take Part of the State to Idaho with Them," National Public Radio, February 24, 2020, npr.org/2020/02/24/808916891/some-oregonians-want-to-leave-and-take-part-of-the-state-to-idaho-with-them. Also see the Greater Idaho website at greateridaho.org.

10. Greater Idaho website, greateridaho.org.

11. *Ibid.*

12. For 2019 Idaho population demographics, "U.S. Census Bureau Quick Facts," census.gov/quickfacts/ID. Quotes are in "Some Oregonians Want to Leave," and bigcountrynewsconnection.com/Idaho/another-oregon-county-to-begin-collecting-signatures-for-move-oregons-border-for-a-greater-idaho, December 14, 2020.

13. Moscow-Pullman *Daily News*, April 13, 2021; Idaho Falls *Post Register*, April 12, 2021; *Idaho Ed News*, November 21, 2019.

CHAPTER 5

1. John Mullan, *Report on the Construction of a Military Road from Fort Walla Walla to Fort Benton* (Fairfield, WA: Ye Galleon Press, 1998), 36.

2. For the quote, T. C. Elliott, "The Organization and First Pastorate of the First Congregational Church of Walla Walla, Washington," *Washington Historical Quarterly* 6:2 (April 1915), 92. Also see G. Thomas Edwards, "Walla Walla, Gateway to the Pacific Northwest Interior," *Montana: The Magazine of Western History* 40:3 (Summer 1990), 29–43, and Robert A. Bennett, *Walla Walla: Portrait of a Western Town, 1804–1899* (Walla Walla: Pioneer Press Books, 1980).

3. Herman Deutsch came up with the very appropriate drooping paunch analogy, "The Evolution of Territorial and State Boundaries in the Inland Empire of the Pacific Northwest," *Pacific Northwest Quarterly* 51:3 (July 1960), 126.

4. J. Gary Williams and Ronald W. Stark, eds., *The Pierce Chronicle: Personal Reminiscences of E. D. Pierce as Transcribed by Lou A. Larrick* (Moscow: Idaho Research Foundation, 1974), 78–79.

5. *Ibid.*, 81; San Francisco *Bulletin*, February 28, 1861.

6. For the first quote, Merle W. Wells, "Idaho's Centennial: How Idaho was Created in 1863," *Idaho Yesterdays* 7:1 (Spring 1963), 52. For the second, Robert E. Ficken, *Washington Territory* (Pullman: Washington State University Press, 2002), 69.

7. Annie Laurie Bird documented Wallace's life in a multi-part biography that appeared in *Idaho Yesterdays* 1:1 (Spring 1957) through 3:1 (Spring 1959). For Mullan, Keith C. Petersen, *John Mullan: The Tumultuous Life of a Western Road Builder* (Pullman: Washington State University Press, 2014).

8. Rebecca E. Zietlow, *The Forgotten Emancipator: James Mitchell Ashley and the Ideological Origins of Reconstruction* (New York: Cambridge University Press, 2018).

9. "Lincoln's State of the Union Address," December 1, 1862, at infoplease.com/primary-sources/government/presidential-speeches-state-union-address-abraham-lincoln-december-1-1862. For Kellogg's resolution, *Congressional Globe*, part 2, 37th Cong., 3rd Sess., March 3, 1863, 1507.

10. The name Idaho for the proposed new territory had been discussed previously, but for some reason Mullan and Ashley referred to their new territory as Montana.

11. For the quote, "Mr. Lincoln's White House: Notable Visitors, Anson G. Henry," mrlincolnswhitehouse.org.residents-visitors/notable-visitors/notable-visitors-anson-g-henry-1804–1865. For the long ties between Lincoln and Henry, see "Mr. Lincoln & Friends: The Politicians, Anson G. Henry," mrlincolnandfriends.org/the-politicians/anson-henry. For Henry drawing Washington's eastern border, Wells, "Idaho's Centennial," 50. For Henry being in Washington, DC, David H. Leroy, "Lincoln and Idaho: A Rocky Mountain Legacy," *Idaho Yesterdays* 42:2 (Summer 1998), 12–13.

12. The best accounts of the political maneuvering come in Wells, "Idaho's Centennial;" Merle W. Wells, "The Creation of the Territory of Idaho," *Pacific Northwest Quarterly* 40:2 (April 1949), 106–23; Merle W. Wells, "Walla Walla's Vision of a Greater Washington," *Idaho Yesterdays* 10:3 (Fall 1966), 20–31; and Leroy, "Lincoln and Idaho."

13. *Congressional Globe*, 37th Cong., 3rd Sess., February 20, 1863, 1127.

14. Both quotes in John R. Wunder, "Tampering with the Northwest Frontier: The Accidental Design of the Washington/Idaho Boundary," *Pacific Northwest Quarterly* 68:1 (January 1977), 7.

15. *Congressional Globe*, 37th Cong., 3rd Sess., March 3, 1863, 1508–09.

16. *Ibid.*, 1513, 1525, 1530, 1542.

17. For the best analysis of the convoluted evolution of the word Idaho, see Merle W. Wells, "Origins of the Name 'Idaho' and How Idaho Became a Territory in 1863," digitalatlas.cose.isu.edu/geog/explore/essay. For a briefer account, see "How Idaho Got Its Name," *Idaho State Historical Society, Reference Series No. 258.*

18. *Congressional Globe*, 37th Cong., 3rd Sess., March 3, 1863, 1542.

19. Idaho's awkward boundaries and the difficulties of governing a territory/state with such significant geographic challenges has been the subject of work by several historians. The best synopsis is Carlos A. Schwantes, *In Mountain Shadows: A History of Idaho* (Lincoln: University of Nebraska Press, 1991). For the impact of Idaho's diverse geography on the development of various regions in the state, see Keith C. Petersen, *Idaho, the Land & Its People* (Boise: Idaho State Historical Society, 2019).

20. Mullan advocated for a new territory in his *Miners and Travelers' Guide to Oregon, Washington, Idaho, Montana, Wyoming, and Colorado* (Fairfield, WA: Ye Galleon Press, 1991), 68–69.

21. The letters of support for Mullan's appointment, Mullan's letter to Lincoln, and the record of the Senators' visit to the White House are in General Records of the Department

of State, 1763–2002, Record Group 59, Series: Applications and Recommendations for Public Office, National Archives and Records Administration, College Park, Maryland.

22. Sacramento *Daily Union*, April 6, 1863. Mullan completed his road project as a lieutenant and then received promotion to captain. He resigned from the Army in 1863.

23. Quote is from the diary of Preston Wilson Gillett, May 12, 1862, in Grangeville *Idaho County Free Press*, June 30, 1899.

Border Story: Survey

1. Alonzo V. Richards Papers, Microfilm no. 412, State Historical Society of Wisconsin.

2. Kris Runberg Smith and Tom Weitz, *Wild Place: A History of Priest Lake, Idaho* (Pullman: Washington State University Press, 2015), 6–9.

3. "Journal of the Survey of the 49th Parallel, 1857–1861," May 9, 1860, George Clinton Gardner Papers, Bancroft Library, University of California, Berkeley.

4. Amherst Barber to "Dear Friend Headgman," December 11, 1901, Barber Letters, M52/129, Idaho State Archives, Idaho State Historical Society. Also see Otto Klotz, "The History of the Forty-Ninth Parallel West of the Rocky Mountains," *Geographical Review* 3:4 (May 1917), 382–87; and for a Canadian perspective, Katherine Gordon, *Made to Measure: A History of Land Surveying in British Columbia* (Winlaw, BC: Sono Nis Press, 2006), 40–72.

5. Richard Urquhart Goode, *Survey of the Boundary Line between Idaho and Montana from the International Boundary to the Crest of the Bitterroot Mountains* (Washington: Government Printing Office, 1900), 19, 60.

6. *Ibid.*, 19.

7. Carpenter's quote is in "Field Notes of the Survey of the Boundary Line between the States of Idaho and Montana," Vol. 3, Howard Carpenter Papers, MG 429, University of Idaho Library Special Collections. *Towers: A Newsletter for Supporters of the University of Idaho Library* (Winter 2000) has a brief biographical sketch of Carpenter.

8. The quote is in R. B. Marshall, *Retracement of the Boundary Line between Idaho and Washington* (Washington: Government Printing Office, 1911), 11. The description of the survey crew is in Rollin J. Reeves, "Marking the Washington-Idaho Boundary," *Washington Historical Quarterly* 2:4 (July 1908), 286.

9. Marshall, *Boundary between Idaho and Washington*, 11. For the *Colonel Wright*, Randall V. Mills, *Stern-wheelers Up Columbia: A Century of Steamboating in the Oregon Country* (Palo Alto: Pacific Books, 1974), esp. 40–43; and Lulu Donnell Crandel, "The Colonel Wright," *Washington Historical Quarterly* 7:2 (April 1916), 126–32.

10. Marshall, *Boundary between Idaho and Washington*, 11.

11. *Ibid.*, 12. The Snake River formed the border between Washington and Idaho for about 30 miles south of Lewiston. That natural feature required no monuments to mark the line, so after their work in Lewiston, the survey crew moved north of that city.

12. Details on the surveying and quotes in the following pages are from Marshall, *Boundary between Idaho and Washington*, and Reeves, "Marking the Washington-Idaho

Boundary." John J. Peebles, "Retracing a Line: The 1908 Idaho-Washington Boundary Resurvey," *Idaho Yesterdays* 13:3 (Fall 1969), 20–25, provides a summary of the Reeves survey and the later resurvey of the border.

13. Keith C. Petersen, *John Mullan: The Tumultuous Life of a Western Road Builder* (Pullman: Washington State University Press, 2014), 236–37. For the significance of the Mullan Road on settlement patterns, 239–56.

CHAPTER 6

1. James R. Thane, Jr., "An Ohio Abolitionist in the Far West: Sidney Edgerton and the Opening of Montana, 1863–1866," *Pacific Northwest Quarterly* 67:4 (October 1974), 151–62, quote p. 152. Also see Thane, ed., *A Governor's Wife in the Mining Frontier: The Letters of Mary Edgerton from Montana, 1863–1865* (Salt Lake City: University of Utah Library, 1976). House description on p. 47.

2. Margaret Day Allen, *Lewiston Country: An Armchair History* (Lewiston: Nez Perce County Historical Society, 1990), 39.

3. Merle Wells, "Idaho's Centennial: How Idaho was Created in 1863," *Idaho Yesterdays* 7:1 (Spring 1963), 56.

4. Council Memorial Number 1, Territorial Council and House Bills, AR1, Box 1, Idaho State Archives, Idaho State Historical Society. For the role of Rheem in crafting the bill, Thane, "Ohio Abolitionist," 153.

5. Annie Laurie Bird, "Portrait of a Frontier Politician," *Idaho Yesterdays* 3:1 (Spring 1959), 23.

6. Thane, *A Governor's Wife*, 56. For the Bannack fundraising, Thane, "Ohio Abolitionist," 153. For Ashley's efforts to create Montana before Edgerton appeared in Washington, DC, Merle Wells, "The Idaho-Montana Boundary," *Idaho Yesterdays* 12:4 (Winter 1968), 6–9.

7. The quotes are from an 1892 Edgerton letter reflecting back on this time, in James L. Thane, Jr., "Montana Territory: The Formative Years, 1862–1870," PhD. Diss., University of Iowa, 1972, 75.

8. For the Nesmith quote, *Congressional Globe*, 38th Cong., 1st sess., May 19, 1864, 2350. For a broader discussion of the congressional debate over the Montana bill, see Thane, "Montana Territory," 79–80, and Quintard Taylor, *In Search of the Racial Frontier: African Americans in the American West, 1528–1990* (New York: W.W. Norton & Company, 1998), esp. p. 121.

9. *Congressional Globe*, 38th Cong., 1st sess, May 26, 1864, 165.

10. Arch G. Turner to William Wallace, May 19, 1864, William Wallace Correspondence, AR0001, Idaho State Archives, Idaho State Historical Society.

11. *Congressional Globe*, 38th Cong., 1st sess., May 26, 1864, 165.

12. Herman J. Deutsch, "The Evolution of Territorial and State Boundaries in the Inland Empire of the Pacific Northwest," *Pacific Northwest Quarterly* 51:3 (July 1960), 128.

13. "The Idaho-Montana Boundary Legend," *Idaho State Historical Society Reference Series No. 156*, 1966.

14. Thane, "Ohio Abolitionist." W. Turrentine Jackson, "The Appointment and Removal of Sidney Edgerton, First Governor of Montana Territory," *Pacific Northwest Quarterly* 34:3 (July 1943), 293–304. Edgerton's daughter, Martha Edgerton Plassman, wrote about the family's trip to Montana and early Bannack, "Biographical Sketch of Honorable Sidney Edgerton, First Territorial Governor," *Contributions to the Historical Society of Montana*, 3 (1901), 331–40.

15. For the Edgerton quote, Thane, "Montana Territory," 77. For "southern territory," see "National Issues in Idaho During the Civil War," *Idaho State Historical Society Reference Series No. 478*, 1975. For background on the 1863 and 1864 elections, David H. Leroy, "Lincoln and Idaho: A Rocky Mountain Legacy," *Idaho Yesterdays* 42:2 (Summer 1998), 8–25; and Ronald H. Limbaugh, *Rocky Mountain Carpetbaggers: Idaho's Territorial Governors* (Moscow: University Press of Idaho, 1982), esp. 33–36.

16. *Washington Standard*, September 9, 1865. sos.oregon.gov/archives/exhibits/constitution/Pages/during-process.aspx

17. Rebecca E. Zietlow, *The Forgotten Emancipator: James Mitchell Ashley and the Ideological Origins of Reconstruction* (New York: Cambridge University Press, 2018); Robert F. Horowitz, *Great Impeacher: A Political Biography of James M. Ashley* (New York: Brooklyn College Press, 1979).

18. Horowitz, *Great Impeacher*, 158.

19. *Ibid.*, 162; Michael P. Malone, Richard B. Roeder, and William L. Lang, *Montana: A History of Two Centuries* (Seattle: University of Washington Press, 1976), 105–06.

Border Story: Big Hole

1. For the Walla Walla Council, see Kent D. Richards, *Isaac I. Stevens: Young Man in a Hurry* (Pullman: Washington State University Press, 1993), 215–26. For the quote, Alvin M. Josephy Jr., *The Nez Perce Indians and the Opening of the Northwest* (New Haven: Yale University Press, 1965), 316.

2. The entire treaty can be found at "Treaty with the Nez Perces, 1855," critfc.org/member_tribes_overview/nez-perce-tribe/treaty-with-the-nez-perces-1855.

3. For the best analysis of the 1863 treaty, see Elliott West, *The Last Indian War: The Nez Perce Story* (New York: Oxford University Press, 2009), 75–120. For the quote, Josephy, *Nez Perce*, 390.

4. West, *Last Indian War*, 106.

5. *Ibid.*, 98.

6. Jerome A. Greene, *Nez Perce Summer 1877: The U.S. Army and the Nee-me-poo Crisis* (Helena: Montana Historical Society Press, 2000), 13–14. The executive order was flawed from the beginning. The intention had been to grant the Nez Perce an area where few whites had settled. But a mix-up at the Bureau of Indian Affairs instead assigned them land settlers had already occupied. The political fallout began immediately. Josephy, *Nez Perce*, 456–57.

7. Greene, *Nez Perce Summer*, 21.

8. The Nez Perce War is one of the best-documented events in Idaho history. I have relied on the following sources. There is never a better beginning place for any Nez Perce topic than Josephy, *Nez Perce*. His exhaustive detail of the war remains the standard interpretation. Also see Greene, *Nez Perce Summer* and West, *Last Indian War*. For the war's beginning at Tolo Lake and the ensuing White Bird Battle, see John D. McDermott, *Forlorn Hope: The Battle of White Bird Canyon and the Beginning of the Nez Perce War* (Boise: Idaho State Historical Society, 1978). For a Nez Perce perspective, see Lucullus Virgil McWhorter, *Yellow Wolf: His Own Story* (Caldwell, ID: Caxton Press, 1940); McWhorter, *Hear Me, My Chiefs: Nez Perce Legend & History* (Caldwell, ID: Caxton Press, 1952); and Scott M. Thompson, *I Will Tell of My War Story: A Pictorial Account of the Nez Perce War* (Seattle: University of Washington Press, 2000). For valuable first-person accounts, see Linwood Laughy, compiler, *In Pursuit of the Nez Perces: The Nez Perce War of 1877 as Reported by General O. O. Howard, Duncan McDonald, Chief Joseph* (Kooskia, ID: Mountain Meadow Press, 1993).

9. *An Illustrated History of North Idaho Embracing Nez Perces, Idaho, Latah, Kootenai, and Shoshone Counties, State of Idaho* (Spokane: Western Historical Publishing Co., 1903), 1146.

10. For the quote, West, *Last Indian War*, 142.

11. For the quote, *Ibid.*, 175.

12. *Ibid.*, 176.

13. Sherman kept up to date on the Nez Perce War while on his western trip. But he did not rush his sightseeing through Yellowstone. He failed to appreciate how fast a group as large as the Nez Perce party could travel once they left Big Hole, and doubted the Nez Perce would enter Yellowstone. He was wrong, and made his safe exit from the park just days before the Nez Perce entered. One can imagine a change in history's course should the Nez Perce have captured him. Sherman, accompanied by Sheridan, continued making their way west. At Fort Benton they arrived at the eastern terminus of John Mullan's military road. They took that highway 624 miles to Walla Walla, stopping at Missoula in early September, where they heard more details about the nearby Big Hole Battle. Mullan's road had suffered from maintenance neglect in places, but Sherman believed it still retained military significance. General Howard, he believed, "could have reached Missoula before the Nez Perces" had he followed Mullan's road, bringing a much earlier conclusion to the hostilities. Sherman ordered the Army to improve the road. He also recommended the construction of a military post in Idaho on Lake Coeur d'Alene—a place that would one day go by the name Fort Sherman. Keith C. Petersen, *John Mullan: The Tumultuous Life of a Western Road Builder* (Pullman: Washington State University Press, 2014), 249–51.

14. West, *Last Indian War*, 187.

15. *Ibid.*, 193.

16. *Ibid.*, 202. The exact number of Nez Perce killed is unknown. Gibbon placed it at 89; Nez Perce estimates range as high as 100.

17. Josephy, *Nez Perce*, 599.

18. *Ibid.*, 630.

19. Theodore Catton and Ann Hubber, *Commemoration and Preservation: An Administrative History of Big Hole National Battlefield* (Missoula: Historical Research Association, 1999), files.eric.ed.gov/fulltext/ED440038.pdf, quote p. 81. Also see Rowena L. Alcorn and Gordon D. Alcorn, "Josiah Redwolf," *Montana: The Magazine of Western History* 15:4 (Autumn 1965), 54–67.

CHAPTER 7

1. T. A. Larson, *History of Wyoming* (Lincoln: University of Nebraska Press, 1978), 36–68; Lewis L. Gould, *Wyoming: A Political History, 1868–1896* (New Haven: Yale University Press, 1968), 1–14.

2. Charles Griffin Coutant, *The History of Wyoming: From the Earliest Known Discoveries* (Laramie, WY: Chaplin, Spafford & Mathison, 1899), 624. Also I. S. Bartlett, *History of Wyoming* (Chicago: S. J. Clarke Publishing Co., 1918), 164–66.

3. Derek R. Everett, *Creating the American West: Boundaries and Borderlands* (Norman: University of Oklahoma Press, 2014), 196.

4. *Congressional Globe*, 40th Cong., 2nd Sess., June 3, 1868, 2793.

5. *Ibid.*, 4345.

6. *Ibid.*

7. *Ibid.*, 467.

8. *Ibid.*, 2793.

9. Quotes are from Merrill J. Mattes, *Colter's Hell & Jackson's Hole: The Fur Trappers Exploration of the Yellowstone and Grand Teton Park Region* (Yellowstone Library and Museum Association, 1962) at nps.gov/parkhistory/online_books/grte1.

10. Carlos Arnoldo Schwantes, *So Incredibly Idaho! Seven Landscapes that Define the Gem State* (Moscow: University of Idaho Press, 1996), 48.

Border Story: Lawless

1. For Kootenai County, see Richard U. Goode, *Survey of the Boundary Line between Idaho and Montana from the International Boundary to the Crest of the Bitterroot Mountains* (Washington: Government Printing Office, 1900), 48. Kootenai County has been divided since this episode, and the ghost town of Leonia is now in Boundary County. For Moyie, see Katherine G. Morrissey, *Mental Territories: Mapping the Inland Empire* (Ithaca, NY: Cornell University Press, 1997), 120–24.

2. Carlos A. Schwantes, *In Mountain Shadows: A History of Idaho* (Lincoln: University of Nebraska Press, 1991), 123.

3. Merle W. Wells, *Anti-Mormonism in Idaho*, 1872–92 (Provo, UT: Brigham Young University Press, 1978).

4. For a summary of Dubois's political rise, and the quote, see Colin Branham, "The Saints Were Sinners: The Mormon Question and the Survival of Idaho," www.boisestate.edu/presidents-writing-awards/the-saints-were-sinners-the-mormon-question-and-the-survival-of-idaho.

5. So potent was anti-Mormon sentiment in the country that the United States Supreme Court unanimously upheld the legality of the morally dubious Test Oath. For disenfranchisement of Mormons in the Idaho Constitution, Dennis C. Colson, *Idaho's Constitution: The Tie that Binds* (Moscow: University of Idaho Press, 1991), 146–59.

6. Russell R. Rich, *Land of the Sky-Blue Water: A History of the L.D.S. Settlement of the Bear Lake Valley* (Provo, UT: Brigham Young University Press, 1963), 147.

7. Dean L. May, "Between Two Cultures: The Mormon Settlement of Star Valley, Wyoming," *Journal of Mormon History* 13 (1986–87), 135.

8. For the poem, see *The History of the Community and Families of Freedom, Wyoming & Idaho* (2008), 34, home.silverstar.com/bbbbbb/Freedom%20History.pdf. For the concentration of Mormons in the region, see Dan Erickson, "Star Valley, Wyoming: Polygamist Haven," *Journal of Mormon History* 26:1 (Spring 2000), 123–64.

9. D. Brooks Green, "The Settlement of Teton Valley, Idaho-Wyoming," MA Thesis, Brigham Young University, 1974, 114–15; James L. Bradley, "History of the Latter-Day Saint Church in the Teton Valley, 1888–1956," MA Thesis, Brigham Young University, 1956.

10. D. Brooks Green, "The Idaho-Wyoming Boundary: A Problem in Location," *Idaho Yesterdays* 23:1 (Spring 1977), 10–14; Franklin K. Van Zandt, *Boundaries of the United States and the Several States, Geological Professional Paper 909* (Washington: Government Printing Office, 1976), 5–6.

11. Green, "Idaho-Wyoming Boundary," 12.

12. *Ibid.*

13. *Ibid.*

14. *Ibid.*, Van Zandt, *Boundaries of United States*, 157.

15. Journalists periodically report on the unusual governmental arrangements for Alta. For a good summary, see Julia Tellman, "How Does Alta Work?" *Teton Valley News*, April 19, 2018.

16. *Congressional Globe*, 40th Cong., 2nd Sess., June 3, 1858, 2793.

17. Michael J. Trinklein, *Lost States: True Stories of Texlahoma, Transylvania, and Other States that Never Made It* (Philadelphia: Quirk Books, 2010), 67–8; Gary Alden Smith, *State and National Boundaries of the United States* (Jefferson NC: McFarland & Company, 2004), 161.

18. Brian C. Kalt, "The Perfect Crime," *Georgetown Law Journal* 93:2 (2005), 675–88; quote 678.

19. *Ibid.*, 678–79.

20. C. J. Box, *Free Fire* (New York: The Berkeley Publishing Group, 2008), 3.

21. *Ibid.*, 37. Thanks to Idaho Senator Mike Crapo, had McCann committed his crime a couple of years later, he might not have had to worry about the misdemeanor, depending on whether he had concealed his weapons. Crapo convinced his friend—Secretary of Interior Dirk Kempthorne, a fellow Idahoan—to delete the regulation prohibiting con-

cealed weapons in national parks. Gun owners are now subject to "more sensible" rules in national parks, according to Crapo. No more misdemeanors for people like McCann. "Rule Change Keeps Gun Law Consistent," Senator Mike Crapo news release, December 5, 2008.

22. Spokane (WA) *Spokesman-Review*, February 6, 2022.

23. For the first Kalt quote, Madison Dapcovich, "Does the Lawless Yellowstone 'Zone of Death' Exist?" January 27, 2021, snopes.com/fact-check/zone-of-death-yellowstone. For the second, Kalt, "Perfect Crime," 685. For the poaching case, *Casper Star-Tribune*, August 26, 2007; March 12, 2009.

24. Dubois's conversion to the Democrats was more complicated than I outline here. Coming from a silver-producing state, Dubois supported the free silver movement that promoted the unlimited production of silver coinage. He left the mainstream Republican Party and joined the Silver Republican faction in 1896. He refused to rejoin the Republicans, and Democrats in the legislature rewarded that by sending him back to the Senate. He then joined the Democratic Party. For a summary of Dubois's wandering political allegiances, see Merle W. Wells, "Unexpected Allies: Fred T. Dubois and the Mormons in 1916," *Idaho Yesterdays* 35:3 (Fall 1991), 27–33.

CHAPTER 8

1. Congressional Record, 49th Cong., 1st sess., February 23, 1886, 1706.

2. For the best synopsis of congressional activity on the Idaho panhandle annexation issue in the 1880s, see Merle W. Wells, "Politics in the Panhandle: Opposition to the Admission of Washington and North Idaho, 1886–1888," *Pacific Northwest Quarterly* 46:3 (July 1955), 79–89.

3. Merle W. Wells, "Territorial Government in the Inland Empire: The Movement to Create Columbia Territory, 1864–69," *Pacific Northwest Quarterly* 44:2 (April 1953), 83.

4. Leonard J. Arrington, *History of Idaho* (Moscow: University of Idaho Press, 1994), Vol. I, 221.

5. Robert Devine, "Leaving Lewiston: Politics and Geography Conspire to Remove the Capital to Boise in 1864," *Idaho Landscapes* 3:1 (Summer 2010), 30.

6. For the quote, Robert E. Ficken, *Washington Territory* (Pullman: Washington State University Press, 2002), 69. Also see Eugene B. Chafee, "The Political Clash Between North and South Idaho Over the Capital," *Pacific Northwest Quarterly* 29:3 (July 1938), 255–67, and Merle W. Wells, "Walla Walla's Vision of a Greater Washington," *Idaho Yesterdays* 10:3 (Fall 1966), 20–31.

7. Herman J. Deutsch, "The Evolution of Territorial and State Boundaries in the Inland Empire of the Pacific Northwest," *Pacific Northwest Quarterly* 51:3 (July 1960), 129.

8. The first quote is in Council Memorial No. 5, January 1866, Territorial and House Bills, AR1, Box 1, Idaho State Archives, Idaho State Historical Society. For Meagher, see Wells, "Territorial Government," 85.

9. The break between advocating for a new territory and annexation to Washington was not quite as clear cut as I have summarized. At first, many northern Idahoans viewed annexation

as but the first step: Break away from Idaho, join Washington, then establish Columbia. Even when that appeared unlikely, people continued to advocate for a new territory. But after 1866, the main thrust of the "get out of Idaho" movement centered on annexation.

10. Deutsch, "Evolution of Territorial and State Boundaries," 130; Wells, "Walla Walla's Vision," 28; Carlos A. Schwantes, *So Incredibly Idaho: Seven Landscapes that Define the Gem State* (Moscow: University of Idaho Press, 1996), 50.

11. Wells, "Politics in the Panhandle," 79–81.

12. *Ibid.*, 86; *Congressional Record*, 49th Cong., 2nd sess., March 1, 1887, 2469–70; *Congressional Record*, 49th Cong., 2nd sess., March 2, 1887, 2553–54.

13. James W. Hulce, "Idaho Versus Nevada: The 1887 Struggle between Nevada's Senator and Idaho's Governor," *Idaho Yesterdays* 29:3 (Fall 1985), 28.

14. *Ibid.*, 26–31; "Edward Augustus Stevenson," in Robert C. Sims and Hope A. Benedict, eds., *Idaho's Governors: Historical Essays on Their Administrations* (Boise: Boise State University, 1992), 219–20.

15. C. S. Kingston, "The North Idaho Annexation Issue," *Washington Historical Quarterly* 21:4 (October 1930), 284–85.

16. Keith C. Petersen, *This Crested Hill: An Illustrated History of the University of Idaho* (Moscow: University of Idaho Press, 1987), 19. For Dubois's alliance with Edward Stevenson against north Idaho annexation, Hulce, "Idaho Versus Nevada," 29.

17. Petersen, *Crested Hill*, 20–21.

18. Kingston, "North Idaho Annexation," 290–92; Benjamin E. Thomas, "Boundaries and Internal Problems of Idaho," *Geographical Review* 39:1 (January 1949), 100–01; Rafe Gibbs, *Beacon for Mountain and Plain: Story of the University of Idaho* (Moscow: University of Idaho, 1962), 106–07, 122; Petersen, *Crested Hill*, 61–2.

19. "Packer John's Cabin," *Idaho State Historical Society Reference Series No. 292.*

20. Merle W. Wells, "Steamboat Down the Snake: The Early Story of the 'Shoshone,'" *Idaho Yesterdays*, 5:4 (Winter 1961–62), 23.

21. *Ibid.*, Randall V. Mills, *Stern-Wheelers Up Columbia: A Century of Steamboating in the Oregon Country* (Palo Alto, CA: Pacific Books, 1947), 81–4; Fred Lockley, ed., "Reminiscences of Captain William Polk Gray," *Oregon Historical Quarterly* 14:4 (December 1913), 321–54.

22. Dale Fisk, *P&IN to the Golden Heart of Idaho: The Story of the Pacific & Idaho Northern Railway* (Council, ID: Writers Press, 2001); Hal Riegger, *The Camas Prairie: Idaho's Railroad on Stilts* (Edmonds, WA: Pacific Fast Mail, 1986).

23. "U.S. 95 and Idaho's North and South Highway," 8, fhwa.dot.gov/highwayhistory/US95; Thomas, "Boundaries and Internal Problems," 106–07; Kingston, "North Idaho Annexation," 288.

24. Thomas, "Boundaries and Internal Problems," 106–07.

25. Nancy Foster Renk, *Driving Past: Tours of Historical Sites in Bonner County, Idaho* (Sandpoint, ID: Bonner County Historical Society, 2014), 165–69.

26. Margaret Day Allen, *Lewiston Country: An Armchair History* (Lewiston: Nez Perce County Historical Society, 1990), 210–11; "Early Nez Perce County," *Idaho State Historical Society Reference Series No. 334.*

27. Carole Simon-Smolinski, *Just Add Water: From Barren Jawbone Flat to Bountiful Clarkston, Washington* (Lewiston: Northwest Historical Consultants, 2019), 15–25, 37–40, 189.

28. *Ibid.*, 189; "U.S. 95 and Idaho's North and South Highway," 3–4.

29. "White Bird Grade," National Register of Historic Places nomination form, 1974, history.idaho.gov/wp-content/uploads/2018/09/White_Bird_Grade_74000740; "U.S. 95 and Idaho's North and South Highway," 4–6.

30. "U.S. 95 and Idaho's North and South Highway," 8–9.

31. *Ibid.*, 9.

32. *Ibid.*, 14.

33. *Ibid.*, 11–15.

34. *Wallace Press*, January 30, 1892, quoted in John R. Wunder, "Tampering with the Northwest Frontier: The Accidental Design of the Washington/Idaho Boundary," *Pacific Northwest Quarterly* 68:1 (January 1977), 1.

EPILOGUE

1. Unless otherwise noted, quotes in the epilog are from Mike O'Brien and Jim Fulmis, *Idaho Boundary Trail Hiker's Guide* (Boise: Mike O'Brien and Jim Fulmis, 2018); O'Brien, *Idaho Counterclockwise: A Walk Around the State* (Boise: Mike O'Brien, 2013); O'Brien's 2012 trail journal at www.trailjournals.com/journal/entry/371213; O'Brien's 2014 trail journal at www.trailjournals.com/journal/entry/440084; and O'Brien's emails with the author in the summer of 2021. Idaho Public Television produced a short video on O'Brien's hikes at www.facebook.com/outdoor.idaho/videos/circumnavigating-the-state-one-of-the-adventure-idaho-stories-airing-thursday-at/2102456293136982.

2. R. B. Marshall, *Retracement of the Boundary Line between Idaho and Washington* (Washington: Government Printing Office, 1911), 11. Also see Rollin J. Reeves, "Marking the Washington-Idaho Boundary," *Washington Historical Quarterly* 2:4 (July 1908), 285–89.

3. Reeves, "Marking the Boundary," 287.

4. For Hunt's own account of the expedition, see *The Overland Diary of Wilson Price Hunt* (Portland: Oregon Book Society, 1973). The classic—sometimes embellished—account of the journey is Washington Irving's *Astoria, or Anecdotes of an Enterprise Beyond the Rocky Mountains*. Originally published in 1836, it has been reprinted numerous times. Much more readable—and accurate—is Peter Stark's *Astoria: John Jacob Astor and Thomas Jefferson's Lost Pacific Empire* (New York: Ecco Press, 2014). Marie Dorion gave birth to another child in present-day Oregon, who died shortly afterward as she made her way to Fort Astoria. In the winter of 1813–14 she followed her fur-trapping husband back to the Snake River in today's Idaho. Bannock Indians killed Pierre Dorion and other members of the party. Marie and her two sons escaped, making their way over the Blue Mountains

to the mouth of the Columbia in winter, surviving on horse flesh, mice, squirrels, and frozen berries.

5. For Stuart, see Kenneth A. Spaulding, ed., *On the Oregon Trail: Robert Stuart's Journey of Discovery* (Norman: University of Oklahoma Press, 1953). Stuart had not been with Hunt's party the previous year. Astor sent two groups to the mouth of the Columbia— Hunt's overland expedition, and another by boat. Stuart had been with the latter, but returned East overland.

6. U.S. Department of the Interior, Indian Affairs, "Frequently Asked Questions," bia. gov/frequently-asked-questions.

7. For the long and complicated history of the establishment and eventual enlargement of the Duck Valley Reservation, see Whitney McKinney, *A History of the Shoshone-Paiutes of the Duck Valley Reservation* (Sun Valley, ID: The Institute of the American West and Howe Brothers, 1983). For Powell, Donald Worster, *A River Running West: The Life of John Wesley Powell* (New York: Oxford University Press, 2000) and Wallace Stegner, *Beyond the Hundredth Meridian: John Wesley Powell and the Second Opening of the West* (Lincoln: University of Nebraska Press, 1981).

8. George Brimlow, *The Bannock War of 1878* (Caldwell, ID: The Caxton Printers, 1938); John W. Heaton, *The Shoshone-Bannocks: Culture & Commerce at Fort Hall, 1870–1940* (Lawrence: University of Kansas Press, 2005); Shoshone-Paiute Tribes of the Duck Valley Indian Reservation, "Our History," at shopaitribes.org/spculture.

9. Meriwether Lewis quotes in this section are from August 12, 1805, in Gary E. Moulton, ed., *The Journals of the Lewis and Clark Expedition* (Lincoln: University of Nebraska Press, 1988), 5: 73–75.

10. Clark, September 16, 1805; September 20, 1805, *Ibid.*, 5: 209, 219, 222.

11. Kris Runberg Smith and Tom Weitz, *Wild Place: A History of Priest Lake, Idaho* (Pullman: Washington State University Press, 2015), 6–9. Reeves, "Marking the Washington-Idaho Boundary."

12. Laura Woodworth-Ney, *Mapping Identity: The Creation of the Coeur d'Alene Indian Reservation, 1805–1902* (Boulder: University Press of Colorado, 2004) and Woodworth-Ney, "Negotiating Boundaries of Territory and 'Civilization:' The Coeur d'Alene Indian Reservation Agreement Councils," *Pacific Northwest Quarterly* 94:1 (Winter 2002/03), 27–41. Also helpful is Rodney Frey, *Landscape Traveled by Coyote and Crane: The World of Schitsu'umsh (Coeur d'Alene Indians)* (Seattle: University of Washington Press, 2001).

13. Woodworth-Ney, *Mapping Identity*, 82.

14. *Ibid.*, 105.

15. For the first quote, Vardis Fisher, *The Idaho Encyclopedia* (Caldwell, ID: Caxton Printers, 1938), 15; for the second, Laura Woodworth-Ney and Tara Rowe, "Defying Boundaries: Women in Idaho History," in Adam Sowards, ed., *Idaho's Place: A New History of the Gem State* (Seattle: University of Washington Press, 2014), 148.

BIBLIOGRAPHY

The following is a partial bibliography of published sources. For more thorough documentation, readers are referred to the endnotes.

Arrington, Leonard J. *History of Idaho*, 2 vols. (Moscow: University of Idaho Press, 1994).

Baker, Marcus. *Survey of the Northwestern Boundary of the United States, 1857–1861* (Washington: Government Printing Office, 1900).

Bemis, Samuel Flagg. *John Quincy Adams and the Foundations of American Foreign Policy* (New York: Alfred A. Knopf, 1949).

Bergeson, Nancy. "History of the Forty-Second Parallel as a Political Boundary between Utah and Idaho," MA Thesis, Utah State University, 1983.

Bird, Annie Laurie. "Portrait of a Pioneer Politician," multi-part biography of William Wallace in *Idaho Yesterdays* 1:1 (Spring 1957) and 3:1 (Spring 1959).

Borneman, Walter R. *Polk: The Man Who Transformed the Presidency and America* (New York: Random House, 2009).

Brant, Leonard Corwin. *Kootenai Indians of the Columbia Plateau: A Gathering of History, Ethnography, and Sources* (Rathdrum, ID: Northwest Research and Publications, 2013).

Brooks, Philip Coolidge. *Diplomacy and the Borderlands: The Adams-Onís Treaty of 1819* (Berkeley: University of California Publications in History, 1939).

Carey, Charles Henry. *Journal of the Constitutional Convention of the State of Oregon* (Salem: W. H. Byars, 1882).

_____. *The Oregon Constitution and Proceedings and Debates of the Constitutional Convention* (Salem: State Printing Department, 1927).

Chafee, Eugene B. "The Political Clash between North and South Idaho Over the Capital," *Pacific Northwest Quarterly* 29:3 (July 1938).

Chambers, Ian. "The Kootenai War of '74," *American Indian Quarterly* 42:1 (Winter 2018).

Cook, Warren L. *Flood Tide of Empire: Spain and the Pacific Northwest, 1543–1819* (New Haven: Yale University Press, 1973).

Deutsch, Herman J. "The Evolution of the International Boundary in the Inland Empire of the Pacific Northwest," *Pacific Northwest Quarterly* 51:2 (April 1960).

_____. "The Evolution of Territorial and State Boundaries in the Inland Empire of the Pacific Northwest," *Pacific Northwest Quarterly* 51:3 (July 1960).

Devine, Robert. "Leaving Lewiston: Politics and Geography Conspire to Remove the Capital to Boise in 1864," *Idaho Landscapes* 3:1 (Summer 2010).

Erickson, Dan. "Star Valley, Wyoming: Polygamist Haven," *Journal of Mormon History* 26:1 (Spring 2000).

Everett, Derek R. *Creating the American West: Boundaries and Borderlands* (Norman: University of Oklahoma Press, 2014).

Ficken, Robert E. *Washington Territory* (Pullman: Washington State University Press, 2002).

Golay, Michael. *The Tide of Empire: America's March to the Pacific* (Hoboken, NJ: John Wiley & Sons, 2003).

Goode, Richard Urquhart. *Survey of the Boundary Line between Idaho and Montana from the International Boundary to the Crest of the Bitterroot Mountains* (Washington: Government Printing Office, 1900).

Gordon, Katherine. *Made to Measure: A History of Land Surveying in British Columbia* (Winlaw, BC: Sono Nis Press, 2006).

Gould, Lewis L. *Wyoming: A Political History, 1868–1896* (New Haven: Yale University Press, 1968).

Green, D. Brooks. "The Idaho-Wyoming Boundary: A Problem in Location," *Idaho Yesterdays* 23:1 (Spring 1977).

Greene, Jerome A. *Nez Perce Summer 1877: The U.S. Army and the Nee-me-poo Crisis* (Helena: Montana Historical Society Press, 2000).

Haynes, Sam W. *James K. Polk and the Expansionist Impulse* (New York: Pearson Longman, 2006).

Hecht, Marie B. *John Quincy Adams: A Personal History of an Independent Man* (New York: The Macmillan Co., 1972).

Horowitz, Robert F. *Great Impeacher: A Political Biography of James M. Ashley* (New York: Brooklyn College Press, 1979).

Hulce, James W. "Idaho Versus Nevada: The 1887 Struggle between Nevada's Senator and Idaho's Governor," *Idaho Yesterdays* 29:3 (Fall 1985).

Jackson, W. Turrentine. "The Appointment and Removal of Sidney Edgerton, First Governor of Montana Territory," *Pacific Northwest Quarterly* 34:3 (July 1943).

Josephy, Alvin M. *The Nez Perce Indians and the Opening of the Northwest* (New Haven: Yale University Press, 1965).

Kalt, Brian C. "The Perfect Crime," *Georgetown Law Journal* 93:2 (2005).

Kingston, C. S. "The North Idaho Annexation Issue," *Washington Historical Quarterly* 21:4 (October 1930).

Klotz, Otto. "The History of the Forty-Ninth Parallel West of the Rocky Mountains," *Geographical Review* 3:4 (May 1917).

Larson, T. A. *History of Wyoming* (Lincoln: University of Nebraska Press, 1978).

Laughy, Linwood, compiler. *In Pursuit of the Nez Perces: The Nez Perce War of 1877 as Reported by General O.O. Howard, Duncan McDonald, Chief Joseph* (Kooskia, ID: Mountain Meadow Press, 1993).

Leonard, Glen M. "The Mormon Boundary Question in the 1849–50 Statehood Debates," *Journal of Mormon History* 18:1 (Spring 1992).

Leonard, Thomas M. *James K. Polk: A Clear and Unquestionable Destiny* (Wilmington, DE: Scholarly Resources, Inc., 2001).

Leroy, David H. "Lincoln and Idaho: A Rocky Mountain Legacy," *Idaho Yesterdays* 42:2 (Summer 1998).

Linklater, Andro. *The Fabric of America: How Our Borders and Boundaries Shaped the Country and Forged Our National Identity* (New York: Walker & Company, 2007).

McArthur, Lewis A. "The Oregon State Boundary," *Oregon Historical Quarterly* 37:4 (December 1936).

McDermott, John D. *Forlorn Hope: The Battle of White Bird Canyon and the Beginning of the Nez Perce War* (Boise: Idaho State Historical Society, 1978).

McKinney, Whitney. *A History of the Shoshone-Paiutes of the Duck Valley Reservation* (Sun Valley, ID: The Institute of the American West and Howe Brothers, 1983).

McWhorter, Lucullus Virgil. *Hear Me, My Chiefs: Nez Perce Legend & History* (Caldwell, ID: Caxton Press, 1952).

_____. *Yellow Wolf: His Own Story* (Caldwell, ID: Caxton Press, 1940).

Malone, Michael P., Richard B. Roeder, and William L. Lang. *Montana: A History of Two Centuries* (Seattle: University of Washington Press, 1976).

Manning, Cynthia J. "An Ethnohistory of the Kootenai Indians," MA Thesis, University of Montana, 1984.

Marshall, R.B. *Retracement of the Boundary Line between Idaho and Washington* (Washington: Government Printing Office, 1911).

May, Dean L. "Between Two Cultures: The Mormon Settlement of Star Valley, Wyoming," *Journal of Mormon History* 13 (1986–87).

Merry, Robert W. *A Country of Vast Designs: James K. Polk, the Mexican War, and the Conquest of the American Frontier* (New York: Simon & Schuster, 2009).

Miles, E.A. "'Fifty-Four Forty or Fight'—An American Political Legend," *Mississippi Valley Historical Review* 44:2 (September 1957).

Morrissey, Katherine G. *Mental Territories: Mapping the Inland Empire* (Ithaca, NY: Cornell University Press, 1997).

Nagel, Paul C. *John Quincy Adams: A Public Life, a Private Life* (New York: Alfred A. Knopf, 1997).

Pace, Paul S. "Brothers: Daniel and John Major in the Trans-Mississippi West," *The Nevada Traverse: Journal of the Professional Land Surveyors of Nevada* 45:3 (September 2018).

Parsons, Hudson. *John Quincy Adams* (Madison, WI: Madison House, 1998).

Pattison, William D. "Beginnings of the American Rectangular Land Survey System, 1784–1800," *University of Chicago Department of Geography Research Paper No. 50* (1957).

Peebles, John J. "Retracing a Line: The 1908 Idaho-Washington Boundary Resurvey," *Idaho Yesterdays* 13:3 (Fall 1969).

Petersen, Keith C. *Idaho, the Land & Its People* (Boise: Idaho State Historical Society, 2019).

_____. *John Mullan: The Tumultuous Life of a Western Road Builder* (Pullman: Washington State University Press, 2014).

Reeves, Rollin J. "Marking the Washington-Idaho Boundary," *Washington Historical Quarterly* 2:4 (July 1908).

Richards, Kent D. *Isaac I. Stevens: Young Man in a Hurry* (Pullman: Washington State University Press, 1993).

Ristow, Walter W. "John Melish and His Map of the United States, *Library of Congress Quarterly Journal of Current Acquisitions* 19:4 (September 1962).

Rush, Richard. *Memoranda of a Residence at the Court of London* (Philadelphia: Carey, Lea & Blanchard, 1833).

Schwantes, Carlos A. *In Mountain Shadows: A History of Idaho* (Lincoln: University of Nebraska Press, 1991).

_____. *So Incredibly Idaho: Seven Landscapes that Define the Gem State* (Moscow: University of Idaho Press, 1996).

Seigenthaler, John. *James K. Polk* (New York: Henry Holt and Company, 2003).

Simmonds, A.J. "Southeast Idaho as a Pioneer Mormon Safety Valve," *Idaho Yesterdays* 23:4 (Winter 1980).

Simon-Smolinski, Carole. *Just Add Water: From Barren Jawbone Flat to Bountiful Clarkston, Washington, 1890–1940* (Lewiston, ID: Northwest Historical Consultants, 2019).

Smith, Gary Alden. *State and National Boundaries of the United States* (Jefferson NC: McFarland & Company, 2004).

Smith, Kris Runberg and Tom Weitz. *Wild Place: A History of Priest Lake, Idaho* (Pullman: Washington State University Press, 2015).

Stein, Mark. *How the States Got Their Shapes* (New York: Smithsonian Books/Collins, 2008).

Sowards, Adam M., ed., *Idaho's Place: A New History of the Gem State* (Seattle: University of Washington Press, 2014).

Thane, James R. Jr., ed., *A Governor's Wife in the Mining Frontier: The Letters of Mary Edgerton from Montana, 1863–1865* (Salt Lake City: University of Utah Library, 1976).

_____. "An Ohio Abolitionist in the Far West: Sidney Edgerton and the Opening of Montana, 1863–1866," *Pacific Northwest Quarterly* 67:4 (October 1974).

_____. "Montana Territory: The Formative Years, 1862–1870," PhD. Diss., University of Iowa, 1972.

Thomas, Benjamin E. "Boundaries and Internal Problems of Idaho," *Geographical Review* 39:1 (January 1949).

Thompson, Scott M. *I Will Tell of My War Story: A Pictorial Account of the Nez Perce War* (Seattle: University of Washington Press, 2000).

Trinklein, Michael J. *Lost States: True Stories of Texlahoma, Transylvania, and Other States that Never Made It* (Philadelphia: Quirk Books, 2010).

Van Zandt, Franklin K. *Boundaries of the United States and the Several States*, Geological Survey Professional Paper 909 (Washington: Government Printing Office, 1976).

Wells, Merle W. *Anti-Mormonism in Idaho, 1872–92* (Provo, UT: Brigham Young University Press, 1978).

_____. "The Creation of the Territory of Idaho," *Pacific Northwest Quarterly* 40:2 (April 1949).

_____. "The Idaho-Montana Boundary," *Idaho Yesterdays* 12:4 (Winter 1968).

_____. "Idaho's Centennial: How Idaho was Created in 1863," *Idaho Yesterdays* 7:1 (Spring 1963).

_____. "Politics in the Panhandle: Opposition to the Admission of Washington and North Idaho, 1886–1888," *Pacific Northwest Quarterly* 46:3 (July 1955).

_____. "Territorial Government in the Inland Empire: The Movement to Create Columbia Territory, 1864–69," *Pacific Northwest Quarterly* 44:2 (April 1953).

_____. "Walla Walla's Vision of a Greater Washington," *Idaho Yesterdays* 10:3 (Fall 1966).

West, Elliott. *The Last Indian War: The Nez Perce Story* (New York: Oxford University Press, 2009).

Wheat, Carl I. *Mapping the Transmississippi West, 1540–1861* (San Francisco: The Institute of Historical Cartography, 1958).

Woodworth-Ney, Laura. *Mapping Identity: The Creation of the Coeur d'Alene Indian Reservation, 1805–1902* (Boulder: University Press of Colorado, 2004).

_____. "Negotiating Boundaries of Territory and 'Civilization:' The Coeur d'Alene Indian Reservation Agreement Councils," *Pacific Northwest Quarterly* 94:1 (Winter 2002/03).

Wunder, John R. "Tampering with the Northwest Frontier: The Accidental Design of the Washington/Idaho Boundary," *Pacific Northwest Quarterly* 68:1 (January 1977).

Young, Karen Ashton. "Kootenai Sustenance Rights: In Fact and In Law," MA Thesis, University of Idaho, 1994.

Zietlow, Rebecca E. *The Forgotten Emancipator: James Mitchell Ashley and the Ideological Origins of Reconstruction* (New York: Cambridge University Press, 2018).